"This is an important book in the annals o [...]
Henry's story is terrifying but true. We sh [...]
his ordeal, and to the author for telling us [...]

founding director, AIDWYC (Association in Defence of the Wrongly Convicted)

"The story of Ivan Henry demonstrates that, when prosecutors and police blindly pursue convictions, they ignore the inherent obligation of the state to be fair and just. This book should be required reading for every law student, prosecutor, defence lawyer, and trial judge in Canada."

UJJAL DOSANJH, Q.C., former premier of British Columbia

"Reading *Innocence on Trial* brought back vivid memories of my own experience of wrongful conviction. There were so many similarities between Henry's case and mine, with many of the same players, that ultimately I found it too painful to finish the book."

THOMAS SOPHONOW, exoneree

"Upon being released in March 2003, I said I would remain 'pessimistically optimistic' that the abuse of power and corruption would someday change. As the Ivan Henry story shows, the stigma of guilt will remain as long as certain representatives within our police forces continue to abuse the criminal justice system. It takes people like Joan McEwen to keep this issue in the forefront, so all these wrongs can be righted and governments can do what is just and fair."

JIM DRISKELL, exoneree

"We are once again reminded that our system is composed of humans who make human mistakes. They resist acknowledgement of those mistakes at great cost to the individuals involved and to society as a whole, as our faith in the justice system is eroded."

RON DALTON, exoneree

"The disastrous trial and subsequent tribulations of Ivan Henry, including a quarter of a century of hard prison time for multiple sexual assaults he likely did not commit, shines light on an appalling miscarriage of Canadian justice. Ivan Henry emerges as stubborn and misinformed; a misguided, self-represented litigant. But there are lots of such people trapped in the courts, and the system needs to do a better job of dealing with them. In Ivan Henry's case, it failed miserably."

IAN BINNIE, former Supreme Court of Canada justice

"With forensic precision, Joan McEwen dissects the 'evidence' that confined Ivan Henry to twenty-seven years of wrongful imprisonment. How could so many stakeholders in the criminal justice system so woefully abjure their duty such that the real offender not only went unpunished but remained at liberty to commit further crimes? Shocking!"

DR. MICHAEL NAUGHTON, founder and director, Innocence Network UK

INNOCENCE
ON TRIAL

JOAN McEWEN

1982
MAY 12
PC 388

6 Feet

5 Feet

INNOCENCE

THE FRAMING OF IVAN HENRY

ON TRIAL

VICTORIA · VANCOUVER · CALGARY

Heritage House Publishing Company Ltd.
heritagehouse.ca

LIBRARY AND ARCHIVES CANADA CATALOGUING IN PUBLICATION

McEwen, Joan I., author
    Innocence on trial : the framing of Ivan Henry / Joan McEwen.

Issued in print and electronic formats.
ISBN 978-1-77203-002-0 (pbk.).—ISBN 978-1-77203-003-7 (html).—ISBN 978-1-77203-004-4 (pdf)

    1. Henry, Ivan—Trials, litigation, etc. 2. Trials (Rape)—British Columbia—Vancouver.
3. Judicial error—British Columbia. 4. False imprisonment—British Columbia. I. Title.

HV6569.C32V36 2014   364.15′320971133   C2014-903467-9   C2014-903468-7

Edited by Gary Stephen Ross
Copyedited by Lara Kordic
Proofread by Karla Decker
Cover and book design by Jacqui Thomas
Frontispiece photo courtesy of by Joan McEwen, from
    the Ivan Henry file in the BC Court of Appeal registry
Cover photo courtesy of Ivan Henry

Distributed in the U.S. by Publishers Group West

This edition is based on information gathered and known to the author as of August 2014.
It is expected that new information will come to light if and when Ivan Henry's civil lawsuit
against the City of Vancouver and the Province of British Columbia proceeds.

This book was produced using FSC®-certified, acid-free paper, processed chlorine free and
printed with vegetable-based inks.

Heritage House acknowledges the financial support for its publishing program from the
Government of Canada through the Canada Book Fund (CBF), Canada Council for the
Arts, and the Province of British Columbia through the British Columbia Arts Council
and the Book Publishing Tax Credit.

 Canadian Patrimoine
Heritage canadien   The Canada Council | Le Conseil des Arts
for the Arts | du Canada   BRITISH COLUMBIA
ARTS COUNCIL

18 17 16 15 14 1 2 3 4 5

Printed in Canada

Angel or devil, a man has a claim to a fair trial of his guilt.
Angel or devil, he has a claim to a fair trial, not of his general social
desirability, but of his guilt of the specific offence charged against him.
Such is the letter of our law. Such also is our law's spirit.

— KARL LLEWELLYN —
Jurisprudence: Realism in Theory and Practice

Perseverance is a trait so powerful that it
can overcome almost any deficiency.

— EKENENYIE UKPONG —
Those Days Are Gone! From Hopelessness to Happiness

CONTENTS

AUTHOR'S NOTE

This book is based on lengthy interviews with Ivan Henry and many of the people involved with his case, as well as people familiar with his life and his decades in various prisons. In some cases I have changed their names to protect their anonymity. Names of all the complainants—in both the Ivan Henry and the Donald McRae (Smallman) cases—have been changed in accordance with court-ordered publication bans.

During the trial, Ivan Henry impugned the credibility of the complainants—saying that, because he had not attacked them, they must also be fabricating the attacks themselves. Unlike Henry, I have never doubted that the women were, as they testified, sexually assaulted at knifepoint. Unless one has been through such an experience, it is impossible to comprehend the pain and trauma that comes with it. I imagine this pain and trauma has only been worsened by the ongoing lawsuit regarding Henry's compensation, his claim of innocence, and, finally—in the event that his innocence is finally established—the prospect that the actual culprit has never been brought to justice.

I have been made privy to only a small fraction of the documentation this case has generated. Apart from a sampling of the documents disclosed after the trial, as well as certain information arising from Henry's 2009 application to have his appeal reopened, I have relied primarily on the preliminary hearing and trial transcripts. The dialogue in the book has been reconstructed either from those transcripts or from the recollections of those persons whom I was able to interview.

Early on in the process, I reached out to Henry's lawyers, but they declined to talk to me. In May 2012, I couriered to them a summary of my "malicious prosecution" argument (including my assertion of fake lineup photos and exhibit substitution), but they did not acknowledge receipt. To date, that assertion has not been made part of their civil claim.

• • •

IT IS LIKELY that wrongful convictions are disproportionately high in two groups of inmates—the first being members of our Aboriginal community. Howard Sapers, who as the Correctional Investigator of Canada serves as the ombudsman for federally sentenced offenders, reported in 2013 that although Aboriginals make up only 4 percent of Canada's population, they constitute 23 percent of inmates in federal prisons. It can only be presumed that the number of wrongful convictions of Aboriginal Canadians reflects this same pattern of over-representation.

The second group involves those innocent persons who plead guilty as part of a plea bargain so as to avoid a harsher sentence. Although the precise numbers or demography of such persons cannot be known, a large proportion of those likely lack the resources to mount an effective defence on their own behalf.

• • •

I WISH TO extend my gratitude, first and foremost, to Ivan Henry. For weeks, months, and, indeed, years on end, he answered my questions with good humour and more than a little forbearance. Although we hit more than a few speed bumps along the way, the bond of trust between us deepened over time.

Big thanks to Gary Stephen Ross. No one could ask for a better editor, friend, and writing mentor.

I extend my gratitude to the many other devoted people who work in the "innocence field"—including Canadian exonerees such as Jim Driskell, Ronald Dalton, and Tom Sophonow. Each of them, in his own way, has helped me understand how an innocent man could end up serving twenty-seven years in prison. A tip of my hat as well to the innocence projects springing up all over the world—and special thanks to Tamara Levy, executive director of UBC Law School's Innocence Project, for her support and encouragement.

I humbly dedicate this book not only to my husband, Irwin Nathanson, and our boys, Cory and Ted—without whom none of this would have been possible—but also to the men and women who have been convicted of, or confessed to, crimes they did not commit.

The case of Ivan Henry shows there is always hope.

PROLOGUE

On March 15, 1983, Ivan Henry, a thirty-five-year-old father of two, was convicted in Vancouver of ten sexual assaults involving eight women. Some criminals are considered too dangerous ever to be released back into society; a dangerous offender designation means that the chances of release are slim to zero. In November 1983, Henry was declared a dangerous offender and handed an indefinite sentence.

Twenty-six years later, on January 13, 2009, the British Columbia Court of Appeal ruled that Ivan Henry's 1984 appeal should be reopened.[1] In June 2009, he was released on bail pending his appeal. Electronic monitors were strapped to his ankles, and he was confined, unless accompanied by certain named persons, from 8:00 p.m. to 6:00 a.m., seven days a week, to the North Vancouver home of his elder daughter, Tanya.

In October 2010, the B.C. Court of Appeal ruled him "not guilty" of his crimes[2] and his ankle bracelets were removed. Far from declaring him innocent, however, the court said there was no certainty that the "other offender" mentioned in the court's ruling (Donald McRae) had committed the Henry crimes. Citing faulty identification evidence as the main reason for the acquittal, the court ruled that, though the eight trial complainants identified Henry as their assailant, that testimony was not reliable.

Appearing on television the day of his acquittal, Ivan Henry was the picture of a bon vivant. His arms draped over the shoulders of his adult daughters, he extolled the virtues of freedom—including the pleasures of Diet Coke and hot dogs. Intrigued, I resolved to meet him. I had been involved for some time in assisting long-term prisoners reintegrate into society, and I am interested in the lives of inmates inside our federal correctional institutions. Having never met a sex offender—let alone a serial rapist—I was especially interested in his story.

Henry is suing all levels of government for malicious prosecution and breaches of the *Canadian Charter of Rights and Freedoms*. In March 2011, after the lawyers in his civil case passed on my contact information, he and I met at a coffee shop in North Vancouver. Dressed in a beat-up jacket and bargain-basement pants, Henry, sixty-four at the time, jumped up to greet me in the noisy café. He squeezed my hand between his meaty paws. Although mostly toothless—"A dentist's offered to put in the bottom row for free," he said, before he'd even sat back down—he was handsome in a weather-beaten way: hazel eyes, soft lines curving up from his generous mouth, an appealing kind of sardonic, wink-wink humour.

"What do you want from me?" he asked, making brief eye contact before resuming his roving surveillance of the room.

When I said that his seemingly calm persona on TV intrigued me, he threw back his head and snorted. "I was madder than hell. It was all an act. I didn't want anyone to think I was dangerous. Yeah, I was calm—three clonazepam, just like the doctor ordered."

"I'm curious how sex offenders, guilty or not, are treated in prison."

"You recording this?" he asked.

"No. I wouldn't do that without asking you."

"See that guy over there?" He leaned closer, lowered his voice. "He's undercover. The police are dogging my every move. They want me to fail."

Clearly oblivious of us, the young man in question stuffed his computer and books into his backpack and sauntered out the door.

"The lineup photo's fake," said Henry. "It's never left my side. It's my ticket to freedom."

"What are you talking about?"

"Forget trying to see it," he said, patting his shirt pocket. "I don't show it to just anyone. I'm innocent," he added, eyes drilling into me, "and I need someone to prove it. Take it or leave it."

"Take what?" I said.

"Either you're writing this book or you're not. If you don't, someone else will. Hell, the lady next door has a nephew desperate for work. Says he passed Grade 12 English with flying colours."

"What book?"

After more of his cryptic statements, I began to get the gist. I was to write a book about his not even being in the police lineup that helped get him convicted—he kept saying something about "a head on a body"—or I was to get the hell out of there.

Two hours later, I promised him I'd give the project serious thought.

Not that I knew much about criminal law. Although I'd been drawn to it in law school, I had an almost-morbid fear of jails—I couldn't stand the thought of a client facing incarceration, being stripped of his freedom even for a day. I had gone into labour law instead. It was also clear that Henry would likely not make for a sympathetic character. Not only did he have a criminal record—he was on mandatory supervision for an attempted-rape conviction in Winnipeg when the Vancouver assaults began—but he was also adamant that the complainants in his case had never even been assaulted. Instead, he was convinced that they had been part of the state's grand conspiracy against him. With an attitude like that, I thought, he wouldn't have made a good impression at trial. Mr. Justice John Bouck, Ivan Henry's trial judge, was renowned for not suffering fools gladly. And there was plenty about Ivan Henry to let you take him for a fool.

I was also frankly concerned about Henry's mood swings—warm and sweet one minute, paranoid and suspicious the next. The thought of spending countless hours interviewing him was not entirely appealing. And, finally, what if, after investing weeks, if not months, of my time, I concluded that he was anything but innocent?

When all was said and done, though, it was his parting shot that intrigued and ultimately hooked me. For weeks afterward, I couldn't get it out of my mind. "If you write my story," he said, "you'll be more shocked each day than you were the day before. Yous lawyers should be ashamed of yourselves."

PART ONE

PRESUMED GUILTY (1982–83)

"Mr. Henry, let me assure you, once and for all, the burden
of proof is, was, and always will be on the Crown. Guilt beyond
a reasonable doubt. Have I made myself very, very clear?"

— MR. JUSTICE JOHN BOUCK, MARCH 9, 1983 —

CHAPTER 1

THE ARREST

May 12, 1982. A bright, sunny Vancouver day, blue canopy stretched overhead. Elbow sticking out the window of his car, the breeze playing havoc with his wavy red hair, Ivan Henry sings along to the radio. Cruising the city—enjoying the snow-capped mountains and glittering ocean—in his little canary-yellow AMC Spirit, he's feeling great. Nothing like a pancake breakfast, spiffy new clothes, and the thought of his two little girls making faces in the mirror that morning while he shaved off his moustache. Nine and seven already. *No way am I ever going back to the joint*, he vows—an eye, as always, on the rear-view mirror.

"Freedom's overrated, kid," his best jailhouse friend, Manfred Cullen, used to say. "Give me a bed to sleep in, food in my belly. If the toughest decision of the day's when to take a crap, so be it." But they were young then; kids, really. Young and full of swagger. Far too young to be locked up, with nowhere to go but down. That was then, and this is now.

Feeling the heat—the bad kind—Henry had spent the past week up north, doing a little fly-fishing with his pal, André, and checking out the area as a possible new home for his family. Not that he hadn't stayed in close touch with his former parole officer. "Conroy," he'd say, "I've got a rotten feeling in my belly. They're out to get me. I can feel it." What he didn't say was that Jessie—his former wife, though they still cohabit when their nerves can stand it—had fessed up and told him about the police paying her a visit. When he pressed her to elaborate, she'd clammed up.

"You're imagining things," Chris Conroy said. "You got through mandatory supervision without a glitch. Except of course for that minor little weed thing."

Just as well the lady never reported the B and E in January, Henry thinks, wiping his brow. He'd be a goner for sure.

Jessie's dealer, Johnnie—a no-good SOB addicted to heroin and who knows what else—has a pipeline to the Vancouver Police Department, no doubt about it. All the while acting like Henry's best friend, telling him—wink-wink, nod-nod—that a red-haired so-called rip-off rapist had attacked yet another woman. Johnnie, like most junkies, would sell his soul for the right price.

Breathing in the scent of summer, Henry rejoices in his freedom. When his sentence for the Winnipeg beefs ended in late January, he'd punched the air with his fist. Never had he felt more hopeful and determined to turn the corner. He waves to the gorgeous woman in the convertible next to him, her chestnut hair streaming in the wind, and counts his blessings. Like his new job, hawking fancy-ass blue jeans from the back of his car. Hatchback open, he barely has time to put up the sign—"Designer Jeans, $12 a Pop!"—and ladies from Smalltown, BC, come running. How sweet is the feel of money in his pocket. One day, he grossed $600. After forking over most of it to the wife, he'd treated himself to the duds he's wearing now, a blue velour shirt and Jordache jeans from his own stock.

Designer jeans today, microwave ovens tomorrow. At fifty bucks an oven, the housewives will be clamouring for them.

Curses—

Another glance in the rear-view and his heart plummets. Unmarked vehicle, two cars back. Knuckles white on the steering wheel, he plays cat and mouse for a few blocks.

Bugger the suspense. He pulls over to the curb, opens the car door, and extends one leg, then the other, onto the pavement. Feigning nonchalance, he begins a slow walk towards a nearby coffee shop, hoping against hope he's wrong.

Behind him, the wail of a siren, the screeching of brakes. More cruisers appear out of nowhere.

"Police! Stop in your tracks, Henry. Now!"

Arms up, he pivots in slow motion. The .38 Smith & Wesson inches from his face almost makes his knees buckle.

"You're under arrest."

Recovering, heating up, he says, "You got a warrant?"

"We don't need one. You want a reason?" says the bull. "Let's try breaking and entering, shall we? Take your pick."

"No way you're cuffing me behind my back," he says, jerking his hands away. "Been there, done that."

Arrested at a hash-for-cash swap near Lake Winnipeg years ago, the police had pounded his mug into a brick wall. Awaiting prosecution, he'd bided his time in the infirmary. His smashed-up face swathed in bandages, teeth broken, he'd vowed that he would insist on being cuffed in front should he ever be arrested again.

They cuff him in front and then yank back his hair so hard that his teeth hurt.

Hunched in the rear of the cage-car, he tries to make himself invisible, like when he was little and his stepdad came at him with a belt. Not that he blames anyone but himself. *Face it, you idiot, thirty-five years on the planet and all you've got to show for it is a pair of handcuffs biting into your wrists, your fancy new velour shirt sweat-stuck to the plastic seat.*

Buck up, he tells himself, *you've always been a fighter. And this time, for once in your life, you've got nothing to hide.*

CHAPTER 2

THE LINEUP

S liding down a sunless alley off Cordova Street, in Vancouver's Downtown Eastside, the cruiser passes slack-eyed junkies and ladies-for-hire strutting their knee-high boots and pockmarked faces. Henry is hustled into an elevator as chilly as a meat locker and up to the third floor. A quick sign-off on personal effects—a couple hundred bucks, a belt, shoelaces—then up to five, where he's shoved, face-first, into the drunk tank. A flare of light behind his eyeballs. He tells his handlers to fuck off and take their bacon smell with them.

The walls, stinking of puke—colour to match—close in on him. Nothing to do but curl up and study the stains and graffiti. He tries not to think about Winnipeg. Tanked up real good, he'd walked right through the lady's open door—payback, in his pickled brain, for his wife's two-timing ways. So drunk he could barely find his zipper, he'd fled like a kicked mongrel when she begged him to leave. His legal-aid grunt lawyer sold him down the river. The plea deal was a joke: five years for attempted rape? Not that he's proud of himself—he'd never harm a woman—but murderers get off with less.

In the penitentiary at Prince Albert, Saskatchewan, he'd been called every name in the book—bitch, diddler, hound, dirty skinner. He was prodded, bumped, poked, jabbed, spat upon. They'd have done any-thing to get him alone—in the shower, his cell, the yard, anywhere. Meanwhile, the bulls stood back, arms crossed, smirking, waiting for the show to begin. The con code, custom-made for baboons: murderers at the top, skinners at the bottom. Good thing he knew how to handle himself. Lucky he got out of there in one piece.

• • •

AROUND 5:00 P.M. that same day, May 12, an officer approaches, flashing his badge through the bars. "Wake up. Make yourself decent. We're putting you in a lineup."

"You got a warrant? And, by the way, I ain't going in no lineup."

"The *Marcoux* case, Supreme Court of Canada, says you got no choice. Start walking."

"*Marcoux* says exactly the opposite, you dummy." *Smart ass*, Henry resists saying. *There ain't a con alive who don't know that since 1975 suspects can't be made to participate in lineups.*

Next thing he knows, they've marched him back down to the third floor, and someone's throwing a numbered placard over his head. Plainclothes cops are everywhere—milling around, chortling, elbowing each other, also wearing placards. Not a redhead among the other lineup paricipants.

"I ain't going in no lineup with you slobs," Henry says. "You can't make me."

Three uniforms—including a smart-aleck ginger—collar him. Hoisting him off the ground, choking him, they propel him forward— his shoeless feet barely skimming the ground—towards the brightly lit room at the end of the hall.

After pushing him into the lineup room, someone grabs his wrists in a Vise-Grip behind his back. A force of some sort clamps down hard on his neck. He can't breathe. A sharp jab in his ribs. He doubles over as the headlock tightens, and he's wrenched upright. Another solar-burst of stars.

Later, back in his cell, he listens to the crash of metal against metal. A massive door clangs shut. Then silence, thick enough to taste. Knees drawn up to his chin, he nods off.

• • •

WITH TREMBLING HAND, half-asleep, Ivan Henry accepts Aspirin from the nurse. "Mr. Henry," she says, "you've been sawing logs for hours."

Before long, Detective Bruce Campbell, a bulky man with a day's growth and elephantine thighs, escorts him into an eight-by-ten-foot concrete room with barred, one-way-mirrored windows.

Campbell tells Henry he'll feel a whole better if he "comes clean." After introducing his partner, Detective Marylyn Sims—a looker with long legs and glossy auburn hair cut in a bob—Campbell straddles a metal chair with those massive thighs. Lighting up, he taps his cheek with his index finger, blowing out smoke rings.

"We're hoping for a straight-up conversation," he says finally, tipping ash into his coffee cup. "You're under suspicion for a pack of sexual assaults. By the way, Detective Sims is our first-ever lady detective. So watch your Ps and Qs." Leaning in so close that Henry can smell his ashtray breath, he says, "Tell us where you've been living."

"All over," Henry says, suddenly soaked in sweat. "Friends, hotels, at home with my wife. I keep track of dates. You're barking up the wrong tree."

"Is that so? Well, how come three girls in that lineup say it's you who broke in and assaulted them? One of them said you wore a turtleneck."

"What lineup?"

"The lineup you were in today at 5:00 p.m."

"Guess how I can prove I'm not the one? Clothes—like that turtleneck that don't exist? Turtlenecks make me too hot. Fingerprints, footprints, you won't find any. How long ago was the first one?"

"Over a year and a half."

"I didn't do nothing."

"Mr. Henry," says the lady detective, "do you need a bathroom break? Some water?"

Ah, isn't she nice. Screw 'em. They've got nothing on him.

"You say you remember where you were on certain days?"

"Show me the dates. I keep track in my mind's diary."

"Why didn't you want to go into that lineup?"

"I'm the only redhead there. The plainclothes police are taller, they're dressed like crap. I might be poor, but I know how to dress."

"You arrived in Vancouver in June 1980. After that, you worked steady?"

"Something like thirteen contractors in the first six months. I don't believe any of them girls said they recognized me."

How long since your front tooth went missing? Since you shaved off your moustache? How often do you cut your hair?

"Oh, and by the way," Campbell says, "do you dye it? Do you own a gold chain?"

"I had the tooth pulled a few weeks ago. Some bull loosened it up real good. Red's my natural colour. I hate gold anything. Are you dopes charging me? I demand to see an arrest warrant."

"I'll start with the first of the three positive identifications. May 5, '81, 200 block West 18—"

"April 1981? A year ago? I was living on Canada Way. In Burnaby. Not even the same city."

". . . act of fellatio, then an attempt at anal intercourse."

"Anal intercourse? Never. You can throw that one out—"

"Here's the next one. March 19, '82, 8700 block of Osler Street—"

"I used to live in the 8700 block of Prince Edward." As if they don't know.

"Lady says the intruder put a pillow over her head. Your former wife says you get off on that sort of thing."

They're making it up as they go. Jessie never told them that. Or if she did, high, she mixed it up with stories about his stepdad, Johnny Vukusha, who used to muffle Henry's coughing by pressing a pillow over his face. Do such a thing to a woman? Never.

"No way Jessie would've sworn that statement under oath. March 19, you say? Two months ago. Let me think. Two days after St. Patrick's Day, so I'd have been in Regina." Stretching his legs, he makes like he's breathing easy. "That's two, and I didn't do either of them. Bring on the third."

"Your attitude is most unhelpful," says Sims, already on her feet. "Detective Campbell, it seems Mr. Henry could use a little thinking time. Take a good hard look at this," she says, sliding a sheet of paper across the table. "I trust you won't be so blasé when we return."

VPD REQUEST FOR BULLETIN (CPIC) -- MAY 8/82
Case # 82-21155 et al
Code 5 - violent, dangerous, carries knife Code 12 - has police scanner
Offences: rape X 18
Warrant numbers:
Description: white male, DOB October 22/46;
POB: Manitoba
5'10"; brown hair; brown eyes. Distinguishing features: may or may not have beard; curly c/l hair; sometimes colours hair with peroxide; gaps between upper front

teeth, tattoos of bugs and dagger with "Jessie" on
right forearm.
Associates: ex-wife lives at < >
Associates with unidentified male living at < >
Remarks: resists arrest violently.
Record: rape, B & E, drugs. If located, hold for
Detectives Sims and Campbell. Do not interview. Seize
and tag any tools for Lab.
Treat as major crime suspect.

Eighteen rapes? Major crime suspect? Forget about the omitted bits—
What "unidentified male"? Why has Jessie's address been whited
out? Is her address suddenly a state secret?—he's read enough that his
fingernails are digging into his palms.

Returning, Campbell restraddles the chair. "If you're so innocent,"
he says, "tell us about that rape conviction back in Winnipeg."

"*Attempted* rape. My lawyer tricked me into a guilty plea. Hell,
man, when you get charged with rape, attempted or not, people spit
at you. I was drunk. I was mad at my wife. It was stupid. I wouldn't do
nothing like that ever again."

"The third woman to positively ID you, twenty-two years of age,
assaulted on August 5, '81, 8700 block of Oak Street. Guy busts in, says he's
looking for someone, puts a pillow over her head. Forces her to fellate him."

"Last summer? I didn't do it. Sure, I rent a postal box near there—
Marine Drive, near the tunnel—but I don't walk around them streets.
You're trying to embarrass me. The only reason I'd ever go into a house
is to take money."

"So you're admitting to B and E?"

"Daytime only—less chance of being caught. I'm not going near
anyone with lights on—not with all the mug shots they got of my face.
I'd have to be a goof, wouldn't I?"

"Would you take a lie detector test on these three?"

"Bring it on. Give me a lie detector. Tell me about the others."

"Chronologically, the first one was November 25, '80, 200 block
West 18th. Between Main and Cambie. A twenty-one-year-old girl."

"Why not set up a sting?" says Henry. "Flush the jerk out."

"Next, a rape on January 14, '81, 900 block West 19th. Male looking
for somebody, mentioned money and drugs. After that, February 19,
1900 block West 2nd. Kitsilano. Attempted rape, her four-year-old son

nearby. Man said he was looking for someone who ripped him off. Not the first time he's used that phrase. Sound familiar?"

"Sure, I've said that. Everybody says that. What else did Jessie tell you?"

"A yellow car was seen speeding off. Did you have a yellow car?"

"I got the clutch fixed at Happy Honda in January."

"How about March 23, '81? Another one in Marpole, 3600 block Oak Street. Rape. Guy said he was looking for someone who ripped him off —"

"It's the same guy doing all of them," says Henry. "And I ain't the guy."

"March 31, '81, 200 block West 14th, upstairs attic room, old house. Another B and E and rape."

"I told you, I was living in Burnaby. The guy's got jam, though, don't he? It takes nerve to go upstairs. Even if you're there just for the purse, once she starts screaming you've got to have exits."

Sims leans forward. "I'm assuming you know," she says, like she's talking to an idiot, "that anything you say here may be given as evidence. You are welcome to call a lawyer."

It occurs to Henry that he should have been read his rights before this fiasco began. How dare they blow this past him like he's being offered a refill on his water? Not that he's got any use for lawyers—not after the botched plea deal in Winnipeg. "By the way," he says, "what's with the tape recorder?"

"So we can have an accurate account of our conversation."

"Okay, record this. Here's how I'd catch him. He must be peeping. He must know they're living alone. How many peeping toms do you think there are in Vancouver?"

"Lots."

"Get your cops into the lanes. The guy's a menace."

"Next," Campbell says, "April 8, '81, 2600 block Prince Albert. Fellow said he got ripped off on a drug deal, put a pillow over her head."

"No way would I do anything on that street," says Henry. "I done time in Prince Albert Penitentiary in Saskatchewan. If you're so sure I'm a pillow man, why not come after me in April? This is pretty fucking serious."

"May 14, '81, Point Grey area. June 2, another rape."

"No way!" Henry objects. "That Winnipeg beef went down on June 2. I wouldn't do such a thing on that date. It would be a superstition with me.

How's the guy getting in—sliding doors or what? When was the last one?"

"Most are insecure windows. April 22, '82. You were living four or five blocks away. Same MO. Guy puts his left hand over girl's mouth, right hand holding a knife."

"I never used a weapon in my life."

"Ah, but didn't you say a smart guy would keep changing his MO?"

He didn't say that. Or did he? They're getting him all mixed up.

"I shouldn't talk to you guys," he says finally, sweat burning his eyes. "You're trying to confuse me. First, you need to get identification. I don't know what you have. Then you need to get the other stuff. It won't match mine, guaranteed."

"One girl described a circumcised penis. Are you Jewish?"

"My great-great-grandfather was from Israel. Why the hell, after all this time, can't you catch the jerk? I'll take your bloody lie detector test. Let's do it."

The cops exchange a glance.

"The guy's really, really sick," Henry says. "If you're doing these things every two weeks, your emotions are gone. There's nothing left. You have to satisfy a guilt. And when the thirst gets too great, you do something to cover up the guilt. I'll tell you what. Put me in a cell for two months and see if it keeps going on. Then come back and say, 'Ivan, we're sorry.' Now take me back to my cell. I'm done."

• • •

CURLED UP, TRYING to get warm, Henry lies awake cursing Jessie—still his wife, really, though she'd divorced him a year ago for the welfare. When little Tanya blurted out something about the police coming by and scaring their mother, he'd pressed Jessie for details. Playing their conversation back in his mind, he tries to remember exactly what she'd told him.

"Two of them came by yesterday, said you're wanted on a bunch of rape charges. Said they'd take the girls away. I got so scared. Is it true?"

The bastards. Six years ago in Winnipeg he did something stupid, and they'll make him wear it forever. Entrapment, whatever, it's what they do. But invading his home, threatening his family?

"Jessie," he'd said, gently rubbing her icy hands, "I didn't do nothing wrong. I wouldn't lie to you. Not about that."

Clutching her cardigan close, she'd looked away.

"Tell me you gave them sons of bitches the boot."

She'd eyed him with the vague, glittery eyes of a junkie.

"They paid you, didn't they?"

"They scared the daylights out of the girls. Made them stay in the living room while we talked."

He lifted her chin to make her meet his eyes. "Tell me everything, Jessie. Chapter and verse. I promise I won't get mad."

"I was under par. It was Shirley let 'em in."

Great. Freeloader Shirley—another junkie ratting out low-lifes for cash. If not for the guilt he lugs around—missing in action while his daughters grew from toddlers into sweet, adorable schoolgirls—he'd have shown Shirley the door long ago.

"Ivan, swear you're innocent. You promised there'd be no more breaking the law."

"I ain't touched no women, I promise. You know I've been working my butt off. The cops twist words; it's what they do best. How could you fall for it?"

"The questions came so fast. I said you never owned a turtleneck. They must not have believed me because they asked me for mine. Are you mad at me?"

"Tell me exactly what they said."

"They asked if I had any pictures of you. I gave them a couple—that nice one of you that was on the shelf above the bed."

"What else did you give them?"

A gulp of air, more plucking at her baggy cardigan. "They asked if you have a beard. I said sometimes yes, sometimes no. I told them you'd been a hairdresser. I said I couldn't be sure, maybe you once had a perm. That's all, I swear."

Pissed as he was with Jessie, he smiled at the mention of that God-awful perm. Hell, two years later, his scalp still hurt. "After all you done for me," his ex-cellmate Salvatore had said, waving curlers and hairpins in the air, "it's the least I can do." Lacking the heart to say no, Henry had ended up with a head full of corkscrew curls. Never again.

"S-s-sorry, Ivan, I got so scared. Ask Shirley. She said your moustache was to cover up your missing tooth. That part's true, right?"

"Yeah, Jessie," he'd said, resisting the urge to say something he'd regret. "That part you got right."

CHAPTER 3

CAT AND MOUSE

The day after the lineup, Henry is marched back down to the booking counter to collect his personal effects. While he counts his money and threads the laces into his shoes, the booking officer tries to snap his picture. "Why you taking my picture? It's past noon," Henry says. "The law says you can't hold me without warrant more'n twenty-four hours. I've been in custody twenty-seven, minimum."

"Start walking, Mr. Henry, before I change my mind."

There would be time enough tomorrow to retrieve his car. For now, all he wants is a hot shower and hugs from his girls. After they settle down for the night, he'll talk Jessie into a quick jaunt up north. Back to André and his family—a little fly-fishing for the men, standing knee-deep in the river, the kids bobbing up and down in inner tubes while the wives yakkety-yak in the kitchen. Split the big city for a few days and clear his head.

Rounding the corner of his street, he sees the dicks parked near his house. Just before their faces disappear behind their newspapers, he gives them the finger. Screw them. While they play their stupid head games, the real culprit gets a free ride.

Next morning, at the police compound to pick up his car, he finds that a tail light has been shot out. His tools have been rummaged through, and someone's removed the lead balances from the wheel wells.

• • •

LATE JULY. SUMMER's halfway over, yet Henry's on edge. He's been followed for the past ten weeks, at least in Vancouver. It's kind of a lark, leading the ghost cars on wild-goose chases: weaving through traffic and down narrow laneways, listening to the screeching brakes when he slams his own, laughing and waving at them in the rear-view mirror. But the fact that they're still dogging him spooks him.

Although Jessie kicks him out as many nights as not, he's putting food on the table and paying the rent. Road trips are lucrative, so he's been selling jeans out of his trunk in the interior of the province. He's made sure to bring someone along every time he could—even Kari, his younger daughter, went with him earlier that month. Growing up fast, that kid. More often than not, she beats him at pitch and putt.

At the end of July, he heads back north. He travels solo this time, but he's planning to hire a helper at the local youth hostel. Four hundred kilometres from Vancouver, in Cariboo country, he passes the "Smile You're in 100 Mile" sign. Straight ahead, there's a roadblock—two RCMP cruisers nose to nose across the road. He's being flagged.

He steps out of his car, and suddenly he's doing a face plant on the hood while officers toss his merchandise willy-nilly onto the ground. Someone must have tipped them off. Someone's out to get him.

Hustled into the local RCMP office, he's presented with a seventeen-count information—an arrest document—that specifies seven rapes, nine indecent assaults, and one attempted rape; it's signed by "Informant, VPD Sergeant Gordon Howland." Loudly, Henry demands to know what reasonable and probable grounds they have. What the hell—two of the complainants say they were raped *after* the lineup. Who do they think he is, fucking Houdini? How could he pull a stunt like that right under the cops' noses, when they've been watching him day and night?

"You dummies know better," he says, as they cuff him and read him his rights. "Just last week two of yous pulled me over—stuck your flashlights in my face. How could I assault anybody when you're watching me? Why you picking me up now?"

• • •

BY THE TIME they hit the road back to Vancouver, the sun is low on the horizon. Before long, they're in the mountains, the narrow highway twisting above the fast-moving Fraser River hundreds of feet below.

For the longest time, no one says a word. Henry, alternately angry and despondent, gazes out at the failing light.

When they pull in to a rest stop, the two detectives in front reach for cigarettes while Sergeant Howland deigns to light Henry's. When they suggest he step out of the car to stretch his legs, he laughs out loud. Thanks very much, but no. One minute they'd be lining him up in the headlights of the specially outfitted Oldsmobile; the next, they'd be gunning him down. There's no one in sight. It's a moonless night, pitch black. He'd spotted a store back along the highway—saw a light flickering in the window—but it's too far off for anyone to hear a gunshot. His mind racing, it's as though he can read theirs. Even better than catching him "escaping," they'll chuck him off the embankment. Fewer questions that way. Later, when they say they did their best to stop him, they'll be hailed for trying to talk down a jumper. "But what could we do?" they'll say, as the TV cameras roll, "The man was obviously racked with guilt."

Henry listens to the low roar of the river below, racing towards the thirty-five-metre-wide narrowing called Hell's Gate, the crunching of footsteps on gravel, and his deep inhalations on the glowing butt. More than once, during the long ride, he'd thought about lunging forward, grabbing the wheel, and forcing the car over the cliff. If it weren't for his faith that God would see him through this, he'd have done it.

Once they get back on the road, he gazes out at the tunnel carved by the high beams. From time to time, an oncoming car appears out of nowhere. The headlights blind them momentarily; then the red tail lights shrink into nothing in the rear-view mirror.

"No way I could've raped those last two," he says finally. "If you got any brains at all, you know it."

Switching on the interior light, Howland looks at him and laughs— abrupt and mirthless. "That's not what the New York girl has to say. On June 8, the lights were on in her suite. She had a lengthy opportunity to view her attacker. And you know what? She says it was you."

He grins at Henry in the rear-view, then douses the lights.

• • •

IN CUSTODY, AWAITING a preliminary hearing, Henry is transferred to Oakalla, a prison farm east of the city. It's a dismal, menacing place, built on a lush, meadowy hill in Burnaby that slopes down to Deer Lake. Overcrowded and dirty, with rudimentary plumbing and heating systems, it's largely unchanged from the time it opened in 1912. It houses an assortment of inmates—many of them Aboriginal—serving time, on remand, or awaiting trial or sentencing. History envelops the place like a dank odour. Before capital punishment was abolished in Canada in 1976, dozens of men were hanged in the gallows in the basement. Their ghosts give Oakalla an eerie, haunted feel.

Paranoid and alone, Henry keeps a low profile. Sex criminals are reviled in every prison, and he knows how quickly news travels through the grapevine. He has to figure things out. There's no way they'll give him bail with so many charges against him, so he needs to get Jessie to find out what happened to the merchandise in his car when he got busted. He tells her to drive up north to retrieve it from the police station there, but she's told that it's "gone missing." *Sure*, he curses the powers that be, *set me up on bogus charges and steal my livelihood while you're at it.*

His preliminary hearing is on the horizon, and he needs to figure out how that's going to work. In the prison library he finds some old law books, and day after day he educates himself. A preliminary hearing, he learns, is intended to test the Crown's case—to determine if sufficient evidence exists to proceed to trial. It's also intended to "protect the accused from a needless and, indeed, improper, exposure to public trial where the enforcement agency is not in possession of evidence sufficient to warrant the continuation of the process."[1]

A legal-aid lawyer will be appointed to help him. This is looking good. Should be able to get this thing thrown out before it even starts. Never mind "sufficient" evidence; they've got no evidence at all—no hair, no fingerprints, no fibres, no semen. They couldn't, because he wasn't there. They've got nothing on him but some hysterical women pointing at the wrong guy.

CHAPTER 4

TO PROTECT THE ACCUSED

T he prelim means nothing," says Legal Aid's offering, John White, a little guy with a lousy suit and a goatee. Henry's been cooling his heels, week after week, waiting for this? "It's when we get to trial that the big show begins."

Great, thinks Henry, *just what I need—a clueless little Jewish lawyer with a defeatist attitude. Probably part of the whole set-up.* Henry imagines White huddling in the hallway with the Crown prosecutor— "my friend" this and "my friend" that. To hell with it; let the show begin. Even a goof like White can't stop him from beating such trumped-up charges. Who says the women were even raped? First chance he gets, he'll sue the ass off the police, the Crown, everyone. The conspiracy, he's convinced, runs right through the whole rotten system.

Escorted into a courtroom in BC's Provincial Courthouse on Main Street, Henry takes the measure of the Crown prosecutor, Michael Luchenko: Brylcreem hair, gold cufflinks, mirror-shiny shoes. Luchenko is regaling the sheriffs with the story of his nickname, Blue 3. "When I was in university," he's saying, "I didn't just finish the circuit faster than anyone; I did so while lifting the heaviest—'Blue 3'—weights."

Yeah, well, good for you, prick. How'd you like to go one on one?

His Honour Judge Wallace Craig—ramrod posture, brush-cut hair, and smooth brow—appears through a door in the front of the courtroom. "All stand," says the clerk, and everyone jumps to attention. After nodding at Luchenko, His Honour climbs the stairs to his bench and sits down.

The first complainant Luchenko calls is Miss Browning. Haltingly, she describes a hand on her throat, a man threatening to knife her.

Henry sits still as long as he can. When he's had enough of her drama, he blurts out, "Pretty hard to make it up, eh?"

"You just shut up," says Judge Craig. "Any more of that and you'll be in some difficulty. You'd be well advised to do what your counsel says. You will not interrupt a witness. You'll shut up."

"Then he removed his penis from his pants," Miss Browning continues, "and I suddenly realized what this was about. I looked up at his face because I thought that, if I lived, I wanted to remember that face forever. The man was six feet tall, with lots of dark, wild hair—very, very thick, wavy or curly."

Dark, wild hair? Six feet tall? Good. His hair's copper-coloured and, according to prison records—for some reason, they chart his height and weight every month—he stands five-foot-nine on a good day. He's off the hook.

"Everyone at the lineup was in handcuffs," she's testifying.

"Bullshit!" Henry says, swatting away White's hand. "There were no handcuffs. The woman's a liar."

"I'm warning you," says Judge Craig. "Conduct yourself with proper decorum, or you'll be down in the cells."

Asked by Luchenko why, after seeing the lineup, she'd marked a foil—someone other than the prime suspect—on her ballot, she says: "In trying to be overcompensating, I ignored . . . the man being dragged into the lineup by three policemen. And then I heard this growl. I knew that voice. No one else could ever make a sound like that. After the police pulled his head back, his face was distorted. I just couldn't—I don't know what happened, I was so scared. I didn't pick him because he didn't have dark hair. I picked #18 instead."

Exactly. The placard they put on him was #12, and she picked #18. When are they going to call an end to this bullshit?

When she says she "thinks" Henry—"the man in green"—is her attacker, he resists the urge to give her a standing ovation. The prize goes to the lady who identifies the one man in court in prison garb!

When she says "The accused's voice is that of my attacker," he fires back, "She's a liar, you know!" The judge glares at him.

A few questions into cross-examination, White pauses. Turning to Judge Craig, he says, in his singsong voice, "The defence demands disclosure of any lineup photos that might exist."

Luchenko waits a beat. "To the best of my knowledge, Your Honour, I'm aware of no such photo."

The judge insists that Luchenko "make inquiries" during the break. A few minutes later, Luchenko returns with a blurry black-and-white photo.

"Will the original be forthcoming at some point?" asks Judge Craig.

"It's not immediately available," says Luchenko. "It will be entered at some point down the line."

"Where is it now?

"The police station, across the street. There's only the one copy that I'm aware of. I haven't seen the original copy myself."

"It should be made available. Your friend needs it for cross-examination."

"My friend can go across. I don't know where it is at this time."

"The police will refuse to give me what they consider a piece of evidence," White protests. "It must come through the Crown."

"They may hand it over if my friend makes the request," says Luchenko.

"Mr. Luchenko," says Judge Craig, "produce it. I'll wait for as long as it's necessary for it to be produced."

Fifteen minutes later, Luchenko returns with a photo in hand and passes it to White. Before Henry can catch more than a glimpse—a head on a body; handcuffs!—White's handing it to Miss Browning, she's identifying Henry as #12, and the clerk's marking it Exhibit One and filing it away. Henry's seen all he needs to, though—enough to know the depth of the conspiracy against him and the extremes to which the state will go to frame him.

Miss Browning testifies that all the women sat around, talking, before the lineup. They kept the discussion general, she says, "so as not to prejudice the case." Denying that it would've been "natural" to focus on the "struggling" man in the lineup, she says that, in her drive to be fair, his struggling "hadn't registered on me in that sense." Agreeing that some of the foils were likely plainclothes police officers, she's asked whether a clue might have been the smiles on their faces.

"They weren't looking like that. They were quite straight, doing their best to present their faces to us."

"Was #12 in a chokehold throughout the lineup?"

"For a long time, he was limp—head down and slouching, legs just sort of hanging there. When they realized we couldn't see him, they pulled his head back—making it distorted and stretched."

Asked again why she originally picked #18, Miss Browning says, "Because he had lots of black hair. Quite honestly, I was terrified."

• • •

LUCHENKO ASKS THE next complainant, Miss Cardozo, whether she sees her attacker in court.

No, she says.

Damn right. Enough is enough.

Asked what she wrote on her ballot, Miss Cardozo says her comment was, "The voice of #12 appears to be that of the person who attacked me." Asked whether #12 is present in court, she says—surprise, surprise—yes.

When White says he'll allow "his friend" to introduce into evidence the statement of Miss Davies, a woman Luchenko didn't even bother asking to identify her attacker, Henry interrupts. Banging his fist on the table, he demands that the preliminary hearing be waived so that he can go straight to trial.

"You'll have to discuss that with your lawyer," says Judge Craig.

"I don't want to discuss it with him," says Henry. "I don't even want him. You guys are making a joke of me. I want the production of statements. I want to see all the statements against me."

"It's not something I can order. It's not something that can be done unless the Crown agrees to it."

"'Cause it's just turning into a joke," says Henry, "and I'm not a joke!"

• • •

ON OCTOBER 29, 1982, day two of the preliminary hearing, Henry's out of his seat before White's finished laying out his pens in perfect symmetry.

Jabbing the air with his finger, the judge goes all red-faced. "You remember what I told you on day one? By your conduct, you're ruining any defence you may have. Act like this in front of a jury, and they'll string you up."

"I don't got no defence. This fucking guy's no help. I got no defence. Fuck off, White! Get away from me."

"What I'm going to do," says Judge Craig, "is recess the court for a short while."

• • •

IN A SECURE courthouse interview room with a sheriff standing guard outside, White tells Henry, "Settle down, my boy." Chuckling, he adds, "If you don't, they'll start covering the courtroom door window with cardboard. They'll make up some excuse—tell you it's to avoid the complainants getting a good look at you before you testify."

Sure, asshole: keep the star chamber proceedings secret. Be my guest.

The rest of the day passes in a blur—four more complainants not even asked by the Crown to identify him. The judge has had it, too— slumped shoulders, drooping eyelids. Henry wishes he could give him a jolt of Oakalla's lead paint fumes—that and all the other revolting prison smells. Better than smelling salts any day. See how Mr. Straight-Lace likes spending a night in a shithole like that.

After adjourning the hearing until Monday, November 1, Judge Craig rises to his feet. Everybody else does, too.

Henry, as he's being cuffed, catches a glimpse of Luchenko. He's miming a jumpshot at a pretend basket. So old Blue 3 thinks it's going to be a slam dunk, does he? Well, Ivan Henry's got news for him. Death and taxes ain't the only sure things in this here life. God knows he's innocent and, in the end, God's plan includes laying bare this conspiracy for all to see.

Bugger them all. Their case has more holes than a sieve. We'll see who gets the last laugh. Was it Yogi Berra who said, "It ain't over 'til the fat lady sings?"

CHAPTER 5

PROBABLE CAUSE

When the preliminary hearing resumes, Miss Fields, a twenty-eight-year-old law student, testifies that she can't "positively identify" her attacker.

At this point, Ivan Henry jumps up and proclaims, "I'm done with this trial."

Shooting him an icy stare, Judge Craig says, "Mr. Henry, this is not a trial. My sole task is to determine whether probable cause exists. I have no rights—"

"Well, I do," says Henry. "I have my *Charter* rights and you're not giving them to me." At Oakalla, he's also been studying the *Charter of Rights and Freedoms*, which came into effect that spring. He's damn near got it memorized.

"And what are they?"

"A full and fair public hearing, for one. I'm entitled to the production of all statements, all the evidence they've got against me. I don't got nothing, just this guy writing down what these people are saying."

"You're asking for what are known as particulars—production of the statements, etcetera. I have no authority to order them. I can't even go into the question of whether these are credible witnesses."

"Well, I'm not getting a fair hearing here."

"The point is not whether you're getting a fair hearing. It's whether you're getting a hearing according to the law."

"No matter who represents my client at trial," says White, bowing and scraping, "he'll want the advantage of having preliminary hearing transcripts."

"Conduct this hearing without me," Henry says. "I don't know these people, and I don't need to be here. I ain't here anyway."

• • •

"IT WAS PITCH dark when he came in," testifies Miss Simpson, regarding her May 1981 attack. "I'm thinking, 'Oh, he's going to rape me,' but you're trying hard to put that out of your mind and hope that it was something else." After describing her assailant as having hair that's "black, very dark—a perm gone wrong . . . crinkly . . . kind of a halo effect," she says he had an odour—just like a man she saw on the bus a day or two later. "He smelled the same," she said, "and it just about made me throw up."

Luchenko asks, "So, you see that man in court today?"

"I can't say I could identify that man a hundred percent sure because . . . the conditions under which I saw him, you know, and he may have changed his appearance somewhat after a year and a half."

"Well, give us your opinion about what you see."

"It could be the man in the green pants. I can't honestly say that was him, and yet it could be. I can't—"

"You're not a hundred percent sure?"

"Well, I do not see a man that I could identify as my attacker in the courtroom at this present time."

Henry draws a deep breath. Gutsy little woman, he'll give her that. No matter how hard the prosecutor leans on her, she ain't budging. Now will they end this charade and admit they got the wrong guy?

Frowning, Luchenko consults his notes. "Did you see your attacker on any subsequent occasion?"

"Yes, sir. Two days later, he got on the same bus as me at Main and 17th. He sat opposite me in the back. He had a book, and he was using an envelope as a bookmark. It had an address on it that I remember."

"What do you remember?"

"248 East 17th."

What the hell? His address! And how could she read the writing on an envelope somebody on the bus is using as a bookmark? Jessie and the girls didn't move there until March 1982. She supposedly saw this when?

"After you got off the bus, what did you do?"

"I phoned Detective Marylyn Sims and reported it."

Two weeks later, she testifies, she saw that same man crossing Main Street at East 16th. And more than a year after the attack, at the May 1982 lineup, she wrote down "#12"—followed by a question mark—"based on voice and build."

During cross-examination, all White asks is whether she was really close enough to read an address on an envelope. When she says, "Mm-hmm," Henry almost loses it.

Nice try, but they screwed up. He didn't live at that address until ten months *after* she says she was attacked. He glares at his lawyer. Trial or not, why the hell ain't he blowing a gasket? Clearly, the bastard's part of the whole damn conspiracy to frame him.

• • •

ON MONDAY, NOVEMBER 1, day three of the preliminary hearing, Miss Horvath testifies that, when awakened by the intruder, she lifted her legs, planted her feet on his stomach, and launched him into the kitchen. When he came at her again, using his teeth to hold his turtleneck over his nose, he tried "forcing entry." But, she added, "he couldn't get an erection."

Quite the show, Henry's thinking. *Give her an Oscar.*

"In suggesting that I get on top," she says, "I was sort of pretending that I was going to try to help it along. I was really trying to get him underneath me so that I could run to the back door and get away. Though I made the break, I slipped and fell and he dragged me back to the chesterfield . . . It was only when I said, 'I'm pregnant, please . . . please don't hurt my baby'—a shot in the dark—that he fled."

Asked about her blank lineup ballot, she testifies that, though the "physique" of #12 was "very similar" to her attacker's, she was "distracted," couldn't get a "clear picture," "was not 100 percent sure."

Yet when asked if she can identify her attacker today, she says yes!

White, in cross-examination, asks how it is that, if she wasn't sure then, she's sure today.

"Because, for the first time, I can see his face full on."

Asked about the lineup, she says, "There was the odd comment, the odd sort of joke, because . . . they kept being jostled back and forth—one of them was being pulled down—because of the one being held by the police."

"And that was because they were all in handcuffs?"

"Yes."

"Have you seen any photographs of #12 between the date of the lineup and today?"

"No."

"Did you ask the prosecutor whether #12 would be in court today?"

"No."

"Was that indicated to you in any way?"

"Yes."

• • •

MISS JACOBSEN IS introduced as an "unmarried female employed as a lab technician." She testifies that, at a lineup in the fall of '81, she'd "selected, with a question mark, a man strictly because of his build."

Wait a minute. What are they talking about? There was a lineup before the lineup they tried to force me into?

At the May '82 lineup, she marked down two numbers—the "violently struggling man," based on "voice and build," and #18—"similar build only."

"Do you see the man whose voice was right?" asks Luchenko.

"Him. The accused."

"During the lineup, was your attention focused on the struggling man?"

"Because I thought it might be a set-up—play-acting—I did my best to concentrate on the other men."

"You concluded the police must have a single suspect for all the women?"

"Yes."

The Crown announces that it's out of witnesses for the day, and the proceedings are adjourned until Thursday, November 4.

This leaves Henry days to stew in his cell at Oakalla over the long-anticipated appearance of Miss Kavanagh—the woman who, according to Sergeant Howland, made a positive visual identification of him while the cops had him under surveillance.

Bring her on. This ought to be good. How could he possibly have raped her right under the noses of the Keystone Cops?

ON THURSDAY, MISS KAVANAGH, eyes downcast, is introduced by Luchenko as an "unmarried lady presently residing in New Jersey." She testifies that she spent the summer of 1982 working for a Vancouver repertory theatre company. On June 8, she fell asleep with her bedside light on. Around 3:00 a.m., she awoke to find a man crouching beside her bed.

Asked about the photo array shown to her on July 27 (see insert 4, top), she says Detective William Harkema told her it may or may not include her attacker. But then, "when my eyes landed on the bottom left, my heart just jumped out of my shirt. It was the man, and I was afraid to look at it again . . . I seemed to be having some kind of receptive aphasia. I couldn't register the photo on my brain. I kept looking at the photo and seeing almost nothing there. Though sure it was him, I knew I was leaving the country so I asked to see another photo, a larger one, so I could be absolutely certain—because of the changes in physical appearance, facial hair, hairstyle."

"Was there any information given as to how photographs are taken?"

"Bill—Detective Harkema—said not to expect your typical black-and-white mug shots. 'We here at the VPD do them a little differently,' he said. 'We take them in different places, we do them in colour, and don't worry about what the photographs look like. All you're looking at is the faces, and all you're thinking about are your reactions to them.'"

When did Harkema visit her? "He came in the morning and left in the early afternoon."

"What happened after he left?"

"I had a very strange sort of . . . like I had been terrified and horrified and, suddenly, I felt very numb and almost exhilarated . . . After eating something, I started vomiting and felt almost convulsive . . . When Bill returned the next day, I told him I didn't need to see another photo. 'Great,' he said, 'because I have no others to show you anyway.'"

In cross-examination, Miss Kavanagh testifies that, after giving the VPD a detailed description right after her attack, her only contact with the police was with Detective Sims, by phone.

"And did she ever indicate to you, in any of those phone calls," asks White, "that 'we think we're getting closer,' or 'we have a suspect,' or anything like that?"

"She said if there was anything, and that if they needed me . . . I called her continually to let her know that I was willing at any point if there was a suspect and she said that, if there was anything, they would get in touch with me."

"What was the gist of these phone calls?"

"I talked to her a great deal about my emotional distress and things like that, and she was very helpful."

"Did you discuss characteristics of the person's identity?"

"She had the statement I had made, and she told me to keep in touch with her if I had anything to add to it, so I just—I went over a few of the things with her . . . But she had the information and I would just say, well, this is something that really sticks in my mind and maybe you want to pay attention to that . . . "

"Did any police officer ask you to come to the police station prior to July 26?"

"That visit was the first contact I'd had with them since it happened. Because I wanted to do everything I could to help catch this man, I agreed to undergo hypnosis."

"When Detective Michael Barnard offered to hypnotize you, what did he say about the process?"

"I wanted to give them more details than they already had, and he said he didn't want to implant any ideas. He didn't, I can assure you. The hypnosis didn't reveal anything more than I already had as a conscious experience and I found it to be rather an emotional experience because . . . it brought back a lot of feelings about the event. I'd taken some psychology courses, so I knew what to expect . . . The next day, July 27, Detective Harkema arrived with some photos."

"You knew one of the photos might be of the suspect?"

"Yes. I had a very strong reaction to that one photo. I wanted to see one with no hair on his face, maybe a larger picture when he might have had a different physical . . . longer hair. When he returned the next day, he said there were no other pictures. I said I didn't need any."

"How long did he stay, and what did you discuss?"

"Though he arrived at 10:00 a.m., he waited until my roommate came home to pull out the folder. He left at 12:30. We chatted about things in general—him trying to relax me, also about the case. Nothing specific."

"Why not sign the photo that same day?"

"I would like to have seen another photograph . . . but I didn't need to. I knew I'd be seeing him the next day anyway, so I just waited. When he said it wasn't possible for me to see another photograph, I said it doesn't matter because I am positive about the other one."

• • •

MISS LARSON, A third-year anthropology student at the University of British Columbia, identifies "the person in the green shirt" as her attacker.

Asked by Luchenko why, at the May 12 lineup, she left her ballot blank, she says that, given her poor eyesight, she'd been "counting a lot on hearing the voice." However, the whole situation "seemed so ludicrous because a lot of people weren't taking it very seriously . . . There was this one man in the middle who was being held back by these two huge policemen. His arms were pulled back, and his head was sort of back, thrashing around, and they could barely contain him."

"Were you able to see very clearly?"

"No."

"Was that because of what was going on, or your eyesight, or a combination?"

"A combination."

"Why the long pause when you identified the accused?"

"Because it's not my life on the line," says Miss Larson. "I tried looking at him in the lineup, but I ruled him out—first, because it was too obvious. Also, I thought my attacker had some good in him. This man clearly didn't, so I decided it wasn't going to be him."

White, in his cross-examination, asks about other attempts at identification. She says that, shortly after her attack, a staff sergeant accompanied her on a walk down Main Street. "The police said there could be a suspect working within a three-block area, so we went into every shop on both sides of the street. It was very random."

"Did you indicate that anyone resembled your attacker?"

"A couple of times I thought there was something really insignificant, but I never said there was anyone I thought it could have been."

"Though you 'decided' at the lineup that #12 wasn't going to be your attacker," says White, "now you say he is?"

"In the lineup, his hair seemed a really sort of shocking red colour, quite bright red. Not as red as that of the policeman who's restraining him, but still pretty red. Plus he was violent."

"I suggest to you," says White, "there's a difference between violence and resisting the rough way he was being handled by the police?"

"No," she replies, "his strength was hyper, as in knocking down walls. The guys handcuffed to him were the only ones not laughing. It was sort of a joke to everyone else . . . A few weeks later, my mom read about a man's arrest. Two and a half weeks later, Detective Harkema phoned, asked me to meet with them. He said someone had been charged. They asked me a couple of times if I had been at the lineup and if I'd identified anyone. I assumed they'd charged the man from the lineup . . . I think they did say it was someone from the lineup who had been charged."

"You didn't seem surprised today to make the connection."

"When I look at the man sitting there and I look at the man in the lineup, I can see they're the same person, but it doesn't seem like the same person who was in the lineup . . . Another reason I didn't recognize him at the lineup was the voice. It didn't seem the same, but then I thought I should probably ignore it because he's got someone's arm around his neck."

When Miss Larson steps down from the stand, Judge Craig declares the proceedings adjourned until Monday, November 8, the date the Crown's next witness is available.

Henry's mind runs in circles. Miss Larson leaves her ballot blank at the lineup, but now fingers him? Bad enough. But Miss Kavanagh's testimony seems the biggest pile of bullshit. She was attacked while the cops had him under surveillance? Then they hypnotize her to brainwash her? If she's being paid to lie, he'll damn well run it to ground. If it's something else, he'll find that out, too.

When the trial rolls around—and White's told him that, based on her evidence alone, there will almost certainly be a trial—he'll go after her first. That should sort out this mess once and for all.

CHAPTER 6

NUMBER 12

When the preliminary hearing resumes, on November 8, 1982, Constable Lloyd Foxx, a VPD evidence technician, describes to Judge Craig the lineup he put together when Ivan Henry was first arrested. To speed things up, he says, he arranged it so that the lineup participants and the women would all enter the room at the same time. Although the usual rule is one witness per cubicle—"so as to ensure isolation"—the women were doubled up in the viewing stalls.

"Why such haste?" asks Luchenko.

"The suspect's obstructionism, Your Honour," Foxx replies, addressing the judge.

All the lineup participants, he says, were in handcuffs. After the lineup, which lasted approximately three minutes, the women left and Foxx took the photo. That's when, he says, the police foils laughed: "I don't believe that, during the lineup itself, they were smiling at all."

Luchenko asks if the photo is an accurate depiction of the lineup after the witnesses left.

"Yes," Foxx replies.

When White suggests it's unusual for the subjects of a lineup to be handcuffed together and/or restrained, Foxx agrees, again chalking it up to Henry's "obstructionism."

White asks Foxx to identify the police foils. He says that #10, #15, and #17 are Major Crime Detectives Esko Kajander, Mike Barnard, and Freddie Johns. The man on Henry's left, #1, is Constable Bob Cooper, while #21 and #18 were suspects on other charges. The four uniforms, including the one peeping out from behind the foils? Members of the jail staff who were on duty that night.

Corporal David Baker, acting jail sergeant on May 12, 1982, testifies that because of Henry's resistance, he had a police constable pick a number at random and place it over Henry's head. After hand-cuffing the participants to each other and confirming that the floodlights were on, he led everyone into the lineup room. During the lineup, "Mr. Henry was performing. He had his head down. He was swearing at one point, very uncooperative. It was a very difficult lineup."

Once the lineup photo was taken, Baker testifies, he led the men back to the booking area and removed their handcuffs.

Asked when the "physical restraint" began, he says, "Immediately after the lineup itself had concluded. When Constable Foxx asked Henry to smile for the camera, the police people smiled."

Yes, he testifies, Exhibit One—the lineup photograph—is accurate.

Asked in cross-examination whether he was acting on instructions from Detectives Campbell and Sims, Baker says he was. When he told them Henry was being "resistant," they instructed him to run the lineup anyway. Asked whether any "formal charge" was laid, either before or after the lineup, he says no.

When White suggests that he failed to consider selecting men with characteristics similar to Henry's, Baker testifies that the police foils were chosen based on availability and for "security reasons," as opposed to their similarities to the suspect. Under the circumstances—given the violence exhibited by Henry—he says it was a "very fair lineup."

"Fair, my ass," Henry snarls, as the sheriffs handcuff him and lead him out. He might as well have saved his breath. White's too busy hob-nobbing with Luchenko to even bother looking his way.

• • •

ON NOVEMBER 10, Miss Nielson describes her attacker's hair as "dark black," and Miss McCarthy testifies that she'd know her attacker's voice if she heard it again. Neither woman is asked to identify Henry.

Miss Pavlovik, who says she was raped in November 1980, testifies that she didn't get a good look at her attacker's face but that the "man over there" possesses the "right colour of hair and about the right build."

Testifying that she was out of town at the time of the May 12, 1982, lineup, Miss Pavlovik says she had attended a lineup in the fall of 1981 (see insert 5, top), at which time she was "certain" that the man wearing #12 was her attacker. "He had the right size, height, hair, voice—they made them speak—everything. When Detective Sims asked me how I could be so certain, I said it was a gut feeling. It looked like him, and his voice was very familiar."

What the hell, she's talking about somebody who wore #12 in a different lineup! If there even was a lineup in 1981, Henry sure wasn't in it. But when he elbows White—*Stand up! This is bullshit!*—the lawyer, barely looking up from his doodling, raises his hand as if to say, "Just hold on."

In cross-examination, White asks Miss Pavlovik whether she and the other women at the 1981 lineup discussed what they'd seen. "Not that night," she says, "but a couple of months earlier, twelve or so of us met."

"For what purpose?"

"Detectives Sims and Campbell suggested we meet with several police officers to see if we could come up with any similarities, anything that would help them identify the guy." She testifies that, based on each woman's recollection of her experience, a police artist drew a composite picture.

What struck her most about #12 in the 1981 lineup?

Why, Henry wonders, *are they talking about a lineup I wasn't in? And why did she pick #12 in that lineup? Did that #12 look like me? If so, who the hell was he?*

"Overall, I thought it was him—hair, height, build, etcetera, and the voice clinched it . . . I told Detective Sims I couldn't swear to it, and she said she'd get back to me."

White asks whether, before this preliminary hearing, she knew she was one of several women who'd be testifying. She replies yes and agrees that she "knew that the person charged with the offences would be in the courtroom today."

"I take it that, when the prosecutor asked if you saw that person in the courtroom today, you'd twigged to the fact that I was defence counsel and the man sitting beside me, in prison greens, was the accused?"

"I figured it out, yes."

"Good for you," Henry mumbles under his breath. "You're a genius."

• • •

WHEN COURT RESUMES on November 12, Miss O'Reilly, whose assault took place on May 14, 1981, and who is now an actress in an amateur theatre company back east, testifies that it was too dark to get a good look at her attacker and that he spoke in a "very measured, slow way, as though either on drugs or disguising his voice on purpose."

Long before the May 1982 lineup, she says, she'd moved to Ontario.

In cross-examination, White asks about the earlier lineup, in 1981. "Did you attend a meeting with the other female persons in your situation where the trauma that you experienced and they experienced were discussed in the same room?"

"Yes, in the summer of 1981."

Miss Ramirez, the next witness, testifies that, although she was in Vancouver in May 1982, no one invited her to the lineup. At the lineup she did attend, in October 1981, she didn't pick anyone.

Asked by Luchenko to describe the man who attacked her, Miss Ramirez says he wore beige cord pants, a brown turtleneck, a brown toque, and brown gloves. A hairdresser by trade, she said the assailant's "reddish-brown," shoulder-length hair was "windblown"—"an ungrown perm or natural curls that haven't been conditioned." Describing him as "twenty-six or twenty-seven" years old and five-foot-nine or five-foot-ten, she says he smelled of cigar smoke. He had a "lisp," but it was "nothing distinct." After poking his genitals through a sheet wrapped around his waist, he made her take his penis in her mouth and "do what he asked."

Luchenko asks if she sees her assailant in court today.

"Yes, I'm sure of it."

Had she seen him again before today? Yes, she says—on January 4, 1982, in Shaw's Market, five minutes from her home in the Mount Pleasant neighbourhood. "The man in the checkout lineup asked, 'Don't I know you from somewhere?' I said, 'No, you don't,' and ran out the door."

Luchenko asks whether she called the police. "No, I was scared. When I looked for him, I couldn't find him anywhere, so I didn't think it would be worth my while."

Cross-examined by White, Miss Ramirez says that, shortly after the assault, Detectives Sims and Campbell took her to three different courtrooms in the Provincial Courthouse on Main Street to see whether she recognized any of the accused. As well, Detective William Harkema and Sergeant Gordon Howland came to talk to her—over a year later, in September 1982.

"You say you got a half-decent look at this person, yet the police never showed you any photos?"

"Except for in September. They showed me twelve to sixteen pictures—not mug shots, more like tiny passport pictures, on a piece of cardboard. I said one of them looks similar. They didn't ask me to initial it."

How many women were at the earlier lineup? "Twelve or thirteen. We went in two groups."

Miss Ramirez agrees with White that it is "obvious" that he is the defence counsel and the accused is the man seated beside him.

White asks about other times she saw her attacker. "Before the supermarket incident," she says, "someone tried breaking into my bedroom window—got it open four to five inches before I woke up. Possibly it was him, I'm not too sure. Though I told the police it might have been my attacker, they didn't come to take fingerprints."

Why didn't she report the supermarket incident? "I had already tried three times beforehand and they hadn't . . . One police officer had said I was hallucinating and didn't know what I was talking about. Another said someone was playing a prank on me . . . "

"How many sightings in total?"

"Five. The first one in November. Someone was at the window, motioning me to come closer. I screamed. I don't know who it was. I called the police, and they brought their dogs. December was the next time, then January. The fifth occurred at the end of March/early April 1982. A man was standing at my kitchen window and didn't have anything on from the calves up to the lower chest."

Miss Ramirez says she called the police and they came.

"So the only time you didn't call the police," White asks, "was the supermarket incident?"

"Yes."

"And that's the time you got the clearest picture of the person?"

"Yes."

"When was the first time you told anyone, other than your mother, about the five incidents?"

"When I met with the prosecutor."

• • •

WHEN LUCHENKO ANNOUNCES the end of his case, Judge Craig notes that the Crown has called no evidence concerning two of the complainants named in the information. After a back-and-forth discussion that's lost on Henry, those two charges are dropped.

At this point, Henry sighs audibly. *What the hell difference does it make how many more women testify? The testimony has already revealed dozens of lies and errors and contradictions. And why are they even talking about a 1981 lineup? Luchenko's got nothing on him. The case against him is a joke.*

The judge asks White whether Henry has anything to say. White tries to stop him, but Henry is having none of it. "I didn't get a fair hearing," he says angrily. "I'll say that. I expect the jury to give me a better hearing. I think twelve people will decide that. And that's really all I got to say. I had lots to say, but I'm just too emotional to say a thing."

"Your assumption about the jury giving you a fair hearing is a proper one. That's what everybody believes. Sit down again."

After the Crown has made its submissions, Judge Craig—who's never once, Henry's sure, put pen to paper—delivers his judgment from the bench:

"There was, throughout the testimony, remarkable similarity of events. It obliges me, then, in considering those counts where a positive identification was not made, to conclude, the only conclusion that could be reached on a preliminary inquiry, that the accused is the person who committed the offence in each of those other counts as well. Accordingly, the Crown has made out its case on this preliminary hearing, and I commit the accused for trial with respect to each of the counts other than the two withdrawn by the Crown and, therefore, discharged."

Committed on all of them? Even the ones that happened when he was nowhere near Vancouver? When he was under surveillance? Even the ones where the women couldn't identify the attacker, or gave descriptions that didn't match his?

Henry watches in disbelief as White and Luchenko shake hands. Taking out their calendars, they huddle together, cordially discussing possible dates for the trial.

CHAPTER 7

KILL ALL THE LAWYERS

L ocked up in Oakalla, Ivan Henry waits in line for the only pay phone. Finally, the con in front of him hangs up and it's his turn.

"John White here."

"It's me, Henry."

"Ivan? How you doing, man? Not to worry, I'm already drafting another demand."

"You're done."

"My letter to Mike's in the mail seeking disclosure of everything: victim statements, particulars, medical and other reports—serology, hair, fibre, you name it."

"You've got no balls, White. You're fired. *Comprendy-vous?*"

"Hold the phone, Ivan."

Aware of the cons lined up behind him—mumbling impatiently, shifting from foot to foot—Henry can't help milking the moment. Finally, after weeks of trying, he's got the little weasel's attention.

"Like I said," White says, in that whiny way that drives Henry up the wall, "preliminary hearings are strictly pro forma—a dry run, so to speak. Once we're in front of a solid judge, a jury, the bedrock of our system, they'll sweep all this nonsense aside."

"You heard me. Send me my file. You know the address."

Henry slams down the receiver. When one of the men in line "accidentally" bumps him, he picks up his pace but otherwise doesn't react. The last inmate who hogged the phone ended up with second-degree butter burns to his face.

In his cell, Henry painstakingly works on a handwritten letter to Legal Aid, explaining why he's done with White. "The man would write something down on paper, then he'd doodle—automatic writing, so to speak. He was only pretending to listen. When the coffee break ended, he didn't cross-examine from that page. He hardly asked a thing. His antics were prearranged and, from what I could see, the witnesses were involved as well . . . "

Henry also works on his alibi statement. Luchenko had told him at the end of the preliminary hearing to file it "ASAP or else."

With no idea where to begin, Henry scours the prison library. The same old definition keeps popping up—namely, that the defence of "alibi"—Latin for "somewhere else"—is a defence based on the premise that the accused is truly innocent. In 1926, a justice of the Quebec Superior Court stated, "Once [the defence of alibi] is introduced, the evidence of the prosecution is, for the moment, suspended, and the judge or jury is bound to examine the evidence offered in support of the alibi, since it is clear that, if the alibi be established, the accused could not be the guilty party."[1]

Unless he files the statement in a timely way, and with enough details to allow the cops to investigate it—the cases are crystal-clear on this—the trial judge has the power to rule inadmissible his alibi evidence.[2]

Henry needs to track down people who will back him up. He starts blitzing every phone book in the joint, but half the pages are missing. No surprise. The grapevine has it that the general-population inmates, infuriated with plans to integrate them with low-lifes (like himself) in protective custody—snitches, rapists, pedophiles, and "bad cops"—are stockpiling all things flammable. Just yesterday, some young bug ran naked through the range, waving a makeshift bomb in the air and hollering, "This dump's on the edge of a volcano!" He was taken down and straitjacketed by the SWAT (Special Weapons and Tactics) team.

Thank God for his memory—he pretty much remembers where he was on the dates most of the crimes went down. The list of people able to back him up is long—contractors he worked for, friends at whose homes he crashed, even the boys at the Honda dealer who serviced his car. He asks them to mail records that show the exact dates he'd been without wheels.

After signing and dating his alibi statement, Henry hands it to a guard for mailing and keeps his fingers crossed that the bastard actually delivers it.

Right after the preliminary hearing, he'd applied to the Supreme Court—by way of something he'd just learned about called a habeas corpus application—to have the lineup photo produced for "examination by a Judge of the Superior Court sitting for his inspection in said case." The usual goal of a habeas corpus (literally "you must have the body") application is to have a person being held in custody brought before a judge to determine whether lawful grounds exist for their continued detention. Henry figures this procedure makes as much sense as anything else. One way or another, he's got to get his hands on that lineup photo and have it tested for tampering.

In mid-December 1982, a Supreme Court justice dismisses the application.

• • •

ON CHRISTMAS DAY, Ivan Henry—sick with a vicious flu, despondent that he's locked up when he should be playing Santa for his girls—closes his eyes, confesses his sins to God, and falls asleep hoping he'll never wake up.

• • •

ON JANUARY 1, 1983, Henry writes to Luchenko demanding full disclosure: particulars of each count, copies of the exhibits, witness statements, forensic reports, etcetera. Forget about the spineless efforts of White; he means business.

Ten days and three unanswered letters later, he sends a copy of his latest demand letter to Vancouver's Regional Crown Counsel office. In it, he explains that production and details of the lineup photograph are necessary "so that the accused may conduct scientific or other test or examination." He might as well have saved his breath.

He does, however, finally get the preliminary hearing transcripts—six volumes in a thick manila envelope, pushed, one at a time, through the food slot in his cell. In his excitement, Henry dumps them onto his bed and sees something fall to the floor. When he takes a close look, his heart almost goes through his chest. Thank God—the lineup photo!

Held to the light, it's even worse than he suspected—in the photo, he looks like a mannequin with a face pasted on. His face. Nothing else belongs to him—not that tightly coiled, iridescent red hair; not the moustache. Except, when he studies it more closely, the work pants. *His* work pants; he'd know them anywhere. He'd bought them for a song because of the kinky seam, which starts at the side and ends up in the middle. They were among his personal effects at the time of his arrest in July. How in the hell did they come to be put on the mannequin ten weeks earlier?

Fired up anew, he drafts an appeal from the order committing his case to trial. If only he can convince the BC Supreme Court that there was no identification evidence on most of the counts, those charges, at least, should be dropped. Having turned the joint upside down for legal authority on the subject, this much he knows: "no evidence" on an essential element of the charge can never amount to "sufficient evidence."[2] That's just the start, though. If he can convince the court that the lineup photo's bogus, the whole case will be thrown out on the basis of state corruption.

Day after day, working by the light of a dim hallway bulb, using scrounged pieces of paper and dried-up felt pens dipped in water, he outlines his case. He slams Judge Craig for depriving him of key documents; slams his lawyer for "conspiring" against him; invokes equal protection, equal benefits—equal everything. He cites case after case from the *Criminal Code*, section after section from the *Charter of Rights and Freedoms*. He saves his trump card for last: "I know positively the lineup photograph is a fraud, a fake and a fabrication."

He seals the homemade envelope with masking tape, and labels it SOLICITOR/CLIENT MAIL: PRIVILEGED. Not that it will make any difference: the guards will mock him for claiming to be his own lawyer and dissect his mail before it goes out.

The preliminary hearing transcripts provide fertile ground for cross-examination at trial. Forget that they're full of errors and omissions. Entire question-and-answer portions are missing. Words have been switched around. Names have been added, other names taken away. Late into each night, Henry works on the questions he plans to ask each witness. He can't wait to expose the duplicity of the women and the police.

•••

JOLTED BY RAPPING on his cell bars, Henry jumps up. His copy of the *Criminal Code* goes flying. Luckily, he's applied enough Scotch tape to hold the cracked spine together.

"Some suits here to see you," the guard says, handcuffing him.

After passing through all the moving barriers and undergoing as many pat-downs, Henry is ushered into an interview room in Centre Block.

"Meet Richard Peck," says Legal Aid's Rod Holloway, "one of the finest criminal lawyers in the country. Consider yourself lucky—he's signed on to represent you."[4]

Henry sizes him up. Rumpled and dishevelled, Peck looks like the sort of the man who mismatches his socks and forgets his briefcase on the escalator. Probably forgets court dates, too. A lock of limp black hair keeps flopping into his eyes.

Henry hands over the photo. "Mr. Peck," he says, "I'm being framed. If the women were raped—a big if, I might add—they've got the wrong guy. That photo you're looking at is fake."

Peck raises his eyebrows. He studies it, impassive, then slides it back across the table. "We need only create a reasonable doubt. Nothing more, nothing less."

"Reasonable doubt," scoffs Henry. "To hell with that. I need you to prove the photo's fake. I wasn't in the lineup and anyone who says otherwise is lying. I need to find out who's involved in this conspiracy against me, and why."

Tenting his fingers, Peck gives a little speech about the "presumption of innocence," the "heavy onus" on the Crown to prove "guilt beyond a reasonable doubt"—the usual legal bullshit. Henry listens impatiently.

"Mr. Peck," he says, "you can be my lawyer, but only on certain conditions. Go after Luchenko, White, the cops—everyone. I was never handcuffed in no lineup, and no rapes occurred. The photo's nothing but a head stuck on a body. I need it placed back into the proceedings because it's fabricated and, as such, would completely contaminate the trial."

"To win," Peck says, "it is not necessary to prove conspiracy. I'm here to discuss realistic strategies regarding how best to achieve an acquittal." Perhaps in response to Henry's skeptical look, he repeats his last sentence: "I'm here to discuss realistic strategies regarding how best to achieve an acquittal."

Jesus, is this guy part of the conspiracy? Won't anyone listen? Cursing under his breath, Henry signals to the guard stationed outside the door: meeting over.

Back in his cell, Henry realizes in a panic that the photo's missing. Did Peck take it? Did he leave it in the interview room? Drop it? A sympathetic guard retraces his steps with him, and he finds it on the floor. *Thank God,* he thinks, clutching it to his chest. *If I lose this, I'll never get out of this shithole.*

• • •

ON JANUARY 17, 1983, Henry meets with Dr. Joseph Noone, the court-appointed psychiatrist. He could have said no to the court order, but he's compos mentis sane, so what the heck? Not that he's thrilled to discuss his background. Indeed, for days after the interview, in the dead of night in his cell at Oakalla, images keep rearing up unbidden—images of Vukusha, his stepfather, smothering him with a pillow; smashing his face into the table when he and Darwyn, his big brother, drank their juice too noisily; stealing the food they'd stashed in the basement. A concentration-camp survivor, Vukusha wasn't always mean. Henry was actually sad when the old man died, only to feel stupid years later when his mother told him she'd filed a restraining order against Vukusha after he'd threatened to kill Ivan and his brother with a knife.

After Vukusha died, their mother—unable to handle her increasingly lawless sons—fobbed them off on an uncle. When the uncle wasn't tanning their hides, he was chasing them into the cellar and locking the door.

Far worse than any of the beatings rained down by his uncle was the day the delivery man walked through the unlocked door of his mother's apartment and found him in the bedroom—just waking up, vulnerable and alone . . .

Fuck Dr. Noone and his probing questions. Ain't a man alive, shrink or no shrink, he's letting peer into his soul.

A few days after the interview, Henry reads Dr. Noone's opinion letter with satisfaction. "Mr. Henry is able," the psychiatrist writes, "to comprehend the nature and object of the proceedings, and to have the capacity to instruct and relate to counsel . . . Mr. Henry wishes to conduct his own defence and, although he describes a somewhat private logic to support his judgment in this regard, there is no evidence of contamination by mental disorder but, rather, that volitionally and of his own free will he believes that this is in his own best interest."

• • •

ON JANUARY 26, 1983, a sheriff delivers Ivan Henry to the new Superior Law Courts in downtown Vancouver "to discuss the appointment of counsel." Led into the courtroom of the chief justice, he breathes in the scent of brass and polished oak and new carpets—a far cry from the recirculated BO and clogged drainpipes at Oakalla.

When Chief Justice Allan McEachern—a red-nosed, heavy-set man—walks in, Luchenko, Peck, and Holloway nod and bow like crows on a fence. Biding his time until everyone's said his piece, Henry finally gets his chance.

"In order for the real truth to be revealed," he says, "I need to represent myself. My lawyers to date have caused me nothing but grief."

"Mr. Henry," says Mr. Justice McEachern, raising his thick eyebrows, "you need a lawyer. You must have one. These charges are very serious. You're ignorant as to the law. The trial will be complex—a multitude of witnesses, difficult legal issues."

"Don't get me wrong, sir," says Henry, "nothing personal, but look where my preliminary hearing lawyer got me. And this here Peck fellow? He refuses to take on the establishment, too. There ain't no one I can trust but myself."

Again, the chief justice cautions Henry about his need for a lawyer. Again, Henry objects.

"Very well, Mr. Henry," says His Lordship, after the discussion has gone around in more circles, "but consider yourself well and duly warned. You're a stubborn man, and a mighty foolish one at that. Enough of all that, let's set aside some dates for the trial."

• • •

IN MID-FEBRUARY, TEN days before the trial, Luchenko advises Henry that the Crown will be proceeding on all counts. Henry feels like he's been sucker-punched. He thought the Crown would drop most of them—those without a shred of evidence linking him to the crimes. He's done no preparation. No matter; he knows their evidence by heart. Besides, his cross-examination of Miss Kavanagh will be worth the price of admission. After White's inept cross-examination, it will be a pleasure to expose her pack of lies.

Then, a few days before the trial's set to begin, he's informed that Miss Kavanagh "will not leave the United States to give evidence." No explanation. Nothing. Subpoenas have no effect outside Canada, and that's that. Or so Luchenko would have him believe.

Kneeling in prayer the night before his trial, Henry presses his hands together. "Please, dear Jesus, keep my photo safe from harm. With Your Blessed Lady's help, let me show the world I'm innocent. In God's name, amen."

He can't sleep. He's pumped. At last, his chance to stand before a jury of his peers, people who will smell the stench of BS from miles away. He's going to win this, the biggest fight of his life, no matter what it takes.

Ivan William Mervin Henry. I.W.M.H. When he was little, before all the horrors, his mother told him what his initials really stood for: "I will make history." He'll make her proud. His mother, Jessie, their girls—he'll make them all proud.

CHAPTER 8

THE MAN ON THE BUS

The Law Courts building in downtown Vancouver is a striking, seven-storey structure designed by legendary architect Arthur Erickson. A green-tinted glass roof covers more than an acre of space devoted to the administration of justice. The public circulation areas are open to the roof, forming a large, naturally lit indoor atrium. On the morning of February 28, 1983, thirty-five courtrooms await the day's parade of miscreants.

Marched along the hallway for transporting prisoners, Ivan Henry tries to catch a glimpse of the Great Hall below. All he can make out through the translucent glass blocks are human-sized smudges of washed-out colour. Some of them, he imagines, are prospective jurors, their names picked at random from voters' lists.

In Courtroom 62, Mr. Justice John Bouck takes his place, robes swishing out behind him. A square-jawed man with trimmed eyebrows and pink fingernails buffed to a shine, Bouck has a little tête-à-tête with Madam Clerk, then frowns in Henry's direction.

Wild-haired and scruffy, Henry makes the best of his civvy duds. When he said no to the prison greens he'd been forced to wear at the preliminary hearing, they handed him back the very same work pants—complete with paint stains and warped seam—featured in the lineup photo.

From the prisoner's box, Henry can barely catch the low hum of conversation between Judge Bouck and Luchenko—something about "severance." In due course, Luchenko hands Henry a ten-count indictment, fresh from the photocopy machine. First seventeen counts, now ten? More smoke and mirrors beyond his comprehension. Henry vows to make them produce every last information and indictment.

He's ushered into another courtroom. This one seems huge. No windows—the air is hot, dry, dusty. Some jurors are seated, and others are still standing; they pretend not to notice as the sheriff removes his cuffs. Henry closes his eyes and sends a quick prayer to the Big Guy upstairs.

One at a time, Madam Clerk—a lady with rouged cheeks and coal-black hair scraped into a tight bun—selects jurors at random: a man with huge knuckle joints; a mousy little lady pressing her handbag into her ribs; a wispy-haired senior holding a bag of wool in her gnarled hands; a man scowling so hard, you'd think he'd been stiffed for his cab fare. Each time, the clerk asks Henry if he wants to "challenge" anyone.

"Why would I?" says Henry. "I don't even know them."

After a dozen people have been chosen, he stands and addresses them. "The only reason to step down is if you're not indifferent as to me and the Queen. Otherwise, yous all is fine."

Henry smiles at them, a jury of his peers. Screw the judges and lawyers and their legal bullshit. After all the subterfuge and manoeuvring, he gets to make a direct appeal to his fellow citizens. Who among them won't see that an innocent man is being framed?

• • •

THE FIRST TWO and a half days of the trial are spent conducting voir dires—mini-hearings during which, in the absence of the jury, the admissibility of contested evidence is debated.

On March 2, Judge Bouck rules, across the board, in favour of the Crown. Ignoring the bad feeling in his gut, Henry tells himself this result is to be expected. All Judge Bouck really said was that, since the victims complained to others soon after they were assaulted, the evidence of those complaints should be admissible.

At last, the jury is recalled and Luchenko opens the case for the Crown: "Testimony will indicate the complainants were attacked by a knife-wielding male intruder in their ground-level apartments late at night, almost always after they had fallen asleep. In most of the incidents, the intruder used a distinctive modus operandi in which he claimed to be looking for a woman who had 'ripped off' either him or his bosses. The intruder would then force the complainant to engage in sexual intercourse or fellatio, often saying her compliance was required as assurance that she would not go to the police. I will henceforth refer to this as the 'rip-off MO.'"

On March 3, the first Crown witness, Miss Ramirez, the hairdresser, is examined by Luchenko. At the close of direct examination, Henry insists that the jury be excused. No one thinks to ask Miss Ramirez to step outside.

Before repeating, for what seems the hundredth time, his disclosure request, he complains that the lawyers in the prisoner elevator make crude remarks about him—especially in front of their female clients. Then he demands copies of the missing arrest forms—the informations and indictments.

"Under what authority do they keep changing?" he asks. "Where's the proof that the other counts have been dropped?"

Luchenko assures the court that the Crown is doing its best to meet the accused's demands. The Crown, he points out, can't protect Henry from taunts. As for the non-indictment charges, they have been severed, not withdrawn. The distinction—the fact that they can spring to life at any time, as opposed to being dropped for good—is mumbo-jumbo to Henry's ears.

"Anything to say about that, Mr. Henry?"

"I don't know what's the excuse," he says. "It seems I never had any charges. I mean all I know is that I'm sitting here, and I keep coming here every day, for what reason? They could be bringing any charges . . . Where are the people? Ramirez doesn't know me. I don't know her from a hole in the head. But if you guys want me, fuck, kill me, it doesn't matter. I mean, you're doing it to my heart every day."

"My Lord," says Luchenko, addressing the judge, "I wonder if the witness should be present while this is going on."

"Well, it is all over now so far as I'm concerned," says Judge Bouck, shooting an apologetic look at Miss Ramirez. "There's nothing I can do about those things. He has been supplied with the evidence . . . Just be quiet now, Mr. Henry. I don't know anything about any alleged conspiracy. I have to have some evidence about that, rather than your allegations."

"I will get some."

When Henry insists that Miss Ramirez produce her social insurance number—to prove her true identity—Judge Bouck tells him to move on.

He begins his cross-examination. "Are you really saying," he asks, "that when the guy poked his pecker through the hole, you didn't know the meaning of 'giving head'?"

"Yes."

Out of nowhere, the image of King Herod beheading John the Baptist springs to Henry's mind. "Well, if John the Baptist were here, he'd probably give you his head."

The judge cautions him.

"How can you be so sure that the man left through the back, as opposed to the front, of the house?" Henry asks her. When she says she'd have noticed someone passing by her window, a mere twenty centimetres above the ground, he says, "Oh, I see, it's the cat we're dealing with now."

"No, we're dealing with the man."

Not sure where to go next, Henry takes a stab at humour. "So your fish died, poor thing. Did you give it to the cat?"

Peering over his glasses, Judge Bouck tells Henry to "get on to something that is relevant."

"Do all voices sound the same to you?" Henry asks.

"No," Miss Ramirez answers.

Well, well, if she's decided to be honest, he'll test it. Speaking as both an apprentice stylist and a one-time barber in Stony Mountain Penitentiary, he asks, "You say you're a hairdresser?"

"I most certainly am," she says, tossing back her hair as if to prove it.

"What if a lady came and said I'd like a right bang done?"

"I'd curl it to the right side."

"If she asked, 'Where is my subconscious gland?' what would you say?"

"I wouldn't be able to say."

"It's in your head," says Henry. "It's a gland that holds all those little things together. In fact," he adds, without missing a beat, "you did give him head in the end?"

"Yes," she says, in a whisper.

"Disgraceful, isn't it," says Henry, "that I must be standing here listening to that. So what did happen to your little fish?"

"My Lord," says Luchenko, "this is intended to embarrass and torture the witness."

"What is the relevance of the question?" demands Judge Bouck.

"She says the fish is the only one she lived with. I want to know what happened to it, because I don't want anyone to be lonely."

Henry asks Miss Ramirez how, when she'd looked at her attacker for "all of six to eight seconds," she could be sure it was him.

"I'm sure."

"I'm happy you are. I will think about you the rest of my days in jail, and I will say, 'She was sure of it.' You're swearing under oath that what you say today is the truth, the whole truth, and nothing but the truth, so help you God?"

"I-I'm—"

"As God always says in His Bible, 'Anybody that uses my Bible to swear an oath shall be cursed for the rest of his life.' Thank you, I've run out of questions."

• • •

WHEN THE NEXT witness, Miss Simpson, takes the stand, associate Crown counsel Judith Milliken, Luchenko's sidekick, wastes no time getting her to "clarify" her preliminary hearing evidence.

"Why," Milliken asks, "did you describe your attacker at the preliminary hearing as having 'black, very dark hair'? Do you recall what colour your attacker's hair was, or what was your impression?"

"I thought it was black," Miss Simpson says. "It seemed very dark."

"I note that you're wearing glasses today. How is your eyesight without glasses?"

"It used to be great, but I have become myopic. If I take them off, I can see those people over there, but not as clearly as if I have my glasses on."

Pointing at Henry, Miss Simpson says she'd know his voice anywhere. "Near the end of my preliminary hearing testimony, the accused was very agitated—his voice was really husky, monotone. That's when it struck me that this was his voice, not so much at the lineup."

"Based on his voice in the lineup, at the preliminary hearing, and at the voir dire, how would you compare it to the voice of the man who attacked you?"

"I'd know his voice anywhere. It's that man. It was at the preliminary hearing when I became sure it was him. At the May lineup, his hair was sort of red. I didn't get as clear a look at his face as I can now, but he is the right size and build, and he is right-handed, which the gentleman was. At the hearing, his face was a lot fuller. He's changed his appearance."

Milliken asks Miss Simpson about her vision as of May 12, 1982.

"Just that week," she says, "I broke my glasses for working up close on things. When I took them to the optician, he said I should be wearing glasses for distance." She adds that her eyes "were apparently very bad."

Receiving a nod from Luchenko, Milliken takes her seat.

Knocking over his chair in his haste to speak, Henry thrusts his photo—the five-by-seven-inch lineup photo Luchenko sent him—in Miss Simpson's face. After she's identified Henry as #12 and Judge Bouck has marked the photo "Trial Exhibit One," the jurors pass it around.

"If you people hold that up to the light," says Henry, "you'll see a shirt's been placed on top of that picture."

"You can't give evidence," says Judge Bouck. "Not unless you take the witness box. The picture speaks for itself."

Turning to Miss Simpson, Henry says, "I might remind you I was never in that lineup [referring to the one that took place in 1981], so whoever you picked certainly wasn't me."

"You can't give evidence from the floor of the court," Judge Bouck repeats.

Miss Simpson testifies that Henry "constantly mouthed off" during the lineup, saying things like "How fucking long does it take to identify someone?"

"Great lines," Henry says. "Who's feeding them to you?" He continues: "You stated that you got on the bus with a guy you thought was your attacker just days after your attack. Was it me?"

"No."

The critical significance of that answer lost on him, he asks, "Somebody like me?"

"Somebody, at the time that—he resembled very closely the man who attacked me, which is why I think it was him."

It's the moment he's been waiting for since the preliminary hearing. "The coincidence of it all, ma'am, is that I never lived at that address—in 1981. Nowhere near East 17th. So whoever you got—"

"Don't give evidence from the well of the court," Judge Bouck interrupts.

Henry fumbles, trying to resume his line of questioning. "But you stated it was 248 East—"

"Well, the reason I brought that back up again was I heard on the television at the time you were arrested, they gave your age and ad—"

Luchenko's on his feet: "My Lord, I question whether this sort of evidence, which is hearsay and probably not admissible, should be in front of the jury."

"Well, perhaps it shouldn't," says Judge Bouck, "but he seems to want answers of that nature."

"I appreciate that, My Lord, but it seems to me he probably doesn't appreciate the rules of evidence about somebody saying what someone else told him. My associate, Miss Milliken, could explain it if your Lordship feels it might assist the jury."

"Well, I can't—. He's got the right to pursue his own cross-examination. If it's against him, that's his burden he has to carry. I can't interrupt his cross-examination."

Henry, oblivious of what just went down, loops back to the beginning. "248 East whatever, that's what you saw on the envelope?"

"Uh-huh."

He takes another stab. "You saw some guy similar to me getting on the bus, is that right?"

"I saw a guy who struck me as so much like my attacker. He had dark curly hair, a beard, a leather jacket and jeans. Quite short—five-foot-seven or five-foot-eight—the same build—not quite as broad as you are, I think . . . Naturally, I told the police."

Henry, confused about where to go next, ends his cross-examination without playing his ace: *Was it me you saw on the bus or someone else?*

CHAPTER 9

THE EIGHT-BY-TEN VERSION

On Friday, March 4, the next witness, Miss Larson, testifies that Ivan Henry is the man who attacked her. She describes her experience: "I felt I had to control myself, not to panic, and I figured this was the only way I was going to get out of this . . . I couldn't fight him because, for one thing, I thought he was on drugs and he had that kind of hyper wound-up energy that is explosive, and is potentially very dangerous . . . I was positive that, if I did react like that, he was going to get violent. A knife can do a lot of damage very quickly and, right from the beginning, I thought that, unless I handle this right, my parents are going to spend tomorrow morning identifying me in the morgue."

She testifies that the police took away her clothes and the bedspread, too. Resisting the urge to bathe, she went straight to the hospital.

When Luchenko asks her why she failed to identify Henry in the lineup, Larson says the only men not laughing "like it was a big joke to them" were the two men handcuffed to #12. At the lineup, Detective Sims announced a change of plans: "Because there was some trouble, she said, we'd all have to go in at once. Number twelve was being held up by two men in uniform. They were trying to force his head up and his back straight. Everybody in the lineup, all the men that were hand-cuffed together, except the two that were handcuffed to the struggling man, were quite sober, but the whole thing, the rest of them were laugh-ing and it was a big joke to them . . . We didn't get a chance to hear them talk. They weren't in the room very long."

Luchenko asks that Larson be shown Exhibit One. After retrieving the five-by-seven photo she'd marked Exhibit One the previous day,

Madam Clerk hands it to Luchenko. Rather than passing it to the witness, Luchenko hands it to Henry, then produces a stack of photos and says, "I have additional copies of Exhibit One that Henry has introduced into evidence. I am prepared to give these to the jurors for their records."

The photos given to Madam Clerk for distribution are eight by ten inches. The photo marked "Trial Exhibit One" is five by seven.

"Fine," says Judge Bouck. "Have you got one for me?"

"I believe I have an additional one for the court as well. I am handing up copies of the lineup photo to the court, My Lord, one for each two jury members and one for the court."

"Thank you."

"I have one, yeah," says Henry.

"I have given an additional one as well to Mr. Henry," says Luchenko. "His is actually the exhibit."

When Henry—eager to get his hands on a larger, hopefully more detailed, version—requests a copy of the eight-by-ten version, Luchenko says: "No need for that; he already has one."

Henry writes on the back of his copy, "Rec'd, March 4, 1983." Unsure why he's feeling seriously spooked, he vows to handle the photo with care.

Luchenko asks Miss Larson why she'd left her ballot blank. "Because everyone was laughing," she says, "I didn't think the lineup was meant to be taken seriously. The man who attacked me wasn't violent. Because I was afraid, I decided that this wasn't going to be him. I'd been afraid of identification anyway."

When Luchenko suggests that she'd never had a chance to view #12's face in repose, she agrees: "He was thrashing about so much I couldn't get a good look at his face. Because they had their arms around his neck, his face was reddened by the blood that rushed to it, and his voice was muffled. His language was surprising, too. Although the man in my apartment used sort of coarse language, it wasn't the kind of language he was using in the lineup. The man in the lineup was much more—sort of vocally and physically aggressive."

"How does the accused's voice at the preliminary and the voir dire compare to your attacker's?"

"It's the same voice."

"Why were you afraid to identify him?"

"It's such a serious matter. Sometimes things can seem to be something they are not. I needed to be absolutely sure . . . There were similarities . . . But, unless I was absolutely positive, I didn't want to make a mistake, put someone through this, and then jail."

In cross-examination, Henry asks Miss Larson what she meant when she said that her bed hadn't been turned down. "Are you English, in the sense that you have one of those beds-in-the-wall— you know, you push the button and it comes out like the Matt Helm series?"

"What I meant was that the bedcovers hadn't been turned down."

When Henry suggests he kept his head down in the lineup for protection, Miss Larson says, "There was no reason to protect oneself in that manner because, if one has . . . Nobody else was protecting himself like that. The lineup's just a procedure."

Guffawing, Henry asks, "If I told you to do something you don't want to—like take off your clothes—would you call that 'just a procedure?'"

Judge Bouck interjects: "That's sort of getting into a legal argument with her. You'll have an opportunity to address that to the jury. Just ask her questions."

• • •

THE NEXT WITNESS, Miss Horvath, is asked by Milliken where she was living on June 16, 1981. She testifies she was house-sitting the caretaker's cottage rented by her boyfriend. When she says she can't recall the address, Henry laughs in disbelief. No way a woman who'd actually been attacked would forget the address of the scene of the crime.

Describing #12 in the lineup photo, Miss Horvath says his face was "contorted by being in a headlock—like he was having a seizure. He was in stocking feet, and his feet were all tangled. My attacker had seemed so much more agile, more physically coordinated."

"Could you hear him at the lineup?" asks Milliken.

"He was speaking, but not at a conversation level. It was more struggling and grunting noises."

"You gave evidence this morning at the voir dire," says Milliken, "at which time Mr. Henry asked you a number of questions. What can you say about his voice?"

Surprise, surprise, the witness rhymes off her answer. "It was the same voice as my attacker."

Chomping at the bit, Henry begins cross-examination. How, he asks, could she possibly have kicked an intruder from the bedroom all the way to the living room?

"I was a jogger at the time," she says, "and my legs were in fairly good shape."

"At the preliminary hearing," he says, "you said that the guy in the lineup had an epileptic seizure. What are you—a doctor?"

"Put the statement to her," says Judge Bouck. "She needs the transcript in front of her—the passage to which you're referring—to ensure accuracy."

"I'd like to, but you guys keep burying me all the time, throwing mud in my face because, every time I look, the discrepancies are so vague and sometimes they are so apart that I kind of wonder if that's just not—. You are not tendering when you really don't have anything to tender. I have got a statement that's got no signature on it, and I give it to her, and you oath it and say maybe I am embarrassing myself. So maybe I'm not even going to ask her about the statement."

When Miss Horvath says she'd had a "few drinks" that night, Henry suggests she's confused about the location of the bamboo curtain in her apartment. Bedroom, kitchen—which is it? At her look of bewilderment, he volunteers that bamboo rollups are usually found in bedrooms.

"Are you asking her about something in the transcript now?" asks Judge Bouck.

"No," says Henry, "I am just putting it out there. So I don't really care what you guys do to me, but you guys want to set me up, you just go for it because I got no time to fuck around here."

"You behave yourself. Otherwise, you will be down in the cells."

"I don't care where I am. I am there anyway."

The judge asks Henry whether he's finished his cross-examination.

"I am trying to think what I can ask."

A few disjointed questions later, he says, "I guess it's not relevant for me to ask questions to bring out the truth, but it's okay for you guys to—to shoot your faces off and have no proof at all. You have no fingerprints, you have no nothing. Absolutely nothing, and you—"

"Madam," says Judge Bouck to Miss Horvath, "you are excused."

"And away she goes," says Henry.

"Any re-examination?"

"No," replies Milliken.

"Garbage," says Henry, watching the witness exit through the courtroom doors.

• • •

MIDWAY THROUGH THE direct examination of Corporal Gary Foster, a fingerprint expert for the Vancouver Police Department, Judge Bouck interjects. "Miss Milliken," he says, "I'm having trouble understanding why we need to hear what Corporal Foster did *not* find. Please elucidate."

The sarcasm isn't lost—even on Henry. Although the evidence regarding the difficulty of recovering decent fingerprints is clearly boring His Lordship, Milliken soldiers on. Corporal Foster testifies that only two fingerprints had been recovered—from a broken wineglass in Miss Horvath's kitchen—and that those two "remain unidentifiable."

"I'm coming to that, My Lord," says Milliken.

"But they don't relate to these crimes," snaps Judge Bouck.

"Apparently not," says Milliken, "but he's testifying as to the general principles, explaining the lack of fingerprint evidence."

"Let's try to move it along."

"You say, Mr. Foster, that the fingerprints you recovered remain unidentifiable?"

"Despite an effort to match the recovered fingerprints with six sets of known prints"—prints belonging to "persons of interest" to the police—says Foster, "they remained unidentifiable."

In cross-examination, Henry asks a single question. "So, Mr. Foster, really what you have said here today is nothing, it's immaterial?"

"My Lord," Foster says, directing his answer to the court, "that is correct. I examined the scene and, though two fingerprints were found, they were not identified."

• • •

THE NEXT COMPLAINANT to testify, Miss Cardozo, is asked by Milliken about Henry's voice "both at the lineup and during the voir dire."

"There's no doubt it's the voice of my attacker."

Milliken has barely sat down when Henry is on his feet. "Why," he asks Miss Cardozo, "did you end your ballot notation, 'by voice only, #12,' followed by a question-mark?"

Miss Cardozo says, "I know it was you in that lineup."

"You don't know that, ma'am."

"You are the man that was in the lineup, sir."

"Well, maybe John the Baptist put my head there, because I was never there—maybe at the threshold to the room, but never actually cuffed and in the lineup. You said nothing at the preliminary hearing about a voice—you said you couldn't identify me—yet now you're certain about the voice?"

"Both to Crown counsel and to your defence attorney, I said it was the voice, or appeared to be the voice, of the man who attacked me—"

"That's—"

"Quiet," orders Judge Bouck. "Let her answer the question."

"As I said to Crown counsel and to the defence attorney, I said it was the voice of the man, or appeared to be the voice of the man, who attacked me."

"Appeared?"

Out of steam, Henry flips through his notes. There are a dozen things he meant to ask, but he can't remember what they are. It's almost 4:00 p.m., the end of the court day. "That's all I've got to ask."

As the jurors shuffle out of the courtroom, he wills them to look his way. Not a single one does.

• • •

SHROUDED IN MIST, the lights of Oakalla cast ghostly shadows as the paddy wagon approaches the gatehouse and the massive front gate. Henry's wrist is handcuffed to another prisoner's wrist. Please, he prays, don't let them give my cell away. When he'd returned from court the day before, he'd been dispatched to the cow barn—a segregation unit accessed by a long set of stairs going deep below ground; a dank, low-ceilinged place reeking of feces and mould.

Today something's up. The joint's in lockdown. A cold supper arrives in a brown paper bag, slung through the bars. No one asks the reason for the lockdown; no one explains it. A butt suitcased with drugs? The latest Native kid swinging from a sheet? Reprisal against some rat? An escape plan in the works? Who knows; who cares. Fires have been set, cells wrecked. Inmates have stocked up on splinters of wood, chunks of concrete, batteries in socks.

Henry says a little prayer, then thinks about the trial. Five women down, two—excluding Kavanagh—to go. Surely at some point he'll get Judge Bouck to see the photo for what it is and end the whole charade.

And even if *he* doesn't, the jury will see that the trial's a joke. What was it that Judge Craig said at the end of the preliminary hearing? People believe in the fairness of the jury system.

Please, God, make it so.

CHAPTER 10

MARCH 7

The witness Miss Jacobsen—stumbling red-faced through words like "intercourse," "erections," and "blow jobs"—testifies that, at the 1981 lineup, she chose one man. In May 1982, she made note of two—#18, based on build, and #12, based on voice and build.

"Why two?" asks Milliken.

"I understood we were to pick out anybody that would give the police an idea."

"Is the man in the lineup in court today?"

"Yes"—pointing at Henry—"it's him."

"From the opportunity you got to hear Mr. Henry's voice at the voir dire, what can you say about his voice?"

"I believe this is the same man that entered my apartment on August 5, 1981."

"What causes you to say that?"

"Just a feeling," Miss Jacobsen says. "The pitch is right, the sound is right. It is husky and I just have a gut reaction it does sound like the same voice. I just felt it . . . . He just appears to be the same person."

In cross-examination, Henry gets her to repeat that she picked #18, a man well above his height, at the lineup. Then he asks, "Do these people look to you like tall people? Going by the top of the door, wouldn't you agree?"

"Going by the top of the door?"

"Yes," he says. "Assuming that the door's at least seven feet tall, the men were all tall. Agreed?"

"Yes."

"I have no further questions."

Had Henry not been at his wit's end, he might have carried on the cross-examination. It wasn't just the height of #18 that set him and Henry apart; they could not have looked less alike.

• • •

CONSTABLE DARYL KEEN testifies about Henry's arrest on May 12. When it's time for cross-examination, Henry has only one thing on his mind: "You cuffed me in front, not behind, correct?"

"Behind," Keen says.

Henry pursues it, but the man won't be budged. *So be it*, thinks Henry, sitting down. *When this prick meets his maker, he'll be accounting for at least one bald-faced lie. You handcuffed me in front, you bastard, and we both know it.* If they'll lie about something so inconsequential, what won't they lie about?

Corporal David Baker, up next, testifies that it wasn't until the women had left and photographer Foxx arrived that the "uniforms" had no choice but to put the struggling Henry in a headlock. Because he needed to be "physically restrained," Henry was taken, after the lineup, to an isolation cell on the fifth floor. Returning an hour later, Baker found him to be "very calm"—a person "completely different" from the one he'd dealt with earlier.

Standing to cross-examine Baker, apparently elevated to "corporal" since the May '82 linup, Henry wastes no time before asking, "Is it VPD policy to drag people into lineups?"

"It depends on the circumstances," says Baker. "This was a very unusual lineup. I have never run one like that before."

"Under what circumstances would you—"

"I am somewhat concerned, My Lord," Luchenko interrupts, "that this might not assist the jury. Certainly, if Mr. Henry wishes to lead it he can, but it's a question of relevance."

"I cannot stop his cross-examination," says Judge Bouck. "Whatever questions he wants to ask that he thinks are going to help his case are up to him."

Henry struggles to regain his thread. "I asked you about physical restraint," he says. "What are the circumstances?"

"There are many different reasons, but security would be the main one. Injury to other people in the lineup, difficult people who are uncooperative going in a lineup . . . "

"Is it not for an individual like myself to be found not guilty until proven guilty, or how do we put that? The other way round or—?"

"Corporal Baker, don't answer that," says Judge Bouck. "Mr. Henry, the corporal is not here to answer legal questions. You can ask him about the facts of what happened at the lineup if you want."

"I was not in that lineup," Henry says, "so I cannot ask about facts."

• • •

AT 11:55 A.M., associate Crown counsel Milliken begins reading into the record the preliminary hearing evidence of Miss Kavanagh. After breaking for lunch, she resumes and reads solidly until the afternoon break at 3:05 p.m. It's all Henry can do to keep from nodding off. Hell, the one time he pries open an eye, the jurors are in la-la land.

After the break, Judge Bouck agrees that the Crown can interrupt the reading to accommodate the schedule of Constable Foxx. "I am going to give you a little relief, members of the jury," Judge Bouck says, "and let you see a real live witness for a few minutes." Several heads snap to attention.

After Foxx gives the same evidence he gave at the preliminary hearing, Henry asks him, in cross-examination, about the whereabouts of the "original" lineup photo.

"It's kept," he says, an answer Henry fails to pursue.

Asked about Henry's shirt in the photo, Foxx says #12 appears to be wearing a dark blue or black shirt. Asked if he can see "like a diamond shape in the bottom by the crotch area that completely blocks off the shirt," Foxx says, "I'm sorry, I don't see what you're speaking of."

"I don't know," says Henry, eyeing the weird handcuffs and phantom legs, "maybe you have a different picture to me, but I have no question I can see like the guy is going to play baseball or something. He has a cap on him, or something like that."

"I don't see what you're referring to."

"When you look at the waistline, aren't there three or four inches missing at the waist?"

"I don't understand what you're getting at—"

"If the shirt were blue, I wouldn't contest what I was wearing. But I sort of wonder how I got into this picture when I'm not really in it. It is amazing."

Out of questions, Henry concludes his cross-examination. It does not occur to him to follow up his speculation—"maybe you have a different picture to me"—by comparing the photo he has to the one in the hands of Constable Foxx.

• • •

ON MARCH 8, Miss Johnson, Miss Kavanagh's Vancouver roommate, testifies that Miss Kavanagh's father died in January, leaving his daughter devastated.

"Did Miss Kavanagh indicate her willingness to return for the trial?" asks Milliken.

"I've decided that she's not going to come," says Judge Bouck. "The rest is hearsay."

Constable Esme Adams of VPD's Identification Squad testifies in direct examination about the silicon cast he made of the fresh tool-mark impression on the inside of Miss Kavanagh's door. In cross-examination, he agrees with Henry that, because the door had no plate in it, a man could have easily used a knife to make the spring mechanism jump back.

"If that's true," says Henry, "the guy was a poor thief, scratching away like that at the wood. Why would the guy scratch at the wood?"

"I have no idea."

• • •

DETECTIVE WILLIAM HARKEMA, a squat, muscular man with narrow eyes and thick arms, testifies that, right after Miss Kavanagh identified Henry on July 28, Sergeant Howland swore the information leading to Henry's arrest.

In his cross-examination, Henry asks Harkema three questions, each more insistent than the last: "Am I correct, sir, that the information sworn by Sergeant Howland pertained only to Kavanagh?" "Can informations be beefed up by adding counts later on?" "If Howland only had knowledge of her two counts, how could I have been charged with seventeen?"

Before Harkema can open his mouth, Judge Bouck intervenes, saying that "questions of law" are not for witnesses to weigh in on.

"Do police usually show victims pictures of people behind bars?" Henry asks, pointing to the image. "Is that a fair picture? My wife gave you a lot."

Harkema says, "It's the only picture I had available, My Lord."

"You can't say this was a fair photo array, that the picture of me is fair. I look nothing like the others. I'm not an Indian, I don't have long hair—"

"Under the circumstances," says Harkema, "I consider it quite fair. I tried to mix up the pictures with as many different backgrounds on it as I could."

"Yes, I can see that, says Henry, waving the photo array in the air. But I don't look twenty years old . . . Why did it take so long to obtain Miss Kavanagh's statement?"

Without waiting for an answer, Henry plows ahead. "Is it because it was a little hard for me to bring the reality criteria to you, or would it be easier if I were to make up the story?"

"My Lord," says Luchenko, "this is conjecture and argumentative only."

Nodding in agreement, Judge Bouck says, "I don't understand that to be a question anybody can answer."

Sergeant Edward McClellan testifies that, around noon on May 13, 1982, Staff Sergeant Kenneth Miles gave him a thirty-five-millimetre camera and told him to take photos of Henry at the third-floor booking counter. He identifies the image of Henry in the photo array as being the one he took of him that day. (See insert 4.)

When Henry asks, in cross-examination, "On what basis was I arrested and detained?" McClellan says he'd been given a document saying Henry was "being held on a burglary charge."

Just as he'd suspected. They'd had no cause to arrest and interrogate him on the rape beefs.

• • •

ASKED BY LUCHENKO to describe her attack, Miss Browning testifies, as she had done at the preliminary hearing, that when the intruder removed his penis from his pants, she spent "several seconds" staring at his face. Why? "Because I wanted to remember his face forever. If I lived, I was going to remember that face. I was going to make a point. So I studied his face."

Before the lineup, she testifies, the women were taken into the lineup room. "The men were handcuffed together," she says, "and, about the middle of the lineup, towards the left side, were these three policemen dragging in one man. They came through the door forwards, then backed up to the wall and stayed there."

Bingo, thinks Henry. *Finally, a woman not prepared to spout the party line. What she just said proves I was never in the lineup. Sure, the bastards might have corralled me past the threshold, but no way did they manhandle me another step further.*

"I was a bit shocked to see someone being restrained like that," Miss Browning is saying, "and I couldn't see his face anyways, so I thought I'm just going to pay attention to the other men and, when I'm prepared emotionally enough to look at that man, maybe I'll see if I can catch his face . . . Then I heard a growl, the growl I'd heard in my room . . . I very quickly looked over, and this man was just fighting and growling and struggling, and I went into shock . . . The policemen had somehow manoeuvred the gentleman so that we could see his face. It was bright red, and very distorted, and I just didn't—I couldn't tell . . . It was terrifying to hear that voice again, and I picked the one with the darkest hair. Why? I wish I knew, but I honestly don't know. I guess I was just terrified."

Asked by Luchenko about Henry's "outbursts" at the preliminary hearing, Miss Browning says, "First, he called me a liar, then, 'It's pretty hard to make this up, isn't it?' The third time, it was, 'You think it's me? Hey, man, it's my life.' That's when I recognized the voice."

During his cross-examination of Miss Browning, Henry stumbles, without apparent purpose, from subject to subject, then sits back down.

CHAPTER 11

THE BURDEN OF PROOF

A t the end of the day on March 8, 1983, after only five days of trial, Michael Luchenko announces the close of the Crown's case. Henry says he won't be calling evidence because he can't properly defend himself. "I don't think there is any point. If you boys want to put me in the joint, go ahead. Enjoy it. Have a good time."

"I am concerned with that comment," Luchenko says. "Mr. Henry has not requested anything further that has not been provided to him. If Mr. Henry wishes more, I would ask him to say so now so that the Crown can take whatever steps it wants."

"Given that no coherent statement can be expected from the accused," says Judge Bouck, "it's best to just carry on."

After the break, Henry announces that he intends to call various police officers as his own witnesses.

"You'll be stuck with what they say," warns Judge Bouck. "The party calling a witness has no right to cross-examine them."

What the hell?

Before Henry can grasp the implications of Bouck's comments, the judge says, "Given that the Crown has closed its case, you, Mr. Henry, might wish to make a 'no evidence' motion."

"A what?"

"Such a motion occurs before the accused decides whether or not to call evidence in his own defence. An accused has the right to argue that, based on the Crown's case alone, there is no evidence upon which a reasonable jury, properly instructed, could return a verdict of guilty."

A surge of adrenalin moves through him. "Your Honour, I do believe there is no prima facie case other than their evidence and whatever IDs. I don't—I think we're wasting our time. We're wasting a lot of time. I mean, you can keep me in jail for another week, or another two weeks, but basically coming down to the point, I will prove these witnesses are somehow mistaken, or somehow we've got on the wrong battle lines."

Gathering himself, Henry attempts to marshal the key points. "They have no fingerprints. Out of so many charges, we should have fingerprints . . . fibres. I mean just anything, because then it would take me off the hook. I'm the guy who has to prove I'm innocent to you people, and that's not fair.

"We're supposed to be in a country where you're innocent until proven guilty, but all this time I've been trying to—you know, I have to stick my head in there, and that's why I'm standing here myself, is because I want to defend myself, completely without any backstabbing or anything, sort of manipulations by anybody, and I don't, I don't feel there is any warrant to continue the trial any farther, and I'd like to go home."

"That's your no-evidence motion?"

"Yes."

"I'm satisfied there is ample evidence to go before the jury, so we'll continue with the defence. Court is adjourned for the day."

• • •

THE NEXT DAY, Luchenko asks that Henry be instructed again about the burden of proof.

"Mr. Henry, let me assure you, once and for all," says Judge Bouck, "the burden of proof is, was, and always will be on the Crown. Guilt beyond a reasonable doubt. Have I made myself very, very clear?"

Henry repeats his request to see every indictment and information; every fake or missing warrant; the names of every corrupt police officer; and, once again, any medical records that may exist.

"Given that medical evidence is not part of the Crown's case," says Judge Bouck, "what possible good could securing the doctors' names do you?"

"Medical evidence might help take charges away from me, even if but only one."

"You think it might? Then you haven't got a clue."

"I keep trying to say I'm innocent. I can't keep repeating it if you don't have doctors proving these people were even raped. There's no proof they were even raped other than what they've said."

"That is proof enough."

"Give me the lie detector test. How many times do I have to ask for it? A voice detector test. Anything."

"Mr. Henry, let's be very clear on one thing. You. Do. Not. Have. To. Prove. Your. Innocence. Do you understand?"

• • •

AS HIS FIRST witness, Henry calls VPD detective Bruce Campbell. With any luck, the man will tell the truth and Henry will get to the bottom of the ever-changing cascade of informations and indictments—charges added and subtracted, charges put on hold and going ahead.

When Campbell denies knowing the meaning of the term "blue curtain"—the unwritten rule among police officers not to report, or testify about, a colleague's errors, misconducts, or crimes—Henry laughs out loud.

Asked how many rape suspects there were, Campbell says, "At one time or other, as many as fifteen."

"When you went to my wife, on April 23 or 24, you suggested she inform on me?"

"I don't recall the date, and I didn't suggest that."

"Did someone phone you to find me, or was it your hypothesis through elimination? Was that how you came to arrest me?"

"It was the result of information received that we requested you be arrested."

"Why was I released?"

"I had a discussion with my partner and my superiors, and also with Crown counsel. As a result, you were released pending further investigation."

Campbell being a witness "adverse in interest" to the accused, Luchenko's "cross-examination" consists of lobbed questions meant to elicit predictable answers. Asked where he first met Mrs. Henry, Campbell says that it was on the corner of East 16th and Main, a block from her home.

"Is her home, 248 East 17th, situated basically in the heart of the area where these incidents were occurring?"

"Yes, it's when we met on the corner that she gave me the striated picture." (See insert 6.)·

"Were there other photographs of the accused?"

"Yes, but not received personally by me. Others were received by Constables Heggie and Rainsley."

Luchenko asks Campbell, "Why not construct a photo array using the striated photo?" Without waiting for an answer, he supplies it: "Would you agree with me, sir, that that particular photograph is not of a quality that you would ordinarily use in a photograph plan?"

"That is correct."

"And that is because of those striations which would make it too obvious a photo if one were to put it in a lineup?"

"That is correct."

"So you only had two photographs before May 12, and neither of them was of a quality you could use in a photo lineup?"

What—who said anything about just two? From what Henry's pieced together, Jessie as good as emptied out half their picture albums.

"That is correct."

"The police's view at the time was to do everything possible to try to curb or stop all these sexual assaults?"

"That is correct."

"So you had only one method to get some sort of identification, and that was a physical, as opposed to a photographic, lineup?"

"That is correct."

"Are lineups normally conducted 'quietly,' meaning in such a way as not to single out the suspect?"

"That is correct."

"And, of course, by following these steps, you avoid any suggestion that the identification of the witnesses is tainted?"

"That's right."

Horseshit, thinks Henry. *Luchenko feeds him the answers, and Campbell nods his head like a dummy on somebody's knee.*

• • •

HENRY'S NEXT WITNESS is Detective Marylyn Sims. After confirming the identities of the lineup participants, Sims says that the four uniformed jail guards were present "for security." Henry asks her why he was not charged at that time.

"You created such a fuss in the lineup," she says, "that we felt that whatever had been said by the witnesses couldn't be objective, and we didn't think it was fair to lay charges under those circumstances. You were the only person creating a fuss. You were the only person standing out in the witnesses' minds."

"You saw Exhibit One being taken. Is it accurate?"

"Yes."

Another liar, Henry thinks. So far, every lineup attendee and every police officer has said the photo is accurate.

After agreeing with Henry that Marpole, the location of some of the assaults, is a "fair distance" from Mount Pleasant, Sims is "cross-examined" by Luchenko.

"Would a person living at East 17th and Main," he asks, "have had, given the bus routes, ready access to every one of the crime scene locations?

"Yes."

"Were Mr. Henry's actions during the lineup the sole reason the women couldn't view his face in repose?"

"From the minute he entered to the minute he left," Sims testifies, "he had to be restrained. That is why his face was contorted, and there was no view of him in repose at all."

• • •

HAVING FIRST TESTIFIED as a Crown witness, Detective William Harkema is now called by Henry to give evidence for the defence. Although it seemed a good idea at the time, Henry's soon not so sure anymore.

Why, he asks, was there such a long delay in investigating Miss Kavanagh's complaint?

"I wasn't assigned to the case until June 17," says Harkema. "I was involved in many other things. I spoke with Sergeant Howland after I got back from vacation and he filled me in as to date and time."

Rather than asking the obvious question—what greater priority did the VPD have than catching a serial rapist?—Henry asks why Harkema conducted his "re-interviews" so long after each assault.

"Because I was assigned to the case a considerable length of time after the crimes were committed, I needed to re-interview." Harkema adds that during those re-interviews, he "took yet more detailed and concise statements."

Sure, thinks Henry. *More tailored to fit the Crown's case.*

• • •

WHEN HENRY ANNOUNCES his decision to take the stand in his own defence, Judge Bouck cautions him. "You are perfectly entitled to give evidence, but I fear that you do not know what you are doing to yourself.

"The witnesses you have called this morning have all, by and large, told a tale indicating your guilt. They have done nothing to help you. I'm afraid that you're going to keep calling witnesses on your behalf, and you think they're going to be helping you, but they are going to be destroying you. That is entirely up to you, whether you wish to call them. The same thing goes for taking the witness stand yourself. You are perfectly entitled to, but you will be subject to cross-examination . . .

"Let me put it another way. The burden of proof is on the Crown to prove its case beyond a reasonable doubt. You do not have to take the stand unless you want to. Would you like the noon hour to think about it?"

"No," Henry says, and the jury is recalled.

After assembling papers and transcripts, notebooks filled with scrawled reminders and underlined extracts, he begins: "I didn't rape any of the women that I'm charged with . . . If I did it, I certainly wouldn't put a bunch of people through a bunch of turmoil like I'm going through.

"It all really started last April. When the police told Jessie I was wanted on rape, I talked to my PO, Chris Conroy. Around April 19, I went to 100 Mile House to get my emotions together. Lived with André and Donna LaBrosse, kept in touch with Conroy. We'd gotten to be friends by then."

It was true: between then and his arrest in May, when he wasn't staying with Jessie and the girls on East 17th, he was crashing up north with André—anything to keep away from the heat.

"Plus I kept phoning downtown, pretending to be a lawyer—except they knew me right away. I'd ask if a warrant had been issued yet. 'No, Mr. Henry,' the switchboard operator would say, and hang up. On

May 11, I thought what the hell. So I got in my car and I thought, 'Well, let's go for it and see what we got.'

"Landing back in Vancouver, I saw my girls, then I got my mail. I'm driving east when I see a car following me. I didn't want to get shot, so I pulled over, made like I was going to a store. Someone stuck a gun in my back. Soon, I was surrounded by cars. They wanted to handcuff me behind my back, but I argued. So they did the front. My parole officer said they couldn't arrest me without a warrant, but they did.

"I was taken to the police station, my shoes removed. I was not handcuffed in no lineup. I was at the door, but I refused to go in further. I don't have to prove I'm innocent. I've always refused to go in lineups. The officer in charge quoted the *Marcoux* case, saying I had to participate. But that case says the opposite. Ask the Supreme Court of Canada. There shoulda never been a lineup. I was put in the lineup for three minutes, but there were no cuffs on me.

"After being released, I went to see my wife, who was hysterical. I didn't get my car until the next day, after another charge of rape went down."

Forgetting that the November 1980 assault of Miss Pavlovik—the woman who identified #12 in a different lineup!— is not even before the jury, Henry asks them to imagine travelling, without a car, the thirteen kilometres from his home in Burnaby to Mount Pleasant. "I bought my first car on December 8," he says. "Ask Happy Honda. I don't care what you're doing—if you're hunting for rabbits, whatever you're doing, you ain't going to walk that far."

Regarding the summer of '81, Henry says: "Sometimes I slept in Colin Bradbury's home in West Vancouver, or in my own home. When I didn't overnight with Bradbury, he picked me up and dropped me off. I'd smashed my car on May 31 and didn't get it back until September 3. My parole officer will verify it."

Describing January 21, 1982, the day his parole ended, as "the biggest thing I've ever completed in my life," he says that, in February, he was living with his pal Clem and working for another pal, Vince, in Fraserview. "I earned $3,500 under the table. When I got out of the pen, I faked my skills and became a builder. I don't want to get into my life too deeply, because I don't think it's anybody's business. I've done a lot of time."

After going quickly through the other charges—saying a couple of sentences about each of them—he slows down when he gets to Miss Kavanagh. "I knew they had a stakeout on me," he explains. "I had quite a few police cars on me and they were—I used to play around, sort of. Maybe I shouldn't have done that. But when I went out, I used to listen for sounds. I was very adept at sounds, and I used to pick up the odd beep or the odd motor starting, which told me I had a tail on me. There was no way I could move, so I'd go out of town, selling jeans—"

His mind's gone blank. Twenty-five minutes, start to finish. All the other things he planned on saying, all the errors and omissions and lies? Gone.

"That's it, members of the jury, I've nothing more to say. You can get at me now."

• • •

ALTHOUGH MADAM CLERK initially said she couldn't find his alibi statement, she eventually discovers it—in the court file, exactly where it would have been all along. Henry's hopes are raised, but just as quickly dashed when Judge Bouck, glancing at it, declares it "inadmissible in that form."

Fine, he'll just carry on, attacking the sham that is the Crown's case. Given a chance to add anything he left out, Henry tells the jury that, when he was under surveillance, he couldn't do a thing without being watched. On June 9, 1982, he points out, the day after Miss Kavanagh's alleged attack, he was pulled over and ticketed.

He goes on about the lie detector test that never happened, and the lack of physical evidence: "If you don't have medical evidence to support your claim of rape, you don't have anything to support that claim, other than verbalization. Like I said, I can't fly and I'm not invisible, nor can I not leave something behind. There must be something I left—be it a fingerprint, be it anything. Surely there's something that I left.

"I don't think there'd be a one in a million chance that a person charged with as many things as I've been would have not left something behind. It's sort of highly suspectible. Plus, if I'd have been going into someone's house to rape somebody, you'd better believe my face would be covered.

"Given my terrible record," he adds, "it would have been irresponsible on my part not to do so."

CHAPTER 12

STING LIKE A BEE

Michael Luchenko, nodding to the jurors, takes up his position behind the lectern. Henry waits calmly in the witness box. Having called himself as a witness, he has no choice but to undergo the Crown's cross-examination.

"Do you cut your own hair?" Luchenko asks.

"Sure, it's cheap and I get to do it my own way."

"Do you smoke? "

"Sure. Players, Export, you name it."

"Do you have access to tools—screwdrivers, knives? Are you handy? What do you know about locks?"

"Mostly, I bought the tools myself. Screwdrivers? I only had a knife, which you people have got. It's all bent. Locks? I never learned anything about them. I couldn't beat a lock if the lock was open for me. Girls probably know more than me. The sites I work on, we only use deadbolts."

"Patio doors?"

"I couldn't break in without being noisy."

"I'm thinking you're the kind of man who likes changing up your appearance," says Luchenko.

"Whenever the whim suits me," says Henry. "Who doesn't get sick of the same old look every day? I change my hair a lot, but never the colour. Colours change in different lights. Hair has eight colours: blue-black, black-brown, red-brown, red, blonde, ash-brown, ash, and white. If someone said mine's red-brown, others plain brown, I'd say they don't know their colours. Me? I'm the expert. I have hairdressing certificates and diplomas to prove it. Plus a year and a half's experience in Stony Mountain."

"How fast could you grow a beard?

"Twenty-five days max."

Questioned about his alibi evidence, Henry confirms that he'd holed up in seedy dumps at various times—the Blackbriar Hotel on Main Street from May to September 1980; and then, after Jessie and the girls came, a few days in a dingy flophouse, the Woodbine, on skid row, followed by a duplex in Burnaby. As of March 1982, he'd been living either with Jessie on East 17th or in 100 Mile House up north. Yes, he'd obtained a postal box address at a location near where the "Marpole crimes" went down.

"Mr. Henry, can you prove that, from September 1980 to January 20, 1981, you stayed every night at the Burnaby address?"

On an unrelated note, Henry replies, "Me and my wife? We never struck each other. We just used to accept it, and go about our businesses. When the tide comes in and goes out, we would come back together again. Most of the time, we were together because of the girls. If I missed more than two weekends with my family at a time, that would be extraordinary. Weekdays, too—depending of course on where I was working.

"You see, I can only—if you were to look back into your life a year and a half ago, and you were sporadic, as I am, running around, and as many jobs as I have done, you sort of try to fit the pieces in as good as you can. I have records that will back up those records."

Asked whether he has proof of where he was on May 5, 1981, Henry says, "Driving back and forth to the job in Chilliwack in the Fraser Valley. I'd have been at the Woodbine Hotel or with my wife. Either place, but no other place."

First, Luchenko points out, Henry said he was in the lineup; then, "I was never in a lineup handcuffed to anybody." Who was viewing the lineup?

"I know Detective Campbell was," says Henry. "He stuck his head around when they were dragging me in."

"You were putting up a fight?"

"No, just going along like a little dog being dragged along on a leash."

"Were you limp, or trying to resist?"

"All I remember is that my blue shirt had long sleeves that covered my tattoos. I was wearing designer jeans. Never had no black thing on top of me. And I'd shaved off my moustache purposefully that day. I was having enough problems, as it was."

After a pause, Luchenko says, "So you were being intentionally deceitful, purposely changing your appearance?"

How can Luchenko accuse him of deliberately shaving off his moustache while pushing photos of him sporting a moustache on May 12 and 13? *Get with it, you bastard. Quit your stupid games.*

"I guess anybody would," he says, "if they were being chased all across Canada for nothing."

Agreeing that Sergeant McClellan took three photos of him in total, Henry insists that Exhibit Five—the photo array showing Henry with prison bars in the background—isn't one of them. "I didn't have a moustache," he says, tracing an invisible line above his lip. "I'd just shaved it off. The pictures on May 13 were snapped while I was counting my money—which I found to be very facetious."

"And the lineup picture, that's not you either?"

"Might be my head, but not my body."

"How could such a picture come to be taken?"

"Not being a professional photographer, I can't say."

"I'm not asking for a theory. Do you recall anyone taking a picture of your head in that position so they could cut and somehow imprint it on that lineup photograph?"

"When I was being dragged away, yes, I did have a photograph taken of me, but I was alone, other than the policemen around me."

Luchenko asks Henry whether Colin Bradbury will be able to confirm Henry's whereabouts on the night of June 16, 1981. Henry says he has a clear memory of Bradbury waking him up early that morning to take a call from his wife. The Burnaby home had been broken into; among the items stolen was her prized stereo.

When Henry says that he and Bradbury were sleeping in different rooms, Luchenko asks, "So you could quite easily walk away without him knowing it?"

"Depends where I'm walking to. The West Vancouver buses shut down at 6:00 p.m. Twelve and a half miles from West Vancouver to downtown Vancouver. Quite a distance to walk."

Asked how he could be sure he'd lived either in West Vancouver or in Burnaby that summer and nowhere else, Henry replies: "While I was living at the Station Hotel, my parole officer and me had a standard practice . . . The deal was I'd phone him every evening, tell him where I was. He'd tell me not to worry, just let him know my whereabouts. Otherwise, I was going back to jail."

Asked where he was between March 10 and 19, 1982, Henry says that as of mid-March, he'd stayed with his wife, on and off, in an up-and-down duplex at Main and East 17th.

"Located at the centre of Mount Pleasant," says Luchenko of the location. "Lots of buses, running every which way?"

"All I know is it's off Main Street. I'd got my yellow Spirit back around September 11, 1981. A week later, I busted the clutch. Got it back two or three weeks later."

Where was he on March 19, 1982? "I bought Jessie a stereo that day to replace the one stolen last summer. It's sort of funny that I'm able to track down that one date positively. It's my stepfather's birthday."

No, he doesn't have the receipt handy, but he can get it if necessary.

That afternoon, in the paddy wagon on the way back to Oakalla, Henry praises God for one thing at least. The papers from Happy Honda had arrived, and he'd passed them to the Crown. At a minimum, they'll drop the three charges occurring during the transit strike in the summer of '81, while he was working, without wheels, in West Van. A minor victory, maybe, but it's a start.

• • •

THE NEXT MORNING, back in court, Luchenko asks Henry whether his wife has "any intention of showing up."

"It's not that she don't want to come, Your Honour," Henry tells the judge, "but she ain't too happy being out in the public eye. I thought she'd come, but now I'm not so sure."

"Subpoena her fast or it will be too late."

Once the jury's been recalled, Luchenko goes at him again. "Isn't the real reason for leaving town in April, and changing your appearance upon your return in May, because you'd been very 'active' in March?"

"No. I'd made $3,500 on a contract I finished in March. I wasn't in need of money. I went up north to get my emotions in order."

"We're talking here about assaults, not money."

"Yes, but most of them are related to robberies, aren't they?"

"Isn't it true you went up north when you heard the police were making inquiries?"

"Well, when police come to your home with guns drawn, I guess you would, too."

"You say you spent the night of May 13 with your wife. Surely, you having just been released from custody and all, there must have been some resentment between the two of you?"

"Maybe you can't understand, but we never had any physical fights or any sort of really deep emotional fights. Some people have a certain thing about their relationship. We never fought. It was more like nitpicking."

Questioned about the stereo receipt, Henry says he asked Jessie to bring it with her. "It was London Drugs, not the Bay," he adds. "I was there. I contributed $200 towards it."

"How can you say the man in the lineup's not you?"

"As I discussed with my friend in the cellblock, it's not me. Even if I cut my hair really short, you won't see tight curls like that. The guy in the picture's got redder hair, and his sideburns are patchy. Mine grow in full—"

"How very interesting," says Luchenko. "I take it you'll be calling your prisoner pals as expert witnesses?"

In response to a question about the May 13 photo—the one showing Henry in front of a jail cell with a police elbow in his face—he says, "My wonderful wife probably gave you that photo, but I wouldn't have changed shirts overnight. I'd still be wearing the blue, long-sleeved one I was arrested in. Also, that's some trick—putting in a cellblock behind me."

"But weren't the pictures taken in front of the cellblock?"

"I don't remember, because I was certainly mad. I was quite upset."

"You're saying that isn't your shirt?"

"Oh, it's my shirt all right, just not the one I was wearing that day. Also, I don't know how an officer could stick his elbow out in front of me. The officer taking the pictures had no one in front of him. He was all alone. Nothing between him and me."

Putting that photo aside, Luchenko asks Madam Clerk for the lineup photo. "Are you suggesting," he asks, waving it for the jury, "that the women are lying about you being in the lineup?"

"My only argument is and was, and always will be, that anybody that says I'm in that lineup is a liar. I'll maintain that till I die. Because I'm not there. I can't be someplace where I'm not."

"Do you have people to back up your alibis?"

"Not everybody goes to bed with each other each night. I like to be—I like my loneliness, too. I don't like to be with people all the time. Not that I'm saying I'm anti-social or anything, but I like my own meditations."

Asked about his criminal record, Henry refrains from whining about the long sentences handed out by Winnipeg judges. What teenager deserves three years in the hooch for stealing a car, a candy bar, and a colour TV? At age twenty-four, he'd snagged a two-year stint for shoplifting, possession of marijuana, and possession of a weapon. Worst of all, at age thirty-one, he'd pleaded guilty to break and enter and— the thought of it still makes him cringe—attempted rape. Five years concurrent. If they hadn't threatened to pile on a whole slew of other charges, he'd have taken his chances with a trial.

"Regarding the Kavanagh assault," Luchenko's saying, "you say you were being followed. But wasn't it pretty much a hit-and-miss thing in terms of keeping up with you?"

"When there are seven or eight cars on you, there's no hitting and missing. You can't get away. Yes, I had a barrage of cars after me." Sure, he'd tried shaking them off. Who wouldn't?

Had he been travelling around a lot? No, he says, after the lineup he wouldn't even take his daughter out after supper for ice cream. "I'd watch the cops as they played their little games on the street below. I couldn't sleep at night because of what they might be doing to my car."

"Did you ever take midnight walks?"

"You kidding me?"

"That's not what your wife said."

"Bullshit! It ain't true. Show me her signature. Show me you oathed her." *They're making it up on the fly*, he thought. *Bastards*.

Asked why he didn't participate willingly in the lineup, Henry repeats what he's been saying all along—"I'm the only redhead, and the other guys were dressed like slobs."

Hadn't he always taken pride in his appearance? Hell, he'd left home at fourteen, not just because of the abuse, but also because he'd heard that people on welfare get a clothing allowance. Little did he know that moving out would mean being slapped around by one foster parent after another.

"You say you didn't know any of these women?"

"I'll state this on the Big Guy right here. I don't know these women to this day."

"So they bear no rancour; they're just trying to be as honest as possible?"

"I don't know if it's rancour or not. But they're playing games with me. I'd rather lay in a hole and have someone shoot me than do that. To hurt somebody, I could never do that."

"You're saying these women knowingly gave false evidence?"

"I'm not inside their bodies, nor am I inside their heads. I don't know who programmed them. I don't know anything about them. If I was to sit down with them and try to figure out their emotions, or try to figure out what they're trying to put across . . . I've lost it, but what I'm trying to say is that I don't know if this is all real. If I'd have hurt these women, I'd know it's real."

"You're saying everyone is lying?"

"I don't know. If they were to take a lie detector test with me, then we'd assume who the liar was quickly, wouldn't we?"

"All of this, you say, is because you can't be in two places at once?"

"If I was asked where I was last night, I would know. But I'm not God, nor am I that guy from France, that priest, who can be in two places at once. All I can put forth—suggest to you—is that, if I was to go into those places, grabbing lamps and all those other little gizmos—"

Henry's lost his train of thought. Scrambling, he starts up again. "You should have grabbed the guy long ago, instead of laying it on me. If it had been me, I'd have taken everyone's wallet. Not that I go around breaking into people's houses, but if I'm starving, trying to survive? Yes."

At long last, he steps out of the witness box. Luchenko, unable to keep from smiling, sits down. Fish in a barrel. There's nothing quite as satisfying as a defendant intent on hanging himself.

CHAPTER 13

THE EXPERT

van Henry is not surprised when his next witness, Colin Bradbury, fails to look his way as he takes the stand. After days of leaving messages from the jailhouse phone, Henry finally reached him. Bradbury was less than thrilled at the prospect of testifying. "My memory's a sieve, man," he said. "I got nothing to say. No offence, Ivan, but I'd rather not be involved."

"Just tell the truth," Henry urged. "Just say when you and me worked together—dates, times—and about how you used to pick me up at my spot in Burnaby. Tell them how long it took for them to fix my car."

Phone time running out, he stopped pussyfooting around. "As much as I hate to do it," he said, "I'll be subpoenaing you. If you don't come, you'll be in contempt of court."

Now, Bradbury sits, white-faced, in the witness box, looking like a man about to be shot. When Henry asks whether he recalls the date they began working on his house, Bradbury says he has no idea.

Dates of the bus strike? "I don't take buses, so I wouldn't know."

How long did I work for you? "Not a clue."

Did I have transport of my own at the time? "No."

Did you pick me up at my home in Burnaby on days I didn't overnight in West Vancouver? "Yes."

Did this go on for weeks on end? "Yes."

Yes, Bradbury recalls getting a call from Henry's wife early one morning. And, yes, the call concerned a break-in at their Burnaby home.

Regarding the lineup photo—at Henry's request, Madam Clerk hands him Exhibit One—Henry asks Bradbury whether it's been doctored.

"No, I wouldn't think so for a minute."

What the hell? "Has the photo been retouched?"

"No, the shadows aren't wonky and, though the shirt area looks odd, the thing overall looks fine."

"So there's no way I could cut the negative out and put a head in there, and do it that way?"

"That hasn't been done."

"But could it be done?"

"Very, very difficult. Not worth someone's time."

"Unless you were serving time—"

"Oh, I see what you mean. I couldn't tell you. That's conjecture."

Henry asks Madam Clerk to hand Bradbury Exhibit Five, the photo array containing the May 13 headshot of Henry; the array from which Miss Kavanagh identified Henry as her attacker. "Is it possible," he asks Bradbury, "to shoot a picture like that, then put a background in the back? Is that not easy to do?"

"No. It takes an immense amount of skill. Nobody has changed it. The whole picture's slightly out of focus, meaning the whole thing was taken at the same time."

"But I could shoot a background in this, and put that picture on top, could I not, and reshoot a picture?"

"Oh, it's possible, but that doesn't mean it's been done in this case . . . "

Returning to Exhibit One, the lineup photo, Henry asks about the weird black thing he appears to be wearing—like a baseball umpire's chest protector. "You use it so you don't get hit with a ball," he clarifies.

After holding the photo up to the light, squinting, Bradbury as much as says that Henry's rants are lost on him.

Holding his own copy of the photo, Henry approaches the witness box. *How else can he make Colin come to his senses?*

Luchenko leaps to his feet: "I appreciate my friend isn't quite up on what he's doing, but perhaps he could describe to the jury, rather than explain to the witness, these points. I think it's being lost on them."

"Yes, it is," says Judge Bouck.

Luchenko says, "I certainly can't follow what's going on."

Confused, frustrated, and angry, Henry takes his seat.

Luchenko rises to cross-examine the witness. "Mr. Bradbury, you're saying that, while it is possible to doctor photos, so far as your eye can see and your expertise can see, these photographs have not been doctored?

"That's correct."

"That an out-of-focus photo is more difficult to doctor than a clear one?"

"Yes, because you couldn't get the out-of-focus consistent."

"You can't say whether, the nights you stayed in West Vancouver, Mr. Henry was there throughout the night?"

"No, I can't."

Jesus Christ. Henry buries his face in his hands. His star witness.

• • •

NEXT MORNING, BEFORE the jury's called in, Henry stands to speak.

"I think I should, Your Honour," he says, shifting from foot to foot, "for my own sake . . . I said to myself downstairs that I'm really into this over my head. I'd rather make my own submission to the jury than have someone else control my life. But when it comes to dealing with the law, about different identifications and whatever, in that respect I should have someone speak for me."

"You should have thought about that before," says Judge Bouck. "I gave you ample chance to get a lawyer. You had a lawyer, and you fired him."

"Well—"

"I said you should have a lawyer. You turned it down. You elected to represent yourself. You take the chances."

"What I need right now," Henry says, "is a little guy over there, sort of a friend—researching new case law, getting my ideas across."

"A lawyer isn't going to be able to do anything for you. He wasn't here during the evidence. He has no idea what the case is about, no transcript of the proceedings. These are all the chances you took when you decided to defend yourself."

"Yes, but—"

"And that's a difficult decision you've put yourself in, nobody else. Now we've given you a copy of *Martin's Criminal Code*. Were we to turn you loose in the library, you'd have no idea what to do. Perhaps the Crown can help—there's an article by Salhany in *Canadian Criminal Procedure on Identification*."

Judge Bouck instructs the Crown to photocopy the article for him.

"Yes, My Lord," says Luchenko.

"I've dug up other stuff for the past eight months," says Henry. "I'll use that, too."

"Oh," says Judge Bouck, "you won't be arguing law to the jury."

• • •

JERRY PHILIPSON—THE John Howard Society liaison between Henry and his former parole officer, Chris Conroy—takes the stand and smiles encouragingly at Henry. It's the first honest-to-God smile he's seen in months. It's as though Philipson—neatly dressed and crinkly-eyed—actually believes in him.

When Henry asks about the Pavlovik assault on November 20, 1980, Philipson says, "You were working in Port Moody. We watched the Grey Cup together at your home in Burnaby. November 23. And what a game that was, eh Ivan?"

Who could forget it? The Eskimos demolished the Tiger-Cats 48–10, one of the most lopsided Grey Cups ever.

Speaking of the alleged Simpson assault on May 5, 1981, Henry asks, "Wasn't I living on Canada Way and working in Chilliwack? Remember that month-long work/travel permit Parole Services issued me on April 24?" *Damn it. He can see the permit crystal-clear in his mind's eye: April 24 to May 24.*

"Sorry, Ivan," Philipson says, "I'm no good with dates."

And so it goes. To the point that, finally, Henry asks him whether he's able to give any particulars at all regarding dates, times, and locations.

"No," says Philipson, "though we mostly maintained contact, and I did see you in the community and so on for short periods, you may have been living somewhere other than the place you told me."

As for the schedule showing the precise times of their meetings, Philipson says he'd long since discarded both it and his official reports. Indeed, he has nothing to offer but four summary reports—general, not specific, in nature.

"Mr. Henry," says Judge Bouck, "you can review those reports over the break."

• • •

JANUARY 21, 1981 — Mr. Henry is employed consistently. Until a week ago, he lived with his ex-wife, Jessie, and their two children in a very dilapidated, run-down duplex on Canada Way. Nevertheless, a great improvement on where they were living before, a single room on skid road.

Mr. Henry bought an automobile with the writer's permission, in December. It was very difficult, if not impossible, to travel around to his various places by bus, and a car became a necessity. Unfortunately, he bought a 'lemon,' which is constantly being sent back for repairs.

MARCH 27, 1981 — Mr. Henry resides at the Woodbine Hotel on Hastings Street. Though they remain separated, he sees his wife and children fairly frequently, and stays overnight occasionally.

Mr. Henry continues to remain self-employed as a construction labourer/house framer. Although this is a precarious business financially, he seems to survive reasonably well.

MAY 26, 1981 — Mr. Henry was traveling to Chilliwack to work on a daily basis (with a special work permit) for several weeks recently. He is now back working in the Vancouver area.

SEPTEMBER 2, 1981 — Mr. Henry's attitude and response to supervision continues to be very good. He keeps in regular contact and is frank. He is currently living in North Vancouver with a person he is helping frame a house.

JANUARY 26, 1982 — Mr. Henry was in constant touch with me, and made a strong and sincere effort to complete.his term successfully, which he did.

He is a much stronger, capable person now than he was twenty-one months ago and this augers well

> for the future. The fact that he completed Mandatory
> Supervision successfully has given his self-esteem a
> real boost, and this cannot hurt.

How proud he'd been for being—save for that one stupid mistake, the unreported B and E—straight up. But that was then. Reading through the reports again, he sees what a bust they are. Missing is any confirmation of his whereabouts at the exact time each crime went down.

• • •

LUCHENKO SAYS TO Judge Bouck, "I take it from the Court's earlier remarks that, so long as there's no delay, Mr. Henry may retain a lawyer?"

"I discussed it with him the first day of the trial," says Judge Bouck. "I mean, you always have the right to hire a lawyer. It's just that I can't adjourn the trial until you get one."

That lying SOB. Never was the subject mentioned. Not thinking to ask why an adjournment wouldn't be in order for something so serious, he says, "Oh no, I wouldn't do that."

"There's no impediment in your procuring a lawyer. But you must get him yourself," says Judge Bouck. "The Court can't get him for you. Similarly, if you want a certain book, you must identify it before we can make arrangements for it to be brought up here."

Milliken says the Crown will be arguing "similar fact evidence"— meaning that factual evidence regarding one offence may be used to prove the commission of others.

"Thank you," says the judge, "Make sure you copy Mr. Henry as well."

Henry fires a parting shot. "I feel I've got my head and I'm ramming it against a wall. I don't know the law from Adam. I'm uncertain about many things, but when I decided to do all this by myself, I did it for a reason and, sometimes, the reason doesn't prove to be the best. So what I am trying to do is keep on talking about everything, but you are absolutely right—it's not doing me any good at all. I'm closing my case, Your Honour. I feel you guys are setting me up. If you guys want to set me up, fuck, go for it."

"You don't want to call more evidence? Would you like a few minutes to think about it?"

"I have no thoughts," he says. "You're all a bunch of assholes."

CHAPTER 14

CLOSING PITCH

I n response to associate Crown counsel Milliken's impenetrable argument regarding similar fact evidence, Henry gives a speech lasting all of four minutes.

When he's done, he asks Judge Bouck to tell the jury that there is no forensic evidence linking him with any of the crimes, that the prejudicial impact of his criminal record outweighs its usefulness, and that he was denied a lie detector test as well as many complainant statements.

On Monday morning, Luchenko announces the Crown's eleventh-hour decision not to argue similar fact evidence after all. Still uncertain about the implications, Henry assumes it's good news. If he recalls properly, Judge Craig, the preliminary hearing judge, used that same "similar fact evidence" to commit him to trial—in the absence of identification evidence—on all counts.

"Don't worry, Mr. Henry," says Judge Bouck, "I'll be sure to tell the jury to consider each count by itself—make it clear that the facts supporting one count can't be used to support charges on the others."

At this point—10:08 a.m. on March 14, 1983—Ivan Henry, grasping the wooden lectern for dear life, begins his final submission. "I'm sorry I was so downright rude," he says, addressing the jury, "but my friends intend to convict me. My defence is reality. The mistake my friends made was the lack of real proof that these women had been raped and assaulted. When no doctors are called, I again suspect they're trying to make me wear this. My learned friend can argue the point until he's blue in the face. My answer to him is that the proof is taken away from me in—by taking the medical evidence, and not giving it to me.

"Yous all is neutral," he says to the jury. "I've never met you, nor you me. The trial started February 28, and we selected yous. I never looked at any of the clothes you wore, nor the way your emotions seemed to be, the way you were standing there. I looked not at your looks, basically at your eyes, and I tried many seconds to figure out who you were, and if there was some sort of truth that you could feel from me."

Referring to contradictions in the complainants' evidence, Henry mentions hair colour—brown to black to blond to red. Facial hair and age? All over the block. The lack of physical evidence? Given that the rip-off rapist wore gloves only once, he must've left fingerprints. Yet there was nothing: no fibres, footprints, tool marks—nothing linking him to the crimes. "In view of these reality criteria," Henry says, "the attacks likely never occurred."

Highlighting the contradictions between Miss Browning's evidence at trial and a police statement with which he'd been provided, Henry is interrupted by Judge Bouck: "You had the opportunity to put the statement in evidence. You did not; therefore it cannot be mentioned."

"But I asked her about it."

"If you're talking about a statement the complainant made that was not put in evidence—and none of those complainant statements were— you cannot use them as part of your argument."

"The judge is supposed to put those statements in as exhibits, isn't he?"

"No."

"Then I'll use the preliminary hearing transcript."

"Only if you've put the questions to the witness on the witness stand—"

"Sorry. I got, like, taken away, like a little lamb, sort of butchered right away, if you understand the term."

"You elected to defend yourself. You carry on."

Henry pushes on, but then partway into summarizing Miss Larson's evidence, he goes silent. "I'm sort of lost," he says, "because you made me lost."

When Judge Bouck offers to take a break, Henry says, "It don't matter. I'll just do what—I'll proceed to—I'll just dump this all in impromptu."

By the time he gets to Miss Kavanagh—he's been eagerly looking forward to poking holes in her testimony—his tank is empty. Too many interruptions about this and that rule of evidence, the meaning of this or that section of the *Criminal Code,* all the legal bullshit they trot out every time he tries to explain himself. Reaching for the preliminary hearing transcript, he starts pointing out Miss Kavanagh's ever-changing identification evidence.

"You can't read in anything from the preliminary hearing that wasn't put to a witness," says Judge Bouck.

"Excuse me, Your Lordship," says Milliken. "I believe he's referring to Miss Kavanagh's evidence, which, of course, is in the form of the preliminary hearing transcript."

"Oh yes," says the judge, "you can refer to that."

Derailed again, Henry loses his way. Where was he? Oh yeah, was the bamboo curtain in Miss Horvath's bedroom or in her kitchen, because if she isn't sure, then she must be making it all up. As for Miss Simpson's testimony, he says: "It loses merit throughout." And what about that address on the envelope?

"If something seems funny," he says, "as funny as it seems in suspicion, then doesn't it seem it's a set-up issue, so to speak? No one other than the police would know that address, and be able to give her that address to say. The odds of this happening in real day-to-day life is, without a doubt, undoubtful. It would never happen to anyone but me.

"If you believe, which you should, that this lineup isn't real, you must conclude I'm not the culprit. The main mystery deepens throughout these proceedings. Why do people change their minds in regards to identifying me? How is it they can identify me in court when they couldn't during the lineup?

"I didn't hide my criminal record," he points out. "I showed it to yous. I don't care about my past. It's got nothing to do with today."

Building to a finale, Henry says: "Are you people real, or is it just— just to make sort of a front so you just put me away, then I can say I had a jury trial? I don't know. If that's right to say, then I guess I said it, because that's the way I sometimes feel. I feel I've been through a lot, I tell you. I've still got it together, though.

"I don't question the integrity behind anything that the Crown has presented. All I know is it's too easy to rely on identification only. We can just send away a guy on identification. Any one of us can be sent away on identification. Come out of a bank, and some guy says, 'That's the guy over there. Take him.' In reality, the Crown failed to produce a good case. They should've had a little more evidence. Should have brought me some medical evidence, so I could substantiate my blood sample. I don't think that's fair.

"I somehow feel I've been taken for a joke. I've been taken for a ride—if Ramirez can identify me within six to eight seconds, then—

"In true reality, I have a tattoo on my right arm. The picture doesn't show it. If you've ever worn handcuffs, you'll know there's no way you can twist your hands over like that . . . . So, as I've stated, that's not me. It might be my face, but it ain't my hands, not the right hand.

"Thank you."

At 10:47 a.m., thirty-nine minutes after he began, Ivan Henry—frustrated, confused, and exhausted—takes his seat.

CHAPTER 15

THE VERDICT

When Luchenko sums up the case for the Crown, Henry's so shaken that he catches only snippets—how Jessie's failure to appear suggests that he's guilty; how Bradbury, "the expert," had undercut his main defence; and how, in resisting the lineup, he'd shown a "consciousness of guilt."

Then it's Judge Bouck's turn. "Members of the jury," he says, "it is necessary that you consider each count separately."

Having commended the complainants for their "courage," he reminds the jurors of their key role as finders of fact. "In the event of conflicts in the evidence," he says, "it is you who must assess credibility."

Instead of outlining the factors relevant to resolving a factual dispute, Judge Bouck spends more time on cussing than credibility: "Regrettably, I may have to refer to four-letter words, because they were the words used by witnesses in their testimony. In doing so, I do not mean to dignify them by reciting them in a court of law. They are just as distasteful to me as I am sure they are to you. Nonetheless, having been spoken by the witnesses, they may have some meaning in the context of each count."

Turning to Miss Simpson's evidence, he says, "Two days after the incident, she saw a man on a bus who looked like the accused, and she told the police."

You're dead wrong, thinks Henry. *The man she saw on the bus didn't look like me. His build differed from mine; Miss Simpson said so herself. The man she told Detective Sims "closely resembled" her attacker was not me! Maybe it was her actual attacker.*

As for Henry's criminal record, Judge Bouck says, "The convictions in this case cannot be used as evidence of guilt, nor can you assume they indicate a propensity on Mr. Henry's part to commit the crimes for which he is now charged. Evidence of such having been led purely to test an accused's credibility, his truthfulness in this regard reflects favourably on one aspect of his credibility.

"However," he adds, focusing on each juror in turn, "it's for you to say whether a person who has such a criminal record is the kind of witness you might choose to believe."

Did Henry miss something, or did the judge just contradict himself?

Judge Bouck says that Henry first said he was in the lineup, then he wasn't; he was living here, then he was living there. Sure, he asked for a lie detector test, but polygraph results are not admissible in courts of law.

Addressing the identification evidence, Judge Bouck says that while honest people can be mistaken and voice identification is subject to error, "you may act on such evidence by itself or together with any other evidence if you are satisfied beyond a reasonable doubt that Henry is the correct person."

That's it? That's all he has to say about all the contradictions in identification?

Referring to what he calls Henry's "main defence"—namely, that no offences occurred—Judge Bouck reminds the jurors that the complainants said "the accused entered their premises . . . As for the two counts of attempted rape, I have decided that the actions of the accused were more than mere preparation to commit the crime of rape."

Wait a minute. The accused *entered their premises; the actions of the* accused? *He's telling the jury the attacker is me! He's got me guilty already when I'm supposed to be innocent until proven guilty. Why not just tar and feather me right here?*

Regarding Henry's request for medical reports, Judge Bouck tells the jurors: "Though the accused repeatedly demanded disclosure of the medical reports, they need not—because the Crown is not relying on them—be disclosed."

Had the Crown attempted to introduce the lineup photo, Judge Bouck says, he would likely have ruled it inadmissible. "However, presumably, Henry wanted you to draw the inference that any identification of him is a farce, since he's the only one being restrained by three police officers. On the other hand, the Crown suggests his obvious reluctance to participate leads to an inference of consciousness of guilt on his part. It is for you to draw the proper inference upon considering all of the evidence."

Calling Henry's alibi evidence "a defence worthy of consideration," the judge says that the onus is not on the accused to establish this defence; rather, the Crown "must prove that Mr. Henry was at the various addresses mentioned in the indictment.

"However," he adds, taking in the jurors, one at a time, "there doesn't seem to be any evidence that I can find that, with respect to any of these counts, the accused can say exactly where he was on the dates in question."

After consulting his notes, he begins his summation. "Trial by jury stands among one of the most successful accomplishments of our democratic society. It is a system that has made us the envy of many of the people in the world. It depends for its strength on the integrity and the honesty of the ordinary men and women called at random to sit on juries. It rests on the proposition that ordinary men and women will be true to the jury oath, and will base their verdict on the evidence and disregard outside influence."

Out of the jury's hearing, Crown counsel and Judge Bouck engage in a conversation that's lost on Henry. After the jury is recalled, the judge tells them, "While I might have been remiss in some of my statements, let me assure you of this. The Crown has not necessarily proved that the assailant was the accused."

● ● ●

AT 9:30 P.M. on March 15, 1983, the jury, after ten hours of deliberation, delivers its verdict. Guilty on all ten counts.

Head spinning, hands trembling, Henry watches Luchenko get to his feet.

"My Lord," says Luchenko, "the Crown will be seeking a dangerous offender designation."

Dangerous offender? DO is reserved for the worst repeat offenders in the country. If the Crown gets away with this, he'll be in jail until he dies. It's happening in slow motion, and it's happening to him. He's living a nightmare.

"Your presence here has helped the administration of justice," Judge Bouck is telling the jurors. "It also, I hope, gives you a better idea of the way in which the system of justice functions from day to day."

Henry doesn't know whether to laugh or cry. *You bastards. You're framing me for something I didn't do.*

"I know it is an onerous difficult task for you," the judge continues, "and we all appreciate what you have done. Please return next Monday, March 21, to be included in the Panel."

Judge Bouck adjourns the sentencing hearing. Ivan Henry, in shock, is handcuffed and led out of the courtroom. In the secure loading area, he steps into the paddy wagon to Oakalla and a future he cannot imagine.

CHAPTER 16

DOWN BUT NOT OUT

Not since the delivery man came through the unlocked door of his mother's apartment has he felt so helpless and disconnected and low. Back then he didn't stand a chance, a boy against a man. Ed's hands were under the covers before he could say no, and Henry fights the memory of absenting himself from his own body, watching from a distance. Not just once, but on and off for . . . how long—weeks? Months? Were it not for crimes that finally netted him a juvie jail term, who knows when the torment would've ended? It wasn't his fault, or was it? Why can't he banish the shame to this day?

No matter what, no way he'll ever play the victim card. *Don't worry, Mom,* he says, sending her a silent prayer of gratitude. *If it's the last thing I do, I'll make you proud of me.* And then, bowing his head, he prays aloud, "Dear God above, I might be down but I sure as hell ain't out. Just help me win my appeal and we'll be good to go."

Henry rolls up his sleeves. Less than two weeks after the trial, working long hours in his cell and the jailhouse library, he's completed an appeal against his convictions. He's discovered that dried-up felt tips dipped in kerosene mixed with ink from the print shop make the best pens, and the backs of prisoner-request forms make for clean documents. He cites, first and foremost, the phony lineup photo and the police who lied about it. As well, he outlines a long list of judicial errors, including the following:

- Despite agreeing not to charge jury on similar fact evidence, treating all offences as one;

- Bias in favour of the Crown and against the accused;

- Failure to take his self-represented status into account;

- Failure to put his alibi defences fairly to the jury;

- Flawed ID evidence—"The judge didn't treat the pretrial confabulation and coaching of the complainants with the contempt it deserved";

- Suggesting to the jury that his criminal record might detract from, rather than enhance, his credibility; and

- Wrongful exclusion of medical evidence.

In conclusion, he says: "The judge's position is one of great power and prestige, which gives his every word great significance. The statements he made amounted to an interference showing no fairness." When he goes back to court—on April 6, 1983, his next mandatory appearance—he hands the submission to the court clerk.

Weeks later, he receives a stamped copy acknowledging receipt. Although he'd asked the Court of Appeal to hear the appeal of his conviction in advance of his sentencing hearing, the court declines his request.

A couple of weeks later, a young buck from Legal Aid pays him a visit at Oakalla—a little prick who has the nerve to suggest that pleading guilty to even one count might help at the sentencing hearing. What's more, says the rookie, if he agrees to a guilty plea, legal aid might see fit to assist with his appeal.

"Why would I do that," Henry says, staring the man down, "when I ain't guilty of any of them?" He hollers for the guard. End of meeting.

Back in his cell, he writes a note to Luchenko. "From this time forward," he says, "no one is authorized to speak on my behalf. This letter is that confirmation of my true intentions of no lawyer."

• • •

WHEN HENRY IS remanded to Riverview Hospital, a mental health facility, for a thirty-day assessment before his sentencing hearing, his worst fears are confirmed. Such assessments are ordered only when the court is considering a dangerous offender designation.

If not for the loonies all over the place, Riverview—a deceptively beautiful, spacious, sylvan property not far from Oakalla—wouldn't be half-bad. Shortly after he arrives, he runs into Manfred Cullen, his old pal from Stony Mountain Penitentiary near Winnipeg. Could it have been that long ago—1968—that they met? Two young bucks full of swagger, temporarily run afoul of the law, certain of their invincibility.

Although Manfred is rumoured to have at least one murder beef under his belt, Henry avoids the topic. Besides, the last thing he needs is for Manfred—renowned for his hatred of deviants—to catch wind of why he's there. Instead, Henry recruits him to help organize a con-versus-security guard game of doughnut hockey.

The game goes well until Henry dekes out some lard-ass bull. When no one's looking, the bastard smashes him in the face, accidentally on purpose. The hit punches out one tooth and leaves another front tooth dangling and bloody. After biding his time—and taking care to hide his mouth from Manfred—Henry hip-checks the bull into the boards, nailing him good. Ivan Henry doesn't take shit from anybody, guards included.

Later, as Henry cleans up, Manfred wants to know who busted his teeth. "Just the name, pal," he says, as Henry discards a blood-soaked wad of toilet paper. "Just tell me his name. That's all I need."

"I ain't never been a rat, and I ain't about to become one," says Henry. "Besides," he adds, cracking a bloody half smile, "no way am I having that goof's demise on my conscience."

• • •

HENRY WRITES TO William Kaplan, the federal Solicitor General, requesting the trial transcripts. Without them attached to his appeal submission, he points out, he doesn't stand a chance. When he hears back, it's not from Kaplan but from VPD's chief constable, Bob Stewart.

"My inquiry reveals it was you who introduced this photo into Court," Chief Stewart writes, "and also provided an expert witness in an attempt to prove that the picture had been altered. The expert witness said, in fact, that the picture had not been altered. The photo was taken after the lineup had been completed, and was part of the usual procedure of photographing the lineup for the purpose of record and scrutiny by interested parties at subsequent proceedings."

Henry gets back to work on his appeal submission. When it's finally done, he reads it over and tells himself it isn't half-bad at all.

On May 14, 1982, I was under heavy surveillance plus, having just been released from jail, I was with my family . . . I didn't want a lawyer at the prelim. I'd had three. Not that I'm choosy, but I didn't like their questions, such as: "Oh, so you want doctors to say these girls were never raped?"

I truly believed I was the fall guy or there'd been some big mistake for sure. The law [Canadian case law] says I have the right to scrutinize statements, but they wouldn't let me. White refused to show me the photo. The transcripts have been altered. Insulting remarks made by the complainants made me pretty emotional, but my lawyer mocked me, just like the rest of them.

At the preliminary hearing, no-one showed me any evidence. I was just told to shut up or I'd be put downstairs.

I stated to Chief Justice McEachern that I didn't want a lawyer. But I needed protection against evidence being put in without the proper rules being adhered to. Yet I was made to feel like an idiot for defending myself at trial—If I was found guilty, so what?

I brought a writ of "prohibition" to stop them from saying, every time I go to court, "go back to remand for two more months. No, go to the (nut-house) Riverview Forensic Unit. No, go to jail."

Certiorari with habeas corpus was to ensure I was able to proceed to the Supreme Court of Canada.

It is beyond truth that none of these charges exist, nor do I know any of the women. Period.

Once again, he files an application—citing Section 533 (1) of the Criminal Code—to have Exhibit One released for scientific testing:

A judge of a superior court of criminal jurisdiction or a court of criminal jurisdiction may, on summary application on behalf of the accused or the prosecutor, after three days' notice to the accused or prosecutor, as the case may be, order the release of any exhibit for the purpose of a scientific or other test or examination, subject to such terms as appear to be necessary or desirable to ensure the safeguarding of the exhibit and its preservation for use at the trial.

In no time flat, the BC Supreme Court rules that such a right is available only to an "accused," not to a convicted felon.

Desperate to get his hands on the trial transcripts, Henry finally receives word from the Official Court Reporters of British Columbia that, until he ponies up $4,000, work won't begin on their production. Great—four grand? He'll just shake the next money tree he comes across.

Meanwhile, Ottawa enacts a plan long in the works—moving offenders awaiting bail, trial, sentencing, appeal, or probation—from Oakalla to the newly opened Vancouver Pretrial Services Centre. A high-tech, antiseptic fortress of reinforced concrete, Pretrial is the highest-security institution in North America and the most high-tech prison in the world. In the words of Michael Yates, a (one-time) prison guard, "It is definitely the wave of the future for criminal justice, in philosophy, structure, and methodology. And location. The downtown districts of large cities are unusual places for prisons."[1] As Yates went on to say,

> When it opened, Vancouver Pretrial Services Centre was the *nouvelle vague* in corrections design: not a skyscraper, but very CN Tower in spirit. It occupies one city block—across the street from the Vancouver police headquarters and across the lane from the provincial court building—and is connected by tunnel to both . . .
>
> At Oakalla, except for the noise the cons made and the televisions, when on, it was quiet. At Pretrial, it was like trying to sleep in a flophouse with the window open—sirens, drunks, traffic, and endless white noise. And deafening unit doors which fired like weapons.

It is at the Vancouver Pretrial Services Centre, in late October, that Henry gets an unexpected visit from Detective William Harkema. Handing Henry a stack of transcripts entitled "Complainants'

Testimony," he says, "You're entitled to these for use in your dangerous offender hearing." Dropping his voice, he adds, "By the way, we don't want you on these. It's not us, it's the Crown."

Before Henry can open his mouth—Why would the cops be ratting on the Crown? Or is he simply being mocked?—Harkema takes a pen from his pocket. "Here," he says. "Put it to good use." A promising omen, that pen—a symbol of freedom fighters everywhere.

• • •

A FULL DAY goes by before Henry builds up the nerve to open the envelope taped to the transcripts. Michael Luchenko's covering letter reads: "At the dangerous offender hearing, the Crown will argue that the offences show Mr. Henry's failure to control his sexual impulses, the likelihood of causing injury, etc. to other persons as a result thereof. In short, the test of 'serious personal injury offences' has been met. The offender has 'displayed a persistent aggressive behaviour which shows a substantial degree of indifference on the part of the offender as to the reasonably foreseeable consequences to other persons of his behaviour—'"

Henry can counter using all the contradictions in the complainants' testimony. He studies the transcripts late into the night, but something's wrong. Where are the questions he'd carefully written down to ask each woman to test her credibility: Did you attend a doctor? Did you obtain a card and file number from the police? Did you attend a lineup and see handcuffs on me? Did you swear on oath that your complaint and statement are true?

The more he reads, the angrier he gets. Huge sections of the transcripts are missing.

CHAPTER 17

HOPELESS CASES

On November 21, 1983—day one of the hearing that will determine whether the Crown has Ivan Henry designated a dangerous offender—Michael Luchenko's acting like he owns the joint. He fusses with his binders, jokes with the court clerk, and consults with the assembled head-shrinkers—the so-called expert witnesses. Henry—back in Supreme Court for the first time since the guilty verdicts—feels disoriented and sluggish. He hasn't slept in days.

Luchenko tells the court he intends to prove that Henry, by his conduct, "has shown a failure to control his sexual impulses and a likelihood of causing injury, pain, or other evil to other persons through failure in the future to control his sexual impulses." The Crown's not just asking for a long prison sentence; it wants Henry put away forever.

Henry listens impatiently as six of the eight trial complainants testify regarding the "severe psychological damage" they've suffered. Sleeping with lights on. Nightmares. Weight loss, weight gain. Failing grades, lost semesters. Constant fear. Self-blame. Thoughts of suicide.

Next up is Dr. Roderick Whitman, the shrink appointed to represent the interests of the Crown. "When I asked Mr. Henry how he was doing, he replied, 'They think I'm buggy. I'm denying the convictions because I'm not guilty. I've asked for a lie detector, and nobody wants to get me one.' He insisted I examine the lineup photo."

Whitman says that, all in all, Henry was friendly. "I could find no evidence of gross thought disorders. His abstract thinking, though, was markedly impaired . . . Based on everything, my opinion is he would probably be considered a personality disorder and an anti-social type."

"What," Luchenko asks, "is the main factor in your assessment that he would very likely inflict injury on others?"

"That he has repeatedly assaulted women. He does not evidence the slightest concern for the impact of that behaviour. He has failed to show remorse. He lacks the quality of insight that would enable him to modify his behaviour."

I didn't fucking do it! Henry wants to shout. *How am I supposed to show remorse for something I didn't do?*

"In your reading of the trial transcripts," Luchenko asks, "did you detect any expressions whatsoever of sympathy or compassion on the part of Mr. Henry towards those victims?"

"No, I did not."

Henry begins his cross-examination. He asks if the psychiatrist's opinion is based solely on the transcripts. Whitman says he also took into account their face-to-face discussion.

"You're saying that in one hour you can tell I'm an anti-social psychopath?"

"I used this other material to satisfy myself that the scope of my examination was adequate."

"If I was to say to you that all the material you read is garbage, what would you think of that?"

"I have already said that I have accepted it—"

"You say I don't have emotions for these women? I do care about their emotions. But at the same time, I don't give nothing for their emotions because my emotions are also on the line; my heart is. My heart is—"

"I was concerned about the fact that you demonstrated no remorse for the victims."

"Well, maybe I was crying deep inside . . . Underneath all this was some real concern."

Dr. Whitman steps down, and the Crown closes its case.

When Judge Bouck asks if Henry wants to testify, he says no. What could I possibly add, he says, that I didn't already say at trial?

The next morning, Judge Bouck insists that Dr. Clifford Kerr—the psychiatrist appointed to be Henry's designate—be called to testify. When Henry argues that Kerr doesn't have his best interests at heart, the judge says, "The law compels me to hear the evidence of at least two psychiatrists, so I have no alternative."

"Like it or not," he adds, "I'm not about to have you later complain that your interests were not protected."

When Dr. Kerr takes the stand, Henry is tempted to turn his back. Sure enough, in response to every question, Kerr parrots the Crown's shrink, Dr. Whitman, pretty much word for word.

While Dr. Kerr drones on in cross-examination about what a despicable person he is, Henry recites the St. Jude prayer under his breath:

> Oh glorious apostle St. Jude, faithful servant and friend of Jesus . . . the Church honors and invokes thee universally as the patron of hopeless cases . . . Pray for me who am so miserable. Make use, I implore thee, of that particular privilege accorded thee of bringing visible and speedy help where help is almost despaired of. Come to my assistance in this great need, that I may receive the consolations and succor of heaven in all my necessities, tribulations and sufferings—especially that the light of truth will soon shine on this injustice . . .

• • •

THAT NIGHT, BACK in Pretrial, Henry polishes his argument, to be delivered the next morning. "I'm not a present danger to anyone," he writes, "not even a bug on the street." But how to prove a negative? Try as he might, he has trouble finding the words to convince Judge Bouck he's not a psycho.

Meanwhile, the mood in Pretrial is ramping up—phones ringing, walkie-talkies crackling, a herd of bulls in flak jackets with ammo rumbling down the hall, the din of a hundred doors firing shut. Someone cranks up a radio. Normal programming's been suspended. According to the grapevine, the powder keg that's Oakalla has finally exploded in riot—roof halfway to being torn off, water mains busted, and flames scorching the ceiling.

At Pretrial, inmates are locked down so that the guards can be evacuated to join their SWAT-team brethren. Trying to focus, hunched over his paper, Henry can't keep his mind from racing. The riot at Oakalla has unnerved him, and he spends a sleepless night trying to imagine what he can possibly say to help his case.

The next morning in court, when he delivers his speech, his voice is oddly lifeless. He stumbles ahead, tripping over his words. He drops his notes and bumps his head picking them up. He forgets things he meant to say and adds things that make no sense, even to him. Hurrying to the end of his statement, eager to get it over with, he sits back down and crumples the paper into a ball.

"Thank you, Mr. Henry, for your time," says Judge Bouck.

Reading from a text prepared ahead of time, the judge renders his decision: "The jury had no difficulty convicting him, partly because he unknowingly put into evidence testimony and exhibits that tended to prove his guilt. Six of the eight complainants testified in these proceedings about how the attacks affected their lives.

"It is devastating enough to be assaulted, but it must be equally repulsive for them to endure cross-examination, at trial and on this application, by the very person who committed these deplorable acts. They are to be commended for seeing this matter through to the bitter end.

"Society must be permanently protected from this man's predatory behaviour. There are no redeeming features to rule otherwise. I therefore sentence him to detention in a penitentiary for an indeterminate period."

PART TWO
HARD TIME (1983–2009)

"What prisoners try to convey to the free is how the presence
of time—as something being done to you, instead of something
you do things with—alters the mind at every moment."

— ADAM GOPNIK —
"THE CAGING OF AMERICA," *THE NEW YORKER*,
JANUARY 20, 2012

CHAPTER 18

CON-AIR

Eight days before Christmas 1983, Ivan Henry was transferred from Vancouver Pretrial to Kent Institution, two hours east of the city. Located in Agassiz, a farming community in the Fraser Valley, Kent is British Columbia's only maximum-security prison. Having been sentenced to a term of two years or longer, Henry was now a federal prisoner under Correctional Service of Canada (CSC) control.

While the paddy wagon bumped down the dirt road, Henry tried tuning out the loudmouth handcuffed to him. The idiot was ranting about how, if not for his old lady's whoring ways, she'd still be alive. Squinting out the tiny, dirty window, Henry caught sight of a sign-post—Cemetery Road, a fitting address. Worried that news of his supposed crimes had preceded him, he knew he'd have to stay on his toes to survive.

Kent Institution is a formidable set of low-slung buildings surrounded by razor wire. It is a dismal place, bleak in the drizzle and fog, cut off from the world by the heavily forested mountains and the public's wilful ignorance of what goes on behind penitentiary walls.

The slate-grey sky covered the prison like an overturned plate as Henry stumbled down from the paddy wagon. After being strip-searched, he shuffled along the range in lockstep with the blabbermouth who was hauling up his oversized grey sweats, feigning swagger. Rubbernecking cons banged on their cell doors, their anger aimed—for now, at least—at the goof beside him. Not for long, though; no one remains anonymous in the slammer.

"Fuckin' lady killer!"

"Wait'll you're alone in the shower."

"Hey, asshole! Suck my cock!"

Henry snuck a look inside one of the cells. A con was laid out like a corpse on his cot—twenty years old, if that. Blue images from a tiny television flickered over the kid's bloodless flesh. Studying the floor as he walked down the tier—eye contact being considered a major offence for new fish—Henry concentrated on the nose-puckering smell of bleach, old sweat, blocked toilets, damp mortar.

Finally, he reached his cell—a concrete platform, a thin mattress to sleep on, a toilet to shit in. The crash of locks tumbling into place. For the moment, at least, he was safe. His time will come, though. It always does in the joint.

• • •

ON CHRISTMAS EVE, he called home.

"Hi darling, it's Daddy . . . I miss you too, dear. Yes, honey, Grandma's feeling much better. She asks about you all the time. You excited about Santa? . . . Who's Glen? . . . You say Mommy gave him my jammies to wear? . . . Look, baby, I gotta run now. Tell Mom I called . . . I love you, darling. And your sister, too. Big hug for her."

Henry hung up the phone, disgusted by the thought of another man in his pajamas, lonelier than ever. With any luck, Jessie actually put his Christmas card under the tree. Maybe she even used the $120.16 he sent to buy something pretty for the girls.

Ho-ho-ho. Merry fucking Christmas.

• • •

BY THE TIME the inmates welcomed in 1984, banging anything they could get their hands on against toilets, sinks, and bolted-down chairs, Henry had finished another submission, this one appealing his indefinite sentence. It was fifty pages long, painstakingly handwritten, and full of meandering argument and outrage.

A couple of weeks later, he received word that Crown counsel Allan Stewart was applying to have his appeal dismissed—not on its merits, but for "want of prosecution." What the hell? They think that, because he hasn't ordered the appeal books—99 percent of which are the trial transcripts—he's not serious about the appeal? Sure, prior to the dangerous offender hearing, they'd given him the transcripts containing the complainants' testimony, but how in the hell's he supposed to drum up money for the rest?

Searching the prison library—shelves of Zane Grey westerns and recovery books for lushes—Henry came up empty. No case law or statute to help him. Undaunted, he swore an affidavit saying he didn't have two pennies to rub together:

> I have spoken to Mr. Wilf Roy, manager, about trial transcripts, and was quoted $4,000 . . . In no way have I shown a delay, disruption, or hindrance towards the court concerning myself. At the end of the sentencing, Mr. Luchenko stated the transcripts would be provided to me but, so far, he only gave me the complainants'. Actual words spoken have been changed in those—a lot of questions are missing or made to sound as though I was muddled up. Parliament requires that transcripts be accurate. These don't meet that requirement.

• • •

A FEW WEEKS later, on January 28, 1984, Henry was transferred, without explanation, to the Saskatchewan Penitentiary just outside Prince Albert, a thousand miles away. On the "Con-Air" milk run across Canada, shackled to a bench bolted to the floor, he kept the lineup photo tucked away. Having folded it to fit his shirt pocket, he'd slipped it into a Christmas card. When the correctional officer asked, "What's that?" he said it was a card from his momma. As soon as possible, he'd make a little waterproof pouch so he can carry it against his skin if necessary.

Saskatchewan Penitentiary occupies a walled, eight-hectare site that was once occupied by a Native residential school. As with most jails in western Canada, the inmate population is disproportionately made up of Aboriginal people. Its atmosphere mirrors Adam Gopnik's description of prisons in the United States: "a note of attenuated panic, of watchful paranoia—anxiety and boredom and fear mixed into a kind of enveloping fog, covering the guards as much as the guarded."[1]

The place was not new to Henry. In 1967, sentenced to a three-year term for stealing a TV and possessing stolen licence plates, he'd arrived at the Prince Albert prison scared and acting tough, only to have his hair buzzed off. After he'd been deloused, they'd handed him a cup, spoon, blanket, and sheet, plus a canteen slip for purchasing purposes.

Asked about it years later, Henry described the scene. "When I was entering the dome area," he told me, "I saw a good two hundred men standing over the barriers speaking to each other as they waited, holding their pails for the hot water needed for washing, to make coffee, etcetera. No comments about the new fish were voiced. These men were solid. They realized that coming into an institution was hard enough without being harassed.

"The showers were given twice a week—six open showers so the guard could holler, 'Five minutes only! Let's get going!' Another volley of men would replace you while you were getting dressed. It wasn't funny at all. It was very compelling because of the lack of privacy and trying to remain calm. Prince Albert was a serious maximum security institution It didn't house a bunch of pansies.

"I worked in the laundry, washing 580 inmates' clothes, plus the kitchen stewards', whose whites needed special care. There was no protective custody unit then, like there is now. Back then, when I was told I was being transferred to Stony Mountain, I was glad to go."

This time around it was different. He wasn't in for theft, and he might as well have had the word "skinner" tattooed on his forehead. Sexual criminals are despised in prison, and harassment and threats, from guards and fellow inmates, were frequent. Henry was a big, strong fellow with forearms like ham hocks and an air of firm resolve, but that doesn't count for much when you're outnumbered or facing down a shiv.

Barely a week after he was processed and given a regular cell, a guard got in his face, provoking him, demanding that he attend an inmate orientation meeting.

"Why should I, when I ain't guilty?"

Declared insubordinate, Henry was given two weeks in the hole, a two-by-three-metre dungeon-like cell without books or papers, or his precious *Criminal Code*. He had no right to any property, to make phone calls, or to have visitors. No mail. No radio or TV. Not much about solitary has changed, really, since Charles Dickens visited one of America's so-called model prisons in 1842. Dickens had this to say about solitary confinement:

I believe that very few men are capable of estimating the immense amount of torture and agony which this dreadful punishment . . . inflicts upon the sufferers.

I hold this slow and daily tampering with the mysteries of the brain to be immeasurably worse than any torture of the body: and because its ghastly signs and tokens are not so palpable to the eye and sense of touch as scars upon the flesh; because its wounds are not upon the surface, and it extorts few cries that human ears can hear; therefore I the more denounce it, as a secret punishment that slumbering humanity is not roused up to stay.[2]

Henry spent his time doing pushups and praying, pushups and praying. Three times a day, a tray of lousy food was pushed through a slot in the door. Pushups and praying. They weren't going to break him, period. He was not going to merely survive; he would triumph. He just needed a strategy to make the world understand that an innocent man had been framed. The minute he got out, he'd place a call to Saskatchewan Legal Aid. Step one was to figure out how to get that "want of prosecution" bullshit tossed out.

CHAPTER 19

GARBAGE

No sooner was Henry out of the hole—dazed and disoriented—than they put him on a Con-Air flight back to the west coast. Although he'd asked to have his appeal dealt with by way of written submission—less chance for monkey business, he figured—the BC Court of Appeal had directed him to appear in person.

On February 24, 1984, he was escorted down the same hidden hallway in the courthouse he'd first travelled along almost exactly a year earlier, the first day of his trial. In the courtroom, he stood impatiently while three judges dressed head to toe in black silk—Justices Seaton, Anderson, and Carrothers, according to the nameplates lined up in front of them—were ushered in.

When Crown counsel Allan Stewart launched into his pitch about want of prosecution, Henry, seized with vertigo, grabbed the arms of his chair to keep from falling over. When the clerk told him it was his turn to talk, he insisted she hand up the lineup photo to the judges. "Here, take a look at it," he said. "Even a fool can see it's fake."

"Mr. Henry," said Seaton, the judge in the middle, "we won't be needing that. The only issue before us in these proceedings is your failure to order the appeal books."

"But the transcripts are garbage."

For several minutes the judges huddled, talking quietly among themselves. Then the middle one delivered the decision of the court: "The conviction was on March 15, 1983, and a notice of appeal was filed on April 6. The sentence was imposed in November 1983, and the notice of appeal followed promptly. No appeal books have been filed or ordered.

"Mr. Henry says if we want to get them he will write some notes in them for us, but that he will not get them, that they are—I think his word was 'garbage'—and he would throw them away. He refused legal aid at his trial and he either does not want legal aid now or he cannot get legal aid now, maybe both. He has expressed an intention not to proceed with these appeals in accordance with the only way in which they can be dealt with. Under those circumstances, I would grant the motions quashing the appeals for want of prosecution."[1]

• • •

BACK IN LOCKUP at Kent, Henry, fighting off rage, wrote to Federal Justice Minister Mark MacGuigan, requesting a mercy hearing pursuant to the *Criminal Code*—"To Whom Pardon May Be Granted."[2] He had reason to hope. MacGuigan had been appointed justice minister in Prime Minister Pierre Elliott Trudeau's Liberal government in 1982, the same year that Trudeau's brainchild, the *Charter of Rights and Freedoms*, was enacted.

Soon after his application was dismissed due to the absence of transcripts, Henry got a bit of good news: his notice of intention to appeal to the Supreme Court of Canada had been filed.

Once again, without notice, Henry was transferred back to Prince Albert. This time he was housed on B3—the special-needs range at Sask Pen, home to the most violent and dangerous inmates.

"You're going down, asshole."

"Gimme your sandwich, you piece of shit."

"Come near me and you're dead meat."

Each night, Henry prayed that the Supreme Court would hear his appeal. In particular, he prayed that the matter would be heard by Chief Justice Bora Laskin, the finest judge in the country, from what he had read. When, on March 26, 1984, Chief Justice Laskin passed away, Henry was so despondent he refused to leave his cell for a week.

A month later, a wafer-thin letter bearing the gold insignia of the Supreme Court of Canada arrived. Reluctantly opening it, almost afraid to begin, he read: "The motion for leave to appeal from the judgment of the British Columbia Court of Appeal, dated February 24, 1984, was heard this day and dismissed."

For hours he sat on his cot, devastated, his head in his hands.

A week later, a letter arrived from the Crown's Ottawa agents. It was postmarked April 2—a solid month earlier! The letter had been forwarded to him from Kent Institution. He opened it and read: "We write to inform you that you have until April 24 to file your material."

Was it lost in transit, or lost while he was being bounced back and forth between facilities, or were they deliberating screwing him over? To the authorities, to the public, to the whole damn world, it didn't matter. The fact was, nobody gave a damn about Ivan Henry except Ivan Henry. Some days, it was almost enough to make him not give a damn, either.

That night, he retrieved his slim little package from its hiding place. He removed the tape and butcher paper, then held the doctored lineup photo up to the dim bulb. Satisfied, vowing never to relent, he tucked it away again. Somehow—God will show him the way—he'll use it to bring down the entire apparatus of the state.

CHAPTER 20

UNLIKELY SAVIOUR

At Sask Pen, Ivan Henry was constantly being bumped and goaded, threatened and taunted. He worried about his safety and slept badly. Then, in the midst of it all, he received some good news. His old buddy, Manfred Cullen—whom he'd last seen at that con–guard hockey game in Riverview—was being transferred to Prince Albert. Not just that, he planned on checking himself into protective custody. Although he said it was to hang out with his old pal, Henry knew it was to protect him from harm. There was no greater act of solidarity that a general-population inmate could show someone in PC— especially given Manfred's abhorrence of sex offenders.

Word about Manfred was out. In prisons across Canada, his name was synonymous with violence and death. Here was a contract killer—top of the heap in the prison hierarchy—thumbing his nose at the unwritten law that the pariahs in PC—the rats, and cops, and sex offenders—deserved punishment, if not death. Only Manfred could pull that off. One problem, though: the Vancouver beefs Henry could explain by showing him the bogus lineup photo, but he had to keep the attempted-rape beef in Winnipeg a secret.

On tenterhooks for days, Henry was joyous when he finally laid eyes on Manfred. Punching each other on the shoulder, they said in unison, as always, "Good to see you, bro. Ain't it the truth?" After supper, they walked the patch of concrete that passed for a yard.

"PC?" Henry said. "Why would you do such a thing? You're crazy."

Manfred, pulling a doobie from his shoulder-length hair, said, "Hey man, we're kindred spirits. Besides, I ain't never getting out. I figure if I'm going to die inside, I might as well have a little fun in the process."

Three tokes later, everything reduced them to giggles. Then Manfred got all serious. "Them rape offences, Ivan. Pretty serious shit."

"I swear," said Henry, "they made the whole thing up." He pulled out the photo, deeply creased along the fold line: "See for yourself. I ain't no skinner, trust me."

Crouching, rocking on his heels, Manfred examined the photo as Henry described the forced lineup, the contradictory identifications, the lack of physical evidence, Harkema and Miss Kavanagh, the useless defence counsel.

"Not that I'm an expert," Manfred said, handing it back, "but it don't take a genius to see it's phony."

"You believe me—no lie?"

"No lie, man," Manfred said. "When I heard you'd been DO'd—such a shock. I assumed you were innocent. No way would a God-fearing man such as yourself, a Catholic to boot, do shit like that." He shrugged. "At least I did the beefs I'm in for."

Henry brought up the doughnut-hockey game at Riverview. "We blew their socks off, huh?"

"Yeah," said Manfred, producing another doobie. "Whenever I asked why you checked that fat dummy into the boards, you clammed up."

"That front tooth is still killing me," Henry said. "I got cavities, too, but if I say I need a filling they'll pull it out instead."

The cannabis buzz making even the gruesome stuff seem hilarious, Henry told him about the Oakalla riot, and about his favourite trick at Pretrial. "Riding the elevator down to the library, I screwed with the fire alarm and telephone systems. Every time there was a false fire alarm, I thought of Horvath."

"Who's that?"

"One of the complainants. She swore she didn't know the address of her boyfriend's house. She's living there, and she don't know the address? If there was a fire, how would she know where to send the fire trucks?"

With Manfred in stitches, Henry recounted his brew-making fiasco—he'd spent days concocting the perfect blend of juice, bread, and sugar, waiting till it was fit to drink. "When it was just about good to go, the damn thing exploded. Louder than fireworks, I swear."

More weed, more laughter. Manfred pinched the roach and ate it. Henry told him how Constable Keen had pulled a gun on him in the street. "Kids and mothers everywhere," he said. "Who pulls that kind of shit? Not just that. When the bastard testified he'd cuffed me behind my back, he perjured himself."

"Breaking news, buddy. Cops do what they do."

Shaking his head and giggling, Henry said, "Call me a conceited prick, but I admit to having a certain affection for my mug."

When Manfred laughed and gave him a bear hug, Henry sent up a silent prayer. Good to have a friend in Sask Pen, and an unlikely saviour at that. Who better than Manfred to help him survive until he could prove his innocence?

CHAPTER 21

A FOOL FOR A CLIENT

Whenever Henry's resolve waned—when his bad teeth were killing him, or he got melancholic about being a thousand miles from his girls—something always seemed to lift his spirits and renew his determination. He injured his back and was down in the dumps for weeks, depressed by the futility of it all; then, on the first day of spring 1985, Rick Hansen set off on his Man in Motion World Tour. Hoping to raise money for spinal-cord research, Hansen, a paraplegic, planned to circle the globe. *Jesus*, thought Henry, *if a guy can go around the world in a wheelchair, I can find a way to get out of here.*

The only problem was that when he hunkered down in the library to review the law, he didn't really know what he was looking for. He could find nothing in the *Criminal Code* that illuminated the depth and complexity of what he'd been through. "Getting case law that's on point is impossible," he groused to Manfred. "*Canadian Criminal Cases* don't trace the laws back to the framers' conception."

"Whatever you say, bro."

One day, a departing inmate bequeathed him a daisy wheel typewriter. It saved up to a certain number of characters, then printed them out in a flurry. Henry ignored the bellyaches up and down the range: "Dummy up!" "Turn that fucking thing off." To dull the clatter of keys and the noise of the driving mechanism, he got a steel locker box from the metal shop and insulated it with cardboard. After inputting the machine's quota of memory, he'd lower it into the box, switch on the typing mechanism, and close the lid.

Every time he filed an action or wrote a letter—to the Federal Court, or Legal Aid, or Centurion Ministries (an American organization dedicated to freeing the wrongly convicted), he enclosed an affidavit swearing the facts to be true. He swore so many affidavits that, over time, wardens and deputy wardens, admiring his perseverance—if doubting his grasp on reality—began witnessing his signature.

"You again? Where do I sign? How long you going to keep this up?"

"My perseverance is ongoing," he'd reply. "Never will I let anything stop me from being released."

It wasn't easy bringing actions in Federal Court. The laws kept changing, and the rules, sections, and case law invariably favoured the government. Still he soldiered on, and though most of his actions came to naught, every so often one of them was upheld. For example, the commissioner of penitentiaries advised him it would be enforcing the policy of barring inmates from accessing, for legal purposes, accounts where the balance had dipped below $350. "On June 19, 1985, you had $19.65 in your Current Account, and $207.34 in your Savings Account," wrote the commissioner. "Because you do not have the minimum $350 balance in your Savings Account, an amount considered essential if you are conditionally released, I regret that your request for funds from your Savings Account cannot be granted at this time."

They wanted him to have at least $350 in his account so he wouldn't be broke in case he was conditionally released? Since when does a DO serving an indefinite sentence get conditionally released? Henry challenged the policy and won. He was entitled to use every last dime in his account for his legal battles after all. It was a small victory, sure, but still a victory.

● ● ●

AT SASKATCHEWAN PENITENTIARY, Henry made everything from mailbags to uniforms. He earned $63 for working twelve eight-hour days; from that, they deducted $14 for rent and $1.50 for the inmate committee. If not for his gambling successes—he had a knack for picking winning teams—he could never have afforded his legal actions. As for tobacco, he scrounged butts whenever he could. Mostly, he abstained.

The only thing wrong with his job was the sewing-shop supervisor, a blowhard named Casey. "You're late," Casey said one day, eyeing a clock known to run fast. Brushing it off—better a late charge than hole-time for lipping back—Henry went to work. Casey followed him to his seat.

"If you're thinking of fighting the charge," Casey said, "I recommend an insanity defence."

Henry held himself in check until Casey walked away. "The bastard would've known my charges," he later told Manfred. "What a dirty thing for him to say."

From then on, every chance he got, Henry hid scissors, unravelled spools of thread, and did what he could to undermine Casey. Casey, in turn, got a half-wit kid named Rabbit to do his bidding. When he was moved to a new cell, Henry found himself double-bunked with Rabbit.

Retiring to his cot one night, Henry heard a loud pop under the weight of his ass. The scent of shit flooded the cell. Somebody had positioned a zip-lock bag under the sheet. Not one for publicity—or the heat it brought—Henry inched the soiled sheet through the peephole at the back of his cell. Once through, it dropped down several storeys between the cell wall and the platform used by the guard patrol. Henry thought of mixing powder from a fluorescent light bulb into Rabbit's orange crystals, but resisted. He kept to himself, studied the law, and ignored the gossip.

Henry didn't watch much television, but a CBC news item about Thomas Sophonow caught his attention. The Manitoba Court of Appeal had overturned Sophonow's conviction and acquitted him. The poor bugger—convicted of the 1981 murder of a doughnut-shop clerk in Winnipeg—had already spent four years in prison. They might have even crossed paths in Sask Pen without knowing it—birds of a feather, both railroaded. Hoping his own stint in prison wouldn't turn into four years, Henry sat on his cot and raised an imaginary glass to his newly freed brother.

As the clock neared midnight on December 31, 1985, Henry told Manfred: "Legal is my only thing. I'm not into games, none of the bullshit that goes down in here. When an inmate tells me someone wrote on the shower wall that I'm a rat, I shrug and say, 'Whoever put it there, take it down.' If it doesn't happen, I take it down myself."

"Hey, if the guards couldn't turn inmates against each other," Manfred said, "how would they get their jollies?"

"You're right, man," said Henry. "In some of my statements of claim, I name certain guards. They hate that, but I'm not scared. To me, everything is a mental exercise. I feel obligated to pursue all avenues— no matter what the result."

"You still sending off all those appeals and that?" said Manfred. "I'll say this for you—you ain't no quitter."

"They say he who acts for himself has a fool for a client," Henry said, guzzling hooch as the clock struck midnight and a celebratory din overwhelmed the range. "Well," he said, raising his voice above the cacophony, "I'm the fool and the client. Together, we work hard. Happy New Year, bro."

CHAPTER 22

DISTANT INFLUENCE

O ne day Manfred was gone. No warning, no announcement. The day before, he and Henry had agreed, over their cold bread and watery cereal, to meet in the gym after work—to pump their muscles "like Sylvester Stallone." Manfred had called in sick, but instead of seeing a nurse, he'd got revenge on another inmate. The minute the punk headed off to the shower, Manfred piled balled-up newspapers to the ceiling and torched the cell. Right on schedule, the inmate returned—to exploding light bulbs and shattering fixtures.

With the prison in shutdown protocol, the SWAT team transferred Manfred to the psych unit. While corrections officers busied themselves with paperwork, Manfred garrotted the con in the next bed. The guy had called him a goof—the most offensive word in the prison lexicon, worse than "skinner," "rat," and even "diddler."

As disturbed as Henry was by the departure of Manfred—undoubtedly destined for the Special Handling Unit in Quebec, last stop for Canada's most hardened criminals—Henry smiled to think of his buddy begging the guards for a little "alone time" with child killer Clifford Olson, the SHU's most infamous resident.

Even in Manfred's absence, his influence was felt. No one dared attack Henry, though inmates hassled him and staff gossiped openly about the contents of his letters, bumped him, and, when no one else could hear, even threatened to kill him. Guards stole his mail, obliterated letters on his typewriter keys, called out the names of the rape victims in his case over the loudspeaker. He was subjected to frequent and unnecessary strip searches, and his light was flicked off and on at all hours. What bothered him most, though, were the frequent suggestions that an insanity plea was his only way out.

Each night, while the rest of the prison slept, he put his thoughts in order. His cell was illuminated by the thin blue light he insisted never be turned off. As he told me years later, after they opened his mail, some wacko would write on the envelope, "Sorry, we did this by mistake." When and if he bothered trying to stop the naysayers, they'd put more restrictions on his outgoing mail. They'd say he didn't sign the form properly, there was not enough money, or the parcel got lost on the way.

"Three times," he told me, "I had to put a trace on statements of claim. Either the package came back or the original got lost, which meant I had to ask for a time extension, plus put in a claim for lost documents. Playing mind games, V&C [visitors and correspondence] added words like "RAPE" and "PERVERT" to letters from my mother.

"Men paraded past my door—coughing, farting, saying things that pertained to me. I tried to live a solitary existence. I did not have a radio or any machine that played music. I was using a fan for background, to block out the noise. When the cell doors were open, the institution was very noisy—the echo was deafening from yelling or doors slamming.

"Going to church and continuing on in my same path made me feel secure. At least the chaplain was real. At all times, I governed myself with meticulous attention to prison rules."

At night, guards hovered by his cell door, stomping their feet and shouting, "What's that smell?" Ignoring, as best he could, their taunts regarding the futility of his legal endeavours, he warned them that if they didn't comply with his requests he'd file a complaint in Federal Court. Because they knew his level of seriousness, not to mention CSC's hatred of publicity, mostly they backed down.

Manfred's reputation helped immensely, as did his practical lessons. When an inmate came at him in the hall one morning, Henry used Manfred's technique—one quick hard shot to the nose. He nailed the goof so sharply that the guy didn't move; he just stood there stunned, holding his nose in both hands, blood gushing between his fingers. On the other hand, when a killer bragged that the man he'd stabbed was a pedophile, Henry got in his face and said, "You idiot. You think getting a life sentence for whacking some dummy makes you solid?"

One day, a trusty wouldn't stop swishing his mop in front of Henry's cell. Henry let loose a volley of curses, and a couple of hours later he got assaulted by two of the trusty's friends. He didn't retaliate, nor did he fight back a couple of days later when a French-Canadian inmate sucker-punched him in the face. Manfred had taught him about choosing your battles. In the end, it came down to survival of the fittest. If somebody caught him off guard and put a shiv between his ribs, that would be that. Although he wouldn't go down without a fight, he wasn't about to do anything stupid.

At the stroke of midnight on December 31, 1986, the punk kids blew off steam by grabbing the bars and shaking them. They whooped and hollered, banged their spoons and cups non-stop for an hour while Henry plugged his ears. For most cons, a new year was a concrete step towards a release date. But Henry had no release date, and celebrating was the last thing he felt like doing, especially after what he'd witnessed in the gym.

Earlier that day, a young con, ignorant of the code, had dared to ask a steroid-pumped older dude a question. No big deal—an innocent query about the tats snaking up and down the older con's arms. Next time the newbie lowered the barbell to his chest, the bodybuilder drove a shiv into his throat.

• • •

ALTHOUGH THE THREAT of violence was constant, boredom was an equally insidious enemy. As the months turned into years, the petty restrictions of prison life, the injustice of it all, sometimes became debilitating. As Henry wrote Manfred in February 1987,

> Being locked up from night to day is more frustrating than ever. Jail can produce the worst feelings imaginable. Mainly because of the death of the night and day. By that, I mean that nobody's alive.
>
> What noises exist come from the inmates. I choose, as do you, to learn to live with them. As always, my only activity is writing notices of motion or statements of claim. The wintertime

is the noisiest in the gym and cellblock. Limited exercise times in the yard.

Canteen nights are, as you know all too well, uncontrollable. Five hundred to six hundred inmates waiting in line, population guys preying on the PCs—lined up, waiting to rip off their purchases. Or else.

When I injured my back, they threatened to charge me with refusing to work. This, after cleaning the kitchen floors for eighteen months, not a single day off! Things of this nature are forced on me because I have no say at all in what transpires. If I chose not to work, I'd get $3.20 every two weeks. I can't afford not to work.

• • •

IN THE SPRING of 1988, Henry's eyes were glued to the television as NDP member of parliament Svend Robinson told the CBC that he was a homosexual. Henry just shook his head—what was the world coming to? As Leviticus 18:22 says, "Thou shalt not lie with mankind, as with womankind: it is abomination." Henry hated double-bunking because he worried a cellmate might tamper with his legal files, but he also feared sexual advances. His own history made unwanted male overtures a sickening prospect.

Some inmates welcomed cellmates as lovers—when released, they'd die before owning up to it—but Henry wanted nothing to do with anyone, man or woman. He was constantly on guard against the women—both corrections staff and contract employees such as psychologists and librarians. Given his status as a sex offender, their presence disturbed him and made him paranoid.

Months after we met, Henry finally opened up to me about female guards, many of whom were hostile to him because of his crimes and some of whom were eager to entrap him into behaving inappropriately. "The male inmates acted different around female staff and/or inmates," he told me. "I chose, for obvious reasons, to stay dormant to all activity by just pretending not to notice this flirty behaviour. Like the day a female bent over in the butcher's shop, wearing no panties. A staff member asked me, in a belittling tone, if I wanted to rape her, seeing as how I'd raped so many other women. I said no, she didn't turn me on.

"When females came on to me, I never embarked on wanton behaviour. My reason was because they might scream rape. Though, I will say this," he added, his eyes taking in every detail of whatever coffee shop we were in that day. "At all times I told the men to stop bothering the female officers.

"Thinking of a woman creeps into your senses," he said. "As the still of the night makes your heart go faster, one doesn't forget those thoughts easily. When one is labelled a skinner, there can be problems with women trying to get you into a confrontation. Which one must avoid in all circumstances. I understood that I was alone in a corrupt society that invests millions of dollars to convict an innocent guy, and now were spending more to set me up—meaning, the women who were coming on to me were fake, their sole aim being to entrap me.

"One day when I was working as a cleaner in one of Stony Mountain's 'private family visit' cabins, there was a certain redheaded guard I liked, maybe even loved. When I asked her, 'Which is more important, love or trust?' and when she said 'love,' I grabbed one of the 'I LOVE YOU' labels I'd made to stick on letters to my daughters. When she came by later that day, I pushed it through the window slot. She reported me to the security officer. I never spoke to her again."

Every day, Henry reminded himself to keep his mind on his ultimate goal: getting his conviction overturned. At such times, one of Michael Luchenko's comments kept coming back to him: "I have given an additional photo as well to Mr. Henry. His is actually the exhibit." Night after night, Henry would take the lineup photo out of its hiding place, study it for perhaps the ten-thousandth time, then tuck it away again. Then he would pray that, one day, the whole world would see what he saw.

•••

TRUDEAU'S CHARTER OF RIGHTS AND FREEDOMS was opening up new possibilities for offenders. Court decisions were coming down, almost weekly, that made it harder for guards to assault inmates. Positive change was in the air. Using the Charter, Henry sued the commissioner of penitentiaries, arguing that, by conducting excessive strip searches on him, they were violating his right to privacy. Although some of his legal papers mysteriously disappeared, the number of searches dropped considerably.

Before long, Henry won another small victory. Poring through federal and provincial statutes, he stumbled on a section of the *Canada Post Corporation Act* providing that no postage is required on non-political correspondence with the federal government. From then on, every letter he sent to Ottawa bore the phrase "Attention: HMPS [Her Majesty's Postal Service]." Every penny counted, and every stamp was a possible ticket to his release. When he learned that not only did he not need stamps but that he could get his past postage refunded, he felt like he'd won the lottery.

CHAPTER 23

THE RAZOR'S EDGE

On February 11, 1990, a crowd of inmates gathered around the TV to listen to Nelson Mandela. After spending twenty-seven years in jail—twenty-seven years!—the anti-apartheid hero, newly freed from prison, gave a speech that was nothing less than a call to action:

> Our march to freedom is irreversible. We must not allow fear to stand in our way. Universal suffrage on a common voters' role in a united democratic and non-racial South Africa is the only way to peace and racial harmony.
>
> In conclusion, I wish to quote my own words during my trial in 1964. They are true today as they were then:
>
> *I have fought against white domination and I have fought against black domination. I have cherished the ideal of a democratic and free society in which all persons live together in harmony and with equal opportunities. It is an ideal which I hope to live for and to achieve. But if needs be, it is an ideal for which I am prepared to die.*[1]

Standing up as one, the inmates—some with tears streaming down their faces—applauded him. Not that Henry equated his situation to that of Mandela, but the man's tireless determination—stronger than ever, after all those years of imprisonment—buoyed his spirits tremendously.

Days later, the Royal Commission on the Donald Marshall, Jr., Prosecution released its report.[2] Marshall, a Mi'kmaq man convicted of murdering his friend in 1971, was acquitted in 1983 following the emergence of, among other items of fresh evidence, eyewitness testimony that identified another man as the murderer. In its Digest of Findings and Recommendations, the first Royal Commission to inquire into a wrongful conviction wrote:

> The criminal justice system failed Donald Marshall, Jr. at virtually every turn from his arrest and wrongful conviction for murder in 1971 up to, and even beyond, his acquittal by the Court of Appeal in 1983. The tragedy of the failure is compounded by evidence that this miscarriage of justice could—and should—have been prevented, or at least corrected quickly, if those involved in the system had carried out their duties in a professional and/or competent manner. That they did not is due, in part at least, to the fact that Donald Marshall, Jr. is a Native.

• • •

FOR DAYS THEREAFTER, Henry was spooked—consumed with thoughts not only about all those innocent people whose lives were being wasted in prison, but also about all those who had died before they could prove their innocence. Like the American Caryl Chessman—sentenced to death in 1948 after a five-day crime spree that ended in a shootout. Convicted on eighteen counts of robbery, kidnapping, and "unnatural acts" (in modern-day parlance, forced oral sex)—Chessman argued that his confinement prevented him from collecting evidence that would prove his innocence. After a prolonged battle with the authorities, he gained access to a typewriter and the library. After that, there was no stopping the man. Writing several books and achieving eight stays of execution over the next dozen years, Chessman counted among his supporters such notables as Eleanor Roosevelt and Reverend Billy Graham. After Chessman's death in 1960, he became a *cause célèbre* for the movement to ban capital punishment.

When a paroled inmate bequeathed a memory-enhanced typewriter to Henry, the same model Chessman had used, he was overjoyed. A pen was one thing, and the daisy wheel had been a huge help, but this Panasonic was gold! And it was timely. The newly enacted *Court of*

Appeal Rules stipulated that future submissions be filed within certain "specified margins." Not long after, another ruling said that legal submissions could no long be handwritten; they must be typed.

When Henry wasn't working in the kitchen, he studied for hours on end in what other inmates referred to as the "Ivan Henry library." Having found this or that legal authority for the proposition he wished to make, he'd start up the Xerox machine. Every document required nine copies. When the gear on the Panasonic wore out, he was fortunately able to get it fixed.

Intimidation from guards and other inmates was frequent, but according to one of Henry's friends in Sask Pen, he became almost oblivious to it. "Despite all the grief he took about it," William Black told me in the visitors' area of the prison in December 2011, "Ivan was mighty proud of that typewriter—not to mention his old galvanized CORCAN locker box. He was the only inmate who kept up its appearance. He'd polish the exterior with so much Brasso, it looked almost chrome-finished.

"Mostly," Black explained, "the locker boxes were for the use of the guards—Henry being the exception. The old locking-wheel system had riveted metal handles that the cleaners polished daily for the staff. You got charged if you pulled a dirty trick, like putting peanut butter, honey, butter, or feces, on the wheels.

"There were typewriters in the library, but Ivan was working on volumes of output. One has to keep copies, as well as send out multiple copies. If you don't keep a copy, and they decide to tamper with it, you could be back to square one.

"If nothing ever happened to the mail, there'd be no need for registered mail, nor insurance of mail or packages. Ivan spent a lot of his wages on stamps, paper, ribbons, envelopes, etcetera. He lived a more spartan life than most, having to finance his fight for freedom on a shoestring budget."

• • •

WHEN HENRY WAS moved to kitchen detail, his job involved cooking for between 550 and 650 men, a task he embraced. The challenge was to cater to people with multiple complaints. One day, when some tough guys complained that the pork was red inside, Henry avoided a confrontation by showing them that the meat had been cooked at the requisite 185 degrees Celsius. When other inmates pressured him to steal food, he explained that it would only bring more heat on them all.

Black described Henry as "the essential cook" and said that a lumber camp would be lucky to have him. "I doubt they'd pay him what he's worth, though. Take him to the Safeway, buy him a turkey and whatever fixings he wants. Then turn him loose in your kitchen. He fattened me up real good over the years. I always said he killed me with kindness when it came to food. After thirty-five years and counting on the inside, I still rate his soups to be the best. Better yet, he gave me extra helpings whenever possible."

"Did I ever tell you my turkey story?" Henry later recalled. "At our Christmas socials at Mountain, I'd cook twenty-two twenty-five-pound turkeys and a bunch of twelve-pound roasts. Before the visitors arrived, I caught one of my men throwing two roasted turkeys out the window. It was my job to make sure we didn't run out. There'd be 440 inmates and 160 guests. 600 people. Four ounces of meat times 600 equals 2,400 ounces, or 150 pounds. Two stolen turkeys would amount to sixty-five to seventy-five servings.

"I gave the idiot hell. Told him he was giving them an excuse to add more security, shut the joint up tighter than ever. A total disrespect for the inmates who died fighting for justice, the inmates we honour every August 10.[2] In time, the men under me came to respect my leadership. They knew positively that I did not demean or make them feel lower than me. I never wavered, never stopped working towards release. When they realized I wasn't just fooling around, that's when the respect came."

Nonetheless, as a skinner, Henry still lived on the razor's edge. Of all the places in the joint, the kitchen and dining room were the least safe. An inmate wielding an industrial knife might be doing time for a murder. In the dining room, a shotgun-toting guard watched the men eat from his perch in the gun cage. In Blood Alley, the passage between the gym and the kitchen, men had been stabbed without anyone saying a word.

It wasn't just the kitchen that was perilous; violence permeated the whole place. As Henry told me, "Friends who called me brave had no idea the half of it. When violence takes over, it escalates. The full moon makes inmates behave like silly children—violent without cause. Drink is the worst thing one can give an inmate—they use alcohol as their nerve. It can result in stabbing, rape of an inmate, or, worse, a riot.

"In normal times, the guards circulate twice a month—looking for injuries, asking to see knuckles, and shirt removed. Some men suffer stabbings without saying a word. Others are found dead during the a.m. count. If you don't stand to when ordered, you invite a charge so as to increase your security rating. Meaning you'll be sent to a max. On the other hand, if you rat out another con, you're a shoo-in for minimum.

"There are stabbings, suicides, and overdoses. The tension is always high—morning to night. I did my best to help restore calm. The safest time was during lockup. You're safe. Safe, that is, until the next day."

• • •

HAD SOME CLOWN not put a screw in the works, Henry's New Year's Day meal of steak with all the trimmings would have been a triumph. Instead, he recalled, "Some dummy stole a piece of the high-end cut of meat and put it in the flytrap. When Officer Martin blamed me, I threatened to beat up the inmate if he didn't come clean. My pay meant survival. Because the nincompoop fessed up in the nick of time, I didn't lose my job.

"Which of course made Martin madder. So mad, he put some fat kid up to entering my cell, pulling down his pants, and asking me to do him up the bum. Though that stunt ended without incident, Martin started dogging my every step. And when some idiot hid the tinfoil, I not only got blamed, Martin called me a 'fucking goof' in front of my helpers.

"One day an inmate came at me with a shiv because of a trickle of blood that was running down my hand. Martin just stood there, arms crossed, smirking. Which is why I let loose. 'Show me the genius,' I said, 'who could cut pork in five hundred identical-sized pieces without the odd nick or two. You know what you can do? You can take your job and shove it.'"

When Henry put in for a new job, they made him vacate F4, the unit designated for kitchen workers. "You got two choices," he was told. "Double-bunk, or move to the glue-sniffing range."

"But F4's my home," he pleaded in triplicate. "It suits my needs. Away from all the loony-tunes, I can type and print off copies without disturbance."

For his insubordination, he drew four months in the hole.

God, not again. All his books and papers, his typewriter, and three locker boxes full of documents were stacked up in the dome, ready for storage. Stuffing outdated material into one of the boxes, he sent it to Jessie for safekeeping. As for the other two boxes, he watched closely as the authorities recorded and signed off on every item—including the Michigan State law book in which he'd cut a hole to hide the lineup photo. That was the hardest part of all—not knowing whether it would go missing.

After being outfitted in dark green polyester pants and a light green shirt reeking of BO, Henry was marched down to a cell as damp and cold as a burial vault. His bed was a wooden board on a concrete slab, inches off the floor. For the first five days, they removed his ten-centimetre-thick foam pad from 8:00 a.m. to 5:00 p.m. "Forget *Canada's Food Guide*," he recalled, "The slop that passed for food arrived via a slot in the door at 4:00 p.m., 6:30 a.m., and 10:30 a.m. The caged light bulb is never turned off, and cold water sputters from a rusted tap."

For twenty-three hours a day, he was confined to his cell—no books, no work, no hobbies, or activities. Pushups and praying; praying and pushups. Eventually, a sympathetic guard gave him a pen and paper; then he was given a single hardcover book a day. Before long, he resumed his law studies—fourteen hours a day.

Officer Martin, meanwhile, continued his harassment, singing "Time Is on My Side" right outside Henry's isolation cell and noisily opening and slamming shut the gate on the food slot. Frustrated by the sound, Henry devised a plan. Next time the slot opened, he pulled down his pants and began jerking off. "From then on," he told me, "Martin's presence was felt only once every hour."

When Henry wrote out complaints, Martin threw them in the garbage. When Martin decided Henry's cell wasn't clean enough, he had him written up. Henry's requests to file grievances or to be visited by his classification officer took days—often weeks—to process. Martin also cancelled a long-planned visit from Henry's mother.

At the end of the four months, he got a pleasant surprise. He was being moved from the hole to F1, bed thirteen. Not only was it a single-occupancy cell, but it meant he'd be spared contact with the glue sniffers, one of whom had threatened to kill him.

CHAPTER 24

FAMILY TIES

t's your wife on the phone," the chaplain said, minutes before chapel one Sunday. "She says it's urgent."

Please, Henry prayed, *don't let it be about the girls.* "Jessie, is that you?"

"Ivan," she said, "you have every reason to hate me, I know that. But never could I have imagined you doing something this horrible."

"What are you talking about?"

Between sobs, she said that, when she'd opened up the locker box he'd sent home, she'd found a note: "Your husband wants to chop you into little pieces and sprinkle them everywhere. Trust me, I have it on good authority. Watch your back."

So much for the hour each week when he felt like somebody, the hour when he could focus on God's love. Back in his cell, outraged, he was consumed with thoughts of revenge. If he ever got his hands on the bastard who did that . . .

Not long after, his mom wrote to tell him that his daughter Tanya, still in her teens, had run off to Mexico with a man. Henry sat on his cot and wept. Steeling himself, he hauled out the handful of letters the girls had sent him over the years and read them for perhaps the thousandth time. The years were going by. His life was going by. His daughters were growing up, and the possibility that he might never see them again chilled his soul.

So did his mother's unexpected visit several months later, in May 1991. She looked smaller than ever, with stooped shoulders and knuckles swollen with arthritis. "Can you get me some water?" she said, wincing as she corkscrewed her frail body into the molded plastic chair. "I'm afraid I bring bad news, dear. Very bad news."

While she dabbed her eyes with a hankie, he drummed his fingers impatiently. There was no hurrying her—not when he was little and begging her to leave Vukusha, and not now, with her burden of bad news.

"Jessie's dead. I should've told you sooner. I wanted to tell you in person. I'm so sorry."

"What happened?"

"They're not saying why."

All the dark thoughts evaporated, leaving nothing but a terrible ache and sweet memories. Jessie's thick, strawberry-blonde hair. The gleam in her eye in their moments together. The day they wed, and how beautiful she looked in her smart black suit cinched at the waist.

• • •

WITH JESSIE GONE, Henry desperately wanted to connect with his daughters. In an action brought before the Saskatchewan Court of Queen's Bench, he demanded to be provided with news. He needed to know their whereabouts, he said, and confirmation of their safety and well-being. "I did not receive any notice of Jessie's death from the ailment called cancer," he wrote in his court application, "nor that my natural children were placed into welfare. Though divorced due to welfare requirements—she was conned by Manitoba Social Services— Jessie and I remained married in God's eyes. I supported her and my children against the judgment of home wreckers. I have received communications from my daughters, have contributed to their birthdays, their exams and, when they wrote asking for money, I have acted as their father."

Less than a month later, Henry had a reply: "Regarding the relief sought, this Court is without jurisdiction."

In order to be reunited with his daughters, Henry reasoned, he had to gain his freedom. He decided his best hope was to apply for a transfer to Kingston Penitentiary in Ontario—almost five thousand kilometres from the west coast. His father, he said in his application, lived near Kingston. And he'd be spared, in the short term at least, what he described as other inmates' jealousy "due to my perseverances to get out. I could name hundreds of people who have been uncouth to me. Every single minute of the day, I've put up with trash: 'mama's boy,' or 'you ain't never getting out.' Idiots running up and down in front of my cell making animal noises. All my efforts to seek redress have gone nowhere. I've gotten nothing from you. No one cares about my well-being."

Actually, the bit about his dad was stretching it. He hadn't laid eyes on the old man since he was seventeen, fresh out of jail on a gun beef— a .38 Winchester, the only piece he'd ever carried. Back then, the first words out of his mouth when he laid eyes on the stranger at the Toronto train station who said, "Hi, I'm Gerry Henry, your father," were, "How come your hair's not red?" When the old man began stealing money from him, Henry moved on.

No, Henry's real reason for wanting to transfer to Kingston was that it was close to Toronto and Edward Greenspan, the famous criminal lawyer. He'd written to Greenspan more than once, pleading for help and even enclosing the lineup photo. Each time, Greenspan suggested he hire himself a lawyer in the west.

With lightning speed, his transfer application was rejected. "There's nothing special," wrote some bureaucrat, "about your offences which should create trouble for you at Saskatchewan. Given that you have no father in Ontario, we conclude that you have no community support in that province." The letter he'd written to his father seeking support for the transfer had been returned unopened.

CHAPTER 25

YELLOW PAGES

Hey, Ivan," said the supervisor assigned to orient him to his new warehouse job. "They say bloodstains stay on cement floors for a long, long time." Sure enough, underfoot were several red, Rorschach-type blotches. Jumping back, Henry crossed himself—twice, for good measure. Not that God was paying much attention to him these days. Still, the prospect of working alone appealed to him. Let the other cons be spooked by the blood; he planned on spending his work hours deep in thought.

You'd have to be superhuman to block out the images. Not that long ago, three inmates had overpowered a bull in the warehouse, cut him up. Cut up an inmate worker, too. After raping and knifing them, the offenders splashed bleach into their cuts.

"While the prisoners were blocking off the windows," some con had told everyone in sight, "the guards rammed the door with a forklift. When the order was given to shoot, the sniper took the leader out with a single shot—the blast ripping off half his face and shoulder. When the second guy survived the next shot, the sniper fired a third one. That guy fell. Had the third con not jumped under a cardboard presser, he'd have been slaughtered as well."

Eventually, the dreadful images at his new workplace faded away, and Henry began to take pleasure in learning a job. He operated a forklift, stocked shelves, and made toys for children. His favourite toy was a replica pull-type '57 Chevrolet he and his pal Black made together. Knowing that the toys amused the little ones and helped moms and dads enjoy their visits made it satisfying.

Less closely supervised than before, Henry began visiting the painting, carpentry, and welding shops arranged along the perimeter, chatting up the more friendly staff members. The shop bosses, dressed in civilian clothes, had casual attitudes to match. One of them made him a little hotpot so he could boil macaroni on the range. Another gave him seeds to plant corn, peas, carrots, and beets.

It wasn't easy work—constructing huge wooden boxes, ten to a pallet, then strapping the pallets onto flatbeds—but it was good exercise, and he took pleasure in seeing the fruits of his labour. He vowed to spring two thousand beds before he resumed working in the kitchen.

• • •

ON APRIL 16, 1992, a former fellow inmate convicted of murder twenty-two years earlier, was released. Henry watched on television as David Milgaard, acquitted due to flawed evidence at trial, waved to the crowd gathered outside Stony Mountain Penitentiary. "I'm a little nervous and confused," he said, "but I'm going home." Good things were happening. Henry told himself there was hope for him as well.

• • •

A MONTH LATER, on May 15, Henry received the Federal Court judgment—the culmination of the lawsuit he'd started seven years earlier. Was this the moment he'd been waiting for, the first step towards exoneration? Twenty-four hours later he'd worked up the nerve to open it.

In her book-length decision,[1] Madam Justice Barbara Reed dismantled Henry's arguments, one after another. Noting the "131 separate court proceedings" he'd filed between May 8, 1985, and December 5, 1989, as well as his massive volume of exhibits—including "Cardboard with 3 18" x 15" photographs" and "Cardboard with 5 photographs"—she said he'd been "remiss" in not retaining counsel through Saskatchewan Legal Aid. What's more,

> Mr. Henry's main complaint in this case is that the Minister of Justice has failed to review 'new evidence' of a fabricated lineup. The photo wasn't a crucial piece of evidence at trial. Henry himself called an expert who said it wasn't doctored. There is no doubt the photo looks bizarre, but it can be explained.

Mr. Henry has never been able to produce any expert opinion that the photo was fabricated, then or now.

After reviewing the evidence—noting that the photo wasn't a crucial piece of evidence at trial, that Henry's own expert said it wasn't doctored—I must dismiss the action.

Fine, you bastards. You want an expert opinion? Henry flipped through the Prince Albert Yellow Pages until he got to "Photography." Closing his eyes, he placed his fingertip on the page and moved it clockwise. When he stopped and opened his eyes, his finger was pointing at Atkinson Photography.

Several weeks later—after much correspondence, reams of red tape, and multiple security checks—the warden authorized a Mr. Lee Atkinson to attend at the jail.

Lee Atkinson described that visit to me as follows:

The warden called me, said I was to bring lighting and other paraphernalia—tripod, camera, flash units. Other than that, I was told very little. I met up with everyone near the Infirmary. When I saw the photo, it seemed surreal. That, and not knowing what was going on, why I was there.

I took pictures with a Hasselblad camera, 70 mm film. There wasn't much discussion with either the guards or with Henry. I understood that one of the guards had offered to analyze the photo himself, but Henry had said no.

At some later point, he wanted an affidavit. I was objective; I knew very little. I thought the photo was odd. Initially, I looked at it like it was a story, a puzzle.

Among the things that don't make sense are the shield, as well as the wrist of the guy at the end. There's a centre of light, yet the shadows and the numbers are all wrong. I didn't know light sources or trajectory of light. I had no idea why he was incarcerated, or what he wanted to do with my affidavit.

I wondered whether images had been combined through physical cutting and pasting. Another possibility was the creation of false imagery—for example, three different negatives of the same image, taken at different wavelengths. Expose them through three colours—false colour.

There's a yellow area—the straight line has yellow alongside it. If the arm is "blooming"—washed out—why not the number? The numbers on the white placard should wash out before the arm.

In the printing industry, they use ruby lithographs to, for example, hide an area, then add new elements over the top. It's part of the mechanical process.

For a couple of years after that, Henry called or wrote me, told me what sizes he needed. I charged him what he could afford, and I took his collect calls.

In an affidavit dated September 2, 1992, Atkinson swore that the lineup photo appeared to be a composite of pictures. Most notably, he opined that the quartet in the middle—Henry and the three police officers—had been somehow inserted into the photo of the foils.

Armed with Atkinson's affidavit, Henry wrote to the Legal Services Society of British Columbia, citing the "fresh evidence" as cause for reopening his appeal. The negative response came swiftly: "I am writing to advise you that your application has been forwarded to the B.C. Legal Aid Plan . . . I understand your concerns are about identification and lineup evidence. Although the law has developed substantially over the past several years, these will not be applicable to your case . . . My general sense, on reviewing the matter, is that there is no reasonable prospect that you will be successful on appeal."

CHAPTER 26

DESPERATE MEASURES

Henry held back tears when he saw the tiny lettering on the envelope. His pipsqueak, Kari. Could she really be seventeen? On welfare, he read, living in a foster home where the people weren't so nice. Her big sister, Tanya, was now married —married!—and living in Mexico. His babies. Life was leaving him behind.

Kari had travelled to Saskatchewan only once, four years earlier, with her stepfather, the man Jessie married not long after Henry's conviction. It hurt, but who could blame her? When his mother told him about the trip, Henry had begged her to bring Kari for a visit. But his mother was adamant. "You wouldn't want your little girl seeing you this way, now would you?" his mother had said. "She'd be having nightmares for years."

Kari's letter went on, "Mom never recovered from the shock of that note you sent her. I tried telling her it wasn't your writing . . . Daddy, did you do what they say you did? I'm scared, Daddy. I know you didn't, but I just need you to tell me."

Next time Henry had access to the pay phone, he called Kari. It took a few tries, but he finally got her on the line. He'd dreamed of this moment, reconnecting with his flesh and blood. If the men didn't like him hogging the phone, too bloody bad.

"A woman name of Karla Moon phoned," Kari said. "She woke me up—five in the morning, Vancouver time. I thought you'd died. She said that, as your classification officer, she was duty-bound to tell me you're never getting out. Is that true, Daddy?"

Henry resisted jumping in—he wanted to throttle the woman who made that call—but it was better to let Kari say what was on her mind.

"She said I'd be wise to move on with my life," Kari said, her voice a whisper. "Is she right? Daddy, is it true I'll never see you again?"

Henry did his best to reassure her before he had to sign off.

The next time he saw Karla Moon, he confronted her. "You got no business frightening my daughter." Moon hit the panic button. Guards arrived out of nowhere and took him down.

"You buggers are so low, you'd take my wife's ashes and urinate on them," he spat, outraged, as they restrained him.

Then they made him strip in full view of Moon and consigned him to another stint in isolation.

• • •

ONE DAY, VICTORY; the next, despair. First, the news that white voters in South Africa had voted to end apartheid. Nelson Mandela, after all his years in prison, was actually changing the world. Justice and freedom could triumph after all.

Then, a day later, an edict from the Federal Court of Appeal saying that Henry could no longer institute proceedings without the court's express leave. Never could he have foreseen such a thing. "Dear Jesus," he prayed, dropping to his knees, "this new order prevents me from dealing with the security of my person. Because this court order has no reviewability, I must accept that I am literally doomed. From here on in, there is nothing I can do. My power over the guards—'Try it, and I'll sue your ass off'—is gone. From here on in, they are free to view me as fair game." Henry felt utterly defeated.

Slowly, over time, his fighting spirit returned. Whether it was a hamburger cooked to perfection, or the sight of a jailhouse cat preening itself in the sun, little moments began to take on meaning again. If he was going to give up, why had he bothered to come this far? Yes, the finish line kept being moved, but it was still up ahead there somewhere.

Somehow, he had to find a way to prove his innocence. One night, lying in his cell, it came to him. Back in 1982, drunk and outraged by Jessie's brazen behaviour towards other men, he'd committed a B and E no one knew about. If he confessed to that act, he'd be demonstrating his honesty to the world. If he showed himself to be completely truthful, all his proclamations and appeals would also be seen to be true. He was desperate, yes, but this was more than an act of desperation. This was his route to exoneration.

In a letter to Saskatchewan Legal Aid, he wrote: "Around 10:00 p.m. on January 14, 1982, I walked through the open door of a suite in Mount Pleasant, intending to steal. From the kitchen, I entered the bedroom where a woman, naked from the waist up, began shouting, 'Don't rape me!' When I said I needed money because someone (I didn't let on it was my wife) had ripped me off, she pointed to a fish bowl. My hands being too big, I covered my head with a shawl while she retrieved the two wedding rings. Grabbing them, I left at once." He explained that he'd been crazy with jealousy, and stoked up on booze. He was sorry he'd frightened a lovely young woman half out of her wits. He sealed the letter, addressed the envelope, and attached a stamp he was able to reuse by licking the frank marks off it.

How could it go wrong? In voluntarily waiving his right to silence, he was establishing his credibility beyond a doubt. And because the woman had never reported the incident, he was to be doubly congratulated for coming clean.

CHAPTER 27

VIKTOR FRANKL

When Jean Chrétien's Liberals defeated the Progressive Conservatives in the 1993 federal election, after nine long years of Conservative rule, Henry was cautiously optimistic. At long last, back to a Liberal government. Not that he'd gotten anywhere with Trudeau at the helm, but the odds of getting treated fairly were much better under the Liberals.

So it was that when he read about Chrétien's new crime law—which included a provision whereby dangerous offenders would be guaranteed a parole hearing every two years instead of every five—he felt a surge of hope. He could use the opportunity to force disclosure of the complainant statements withheld from him at trial.

Henry worked diligently on the parole application, sent it off, and waited. Eventually, he was called to appear before the three members of the parole board panel. Their message was basically: You want out? Keep refusing to acknowledge your guilt—to provide some evidence at least of your potential for rehabilitation—and you'll never get out. You haven't enrolled in a single treatment program.

"Yeah, but I tried," he told the panelists. "They wouldn't let me enroll. No one who says they're innocent is allowed to participate."

"Ah, Mr. Henry, and for good reason."

"As in?"

More blather—he who "fails to show contrition" doesn't have "the right mindset" to succeed. "We mustn't allow disruptive influences in our classes, now must we?"

Noting his history of "insubordination," his "intransigence to treatment," and his "psychopathic tendencies"—the same language found in the majority of inmate files across Canada—the parole board turned him down flat.

"And when exactly," one of the panel members asked, peering up over his glasses, "can we expect you to take responsibility for your actions"?

"Never," snapped Ivan Henry. "I didn't do the crimes I'm in for."

• • •

AS HENRY'S DAUGHTERS came of age, they learned more and more about his case and took up his cause. In an April 4, 1994, letter to Sask Pen's deputy warden, Kari wrote that her dad had gone to jail when she was seven. Because the girls' mother "did not and could not take me and my sister to visit him because we couldn't afford to upset ourselves no more, communication was little. I know my father is not the best of an image to people in society, but he is my father and we need to be near each other.

"If made to stay in Saskatchewan," she continued, "he will go nuts not having someone to hug, kiss, and talk to him like a human being. It's hard, even for a dangerous offender, not having someone talk to him with respect. Even if a person is a prisoner doesn't mean they don't deserve a family that loves him dearly. My father was very affected by our mother's sudden death, and he has not been able to talk to us face-to-face about it. He's missed so many years of father/daughter bonding. Dad has been in and out of jail since we were babies, and our relationship is just like strangers.

"Writing and talking on the phone does nothing to help after twelve long years without each other. I am in full support of my father, and will help him get a transfer to a British Columbia prison, even if I have to walk on broken glass for miles and miles. We need each other, and I will do anything I need to do to get him here."

A few months later, when Henry's transfer back to the west coast was approved, he had deeply mixed emotions. Yes, he'd be nearer his daughters, but saying goodbye to the only friends he'd had for twelve years—kitchen staff, the chaplain, certain inmates—wouldn't be easy. Sask Pen had become his home, and over the years he'd grown into an elder statesman, helping others with legal matters, arbitrating disputes, teaching new fish how things were done. Even those who thought his proclamations of innocence were bullshit grew to admire his tenacity. There were a few bad apples, sure, but they were good people by and large. People he'd do anything for, and vice versa. As he watched his locker boxes being hoisted onto the green, four-ton Corrections truck, he prayed his things would arrive intact. And that Manfred's influence would still be felt so far away.

He'd read up on Mountain Institution in BC. Constructed in less than three months in 1962 at a cost of just under $300,000, the prison was built to be fireproof—metal buildings, metal beds, metal cupboards, metal stools, flame-resistant blankets, fire-retardant mattresses. The Doukhobors had been famous for trying to burn the place down. In 1969, it became a federal prison for offenders and inmates requiring protective custody.

As the paddy wagon approached, Henry gazed out at row on row of galvanized steel Quonset huts on cement-slab foundations. He and the other prisoners were herded to an area where the keeper, a grey-haired man with soft creases around his eyes, ordered their manacles removed. Calm and respectful, he assigned Henry a cell in East 13, Cubicle 8.

Henry marvelled at his new surroundings. No bars. Just rooms—partitioned, dormitory-style rooms. No locks on the doors. A window in almost every room and a heat vent under the bed. If it got too hot, he had two choices—choices! Either cover the vent with a piece of ply-wood or open the window and let the chilly mountain fog roll in. When his neighbour suggested a swap—cigarettes in return for a mattress and curtain—Henry leapt at the offer. How many smokes in return? "As many as you can afford today, maybe more after they clear your property."

Most inmates had little use for jailhouse shrinks—it was clear they blabbed direct to the Man—but Henry had been reading about Viktor Frankl, a Nazi concentration-camp survivor who'd found reason, among the most hideous circumstances, to go on living. And so, a few weeks after his arrival at Mountain Institution, Henry asked to see the prison psychiatrist. After waiting for months, he finally got an appointment with Dr. Ross Bulmer. When Bulmer asked what Henry wanted more than anything else in the world, he said, "access to a logotherapist."

"Logo what?"

"It's a movement dreamt up by Viktor Frankl," said Henry. "The man studied concentration-camp survivors. You heard of him?"

"Yes," Dr. Bulmer said. "What's your point?"

"The question Frankl most struggled with is this: When the basics of life—forget the comforts; I'm talking basics—are beyond reach, what makes one person endure while others give up? God has abandoned me, like he abandoned Frankl. If I can figure out how best to survive—how best to rise above those intent on oppressing me—I'll be well on the way. Doctor, can you help me?"

At the end of the session Dr. Bulmer placed a note in Henry's file: "This man has a very unique presentation in interview. He has served twelve years while claiming his innocence. His thinking processes are not entirely logical and coherent, but contain certain leaps and shifts that are quite unique. Despite a fairly lengthy interview, I am not clear what it is he is requesting."

CHAPTER 28

A FRIEND IN NEED

L ike Ivan Henry, Keith Vancamp was declared a dangerous offender after being convicted of multiple sexual assaults he claimed not to have committed. After Peter Ryan, Vancamp's lawyer, heard Henry's story, he helped him draft a letter to BC Legal Aid:

> Please find attached the Affidavit containing the expert analysis of the lineup photo.
>
> The highly qualified expert, Mr. Lee Atkinson, makes observations in his Affidavit that lead to the conclusion that the photograph was altered, fabricated or doctored.
>
> As this was strictly an identification case, and given the strong character of the Affidavit evidence, the applicant very likely would be successful in the B.C. Court of Appeal using the Palmer[1] test for fresh evidence [evidence that existed at the time of the trial, but that for various reasons could not be put before the court].

In his cell that night—under his faithful blue light—Henry reflected on the words of Her Ladyship Reed:

> Mr. Henry's main complaint in this case is that the Minister of Justice has failed to review "new" evidence of a fabricated lineup. The photo wasn't a crucial piece of evidence at trial. Henry himself called an expert who said it wasn't doctored.
>
> There is no doubt the photo looks bizarre, but it can be explained. Mr. Henry has never been able to produce any expert opinion that the photo was fabricated, then or now . . .

That final line was no longer true. Not only had he now produced a proper expert, but in Peter Ryan he'd found a lawyer who believed him and who seemed ready to help him advance his case.

Henry was also immersing himself in the *Weekly Criminal Bulletin*, a periodical of unreported criminal cases across the country, which he'd just discovered. He'd been profiling sex criminals, trying to figure out who committed the rapes he was in for, and he set out to gather scuttlebutt on fellow inmates who'd been making his life miserable. The more he knew about his harassers, the less likely they'd be to bother him.

Henry also documented the harassment he suffered at the hands of corrections staff. When he saw a guard in his mobile unit twirling the AR-15 rifle he'd stuck out the window, he recorded the licence number and reported him. "If he's not disciplined," Henry wrote, "I'll go to the Commissioner of Penitentiaries." The guard was transferred soon after that. Another guard regularly taunted him, saying his only way out was in a coffin and flashing a light in his face while he was sleeping. An inmate reported seeing a female guard search Henry's cell when he wasn't there, violating the rule that said two staff must be present at a cell search. And in response to his request for VPD surveillance reports—he argued there was no way he could have raped Miss Fields or Miss Kavanagh while being watched—the Privacy Commissioner said that such disclosure would "seriously harm the effectiveness of police surveillance techniques and procedures in future investigations."

Not every day brought bad news, though. Henry quietly rejoiced in his cell when he learned that Guy Paul Morin, who had spent ten years in jail for the murder of a nine-year-old girl near Toronto, had been excluded as the culprit as the result of DNA testing.

• • •

THE LONGER HENRY spent in prison, the more he threw himself into helping his fellow inmates, whether it was convincing a fish not to go off half-cocked on some real or imagined grievance, or talking down a con after a serious event in his life—the death of a child, or a cheating wife. Henry sought to live as Jesus would have him live. During my visit with Manfred Cullen in Mountain Institution in 2013, I asked him to write down a story about Henry. Soon after, I received a letter about an incident involving "a twenty-five-year-old inmate with the capacity of an adolescent":

A lumbering, six-foot-tall man, Jonathan was full of laughter, an awestruck child experiencing his first trip into the unknown. His family having turned him in for lighting a fire in a town-house complex—destroying fifty to a hundred units. After they declared him a dangerous offender, Jonathan went around the joint hollering, at the top of his lungs, "Problem solved!"

That Jonathan didn't belong in a prison setting was obvious to everyone. Yet, day after day, he sat watching the TV that Ivan, in his role on the Inmate Committee, had got for him.

The day Jonathan was caught sniffing glue came as no surprise to anyone. Glue-sniffing was his drug of choice. Nor did jaws drop to learn he'd refused to cough up the name of his dealer. Single-mindedly, Ivan waited and waited until, finally—everyone knew who it was—he confronted the leech.

Whatever it was Ivan said, the leech complied.

Cut off from his supply, Jonathan vowed to seek revenge. Targeting the Inmate Committee as the most likely suspect, he vowed to lock up its members, torch their meeting-place.

Security having caught wind of it, Jonathan was detained in segregation while they sent for Ivan. Before long, Jonathan was offering assurance, amidst a great flood of tears, that it would never, ever happen again. Though the last thing Jonathan wanted was to be transferred to a mental institution, Ivan convinced him he needed looking after.

In the end, the kid, threatening violence to no end, relented and agreed to be transferred to the Regional Psychiatric Centre in Saskatoon.

When I asked Henry about this, he said, "I maintained honesty and never told anyone something I didn't know. I always helped everyone, young and old. I was self-taught from the old men and inmates of long ago. I always asked the older men what to expect from whatever I was about to do, or was doing. I listened to them as though they were my father.

"When I got older," he said, "the men started coming to me with their legal problems. In the course of doing several court applications for one man, I spotted the difference in his sentencing transcript between "concurrent" and "consecutive" years. They let him out early.

"I did whatever I could for whoever I could. I chose no discrimination in black or white, or any other racial difference. I knew what it was like to be the black sheep—no matter who one was, or their colour."

On October 22, 1996, Ivan Henry turned fifty. Looking back on that day years later, he said, "Birthdays, whether those of relatives or your own, could be heartbreaking. 'Another year gone, and I'm still in here.' I did my thirty-five to sixty-three in jail. Turning forty wasn't so bad, but years turn into decades, and you know you'll never get those decades back."

• • •

BASED ON HENRY'S "proven track record as a hardworking inmate and a dependable Inmate Committee member," the warden agreed to transfer Manfred from Kent Institution to Mountain. Not just Manfred, but also his drag-queen girlfriend, "Miss Chablis." Having been shacked up for months in a single bed in Kent's isolation unit, the couple shared Henry's elation at the move.

Recently, I asked Gerry Ayotte, a beloved, veteran prison chaplain, what he made of the complicated relationship between Henry and Manfred. "On the one hand," I said, "Manfred has an ingrained hatred of skinners. Yet, from the beginning, he loved Henry unconditionally—to the point of checking into PC, even before he'd formed an opinion about the Vancouver rapes. Henry had never told him about the Winnipeg attempted rape conviction, but I inadvertently let it slip during one of our interviews in Mountain. Manfred paused no longer than a heartbeat before brushing it off.

"On the other hand, there's Henry with his visceral, Catholic-based distaste for homosexuals. Given the exploitation he'd endured as a youth, it's no wonder he views homosexuality as repulsive. Yet, when he hears that the warden has arranged for the transfer of Manfred and his male lover? He couldn't have been more thrilled."

Tenting his fingers, Ayotte placed palm against palm, bowed slightly, and said, "Namaste"—the divine soul in me recognizes the divine soul in you. "It's a wonderful story," he said. "On the one hand, Manfred is a man rightly convicted, albeit long ago, of despicable crimes. On the other hand, he's a guardian angel of sorts. He, of all people, saw the goodness in Henry from the beginning, never doubted his innocence. Without him—and Henry grasped this important, human fact in a minute—Henry almost certainly would never have survived as a sex offender. Believe me, guardian angels abound in the prison system.

"He who has eyes, let him see."

• • •

IN THE FALL OF 1997, Henry reflected on all the good news he'd had recently. The Supreme Court of Canada had granted Réjean Hinse—convicted, despite proof that he'd been far from the crime scene, of armed robbery in Quebec—a full acquittal. In July, a DNA laboratory in the United Kingdom released a report confirming that semen samples on the clothing of David Milgaard's supposed rape/murder victim did not originate from Milgaard—for all intents and purposes clearing Milgaard of the crime. And retired Court of Appeal of Quebec judge Fred Kaufman—acting as inquiry commissioner—had found Guy Paul Morin to be factually innocent, "beyond a shadow of a doubt," of the murder of Christine Jessop. After citing evidence of police and prosecutorial misconduct, and of misrepresentation of forensic evidence by the Centre of Forensic Sciences in Ontario, Commissioner Fred Kaufman, acknowledging the taint of guilt still hanging over Morin in the minds of the public, said that although the inquiry was not aimed at establishing Morin's actual innocence, he was pleased to note that it had served such a purpose.

Henry had more reason than ever to hope. Undeterred by Legal Aid's refusal to fund his appointment, Peter Ryan was helping Henry, gratis, to prepare his argument that he had effectively been denied his right to due process under the *Charter of Rights and Freedoms*. His appeal had been dismissed based on a condition he could not comply with—he lacked the necessary funds. As well, the lineup photo had been doctored and the police had perjured themselves.

Ryan had reason to be optimistic. In a remarkably similar case that he had argued, BC Court of Appeal justice Michael Goldie had decided that counsel must be appointed to "ensure that this appeal is properly prepared."[2] Since Henry had been unrepresented at his original trial, the court was more likely to hear his appeal. Henry tried never to let his hopes get too high, but maybe things were finally going his way.

On December 16, 1997, BC Court of Appeal rejected his application.[3]

CHAPTER 29

GONE IN A FLASH

I n 1999, Henry's daughter Kari, ever more committed to her father's case, was looking through recently disclosed police documents when she came across VPD 'Confidential Bulletin' Re Marpole Sexual Assault Update, dated December 24, 1983. The bulletin listed, as one of a half-dozen sexual assaults, charge #82-17341.

"But how can that be?" she wrote her dad. "Charge #82-17341 belongs to Miss Cardozo, the woman they say you raped on March 19, 1982."

She was right. Henry had been found guilty of assaulting Miss Cardozo in March 1982—nine months before the issuance of the bulletin. Kari wrote to Legal Aid, citing the bulletin as "solid evidence proving they had convicted the wrong man.

"My father was jailed in July 1982, convicted in March 1983, meaning the wrong man was behind bars, and the real man was still committing these crimes. This 'Cardozo' case should have been closed. The other five numbers listed in the Bulletin were all committed in 1983, long after my dad was jailed. Like I've said, my dad was wrongfully convicted. For the police to make a mistake like that, for more rapes to have occurred after his convictions, the real perpetrator might still be out there, running free."

Henry felt deeply grateful to his daughter.

And to his mother, for coming to visit him again. How frail she seemed, being frisked and buzzed into the visitors' area, and how insubstantial—like a good breeze might blow her over. She was more stooped now, her face more lined with worry. When he embraced her, she put on a brave front and handed him a chocolate bar from the vending machine. "Your favourite kind."

"You mean the only kind," he said, and they both did their best to laugh.

They took turns reassuring each other. Henry said nothing about his legal setbacks or the daily harassment—she had had more than her share of grief. And certainly nothing about the move from Mountain's Quonset huts into concrete cells. CSC had undertaken an extensive rebuilding of the site—enlarging it and replacing the old living units with three modern buildings, sixty units of which were double-bunked. Also replaced were the dining hall/kitchen, school, and health-care facilities. It was depressing to move from a cubicle he could leave any time to a locked cell, and from having windows that opened wide to ones that barely opened at all, especially when the staff played games with the temperature.

"Where's Darwyn?" he asked his mother. A month ago, his big brother had written to say he'd finally built up the courage to apply for a visitor's permit. Twenty years and counting since they'd laid eyes on each other.

"He's waiting for me in the parking lot," his mother said.

Henry pictured Darwyn outside in his truck, cowboy hat pulled low over his eyes. Given his brother's troubles south of the border, CSC must have rejected his visitor's application.

After his mother said goodbye, memories of his brother haunted him. Like the time Darwyn reached across the table and grabbed food. When their mother jabbed her fork at his hand, he'd jumped up and pushed a fistful of squash in her face. Not long afterwards, she'd had Darwyn carted away and made a ward of the state.

• • •

IN JANUARY 2000, when Larry Fisher was handed a life sentence for the murder of David Milgaard's supposed victim, Gail Miller, on a DNA matchup, the news spread like wildfire. Pacing his cell that night, Henry repeated one of his mantras: *My day will come, my day will come.*

A few months later, the CBC's *The Fifth Estate* aired the episode "His Word against History: The Steven Truscott Story." The next day, Peter MacKay—then justice critic for the opposition Conservatives—

described Truscott's wrongful conviction as a "festering wound on the psyche of this nation, one which casts a shadow over the entire justice system."[1] Within hours, James Lockyer, the founding director of the Association in Defence of the Wrongly Convicted (AIDWYC), held a press conference to announce Truscott's application for ministerial review.

Fearful that his own wrongful conviction might never come to light, Henry sank into depression. Then he received a letter from his old pal in Sask Pen.

"Dear Ivan," Bill Black wrote, "I'm not always strong, and sometimes I get overcome with fear. Just to let you know you're not forgotten, friend. I often felt like you were my rock. I'd have probably whistle-blown or ratted out anyone who hurt you. I'd never have stood idly by and watched you fall. It's difficult in jail because, if I'd have interceded too quickly, it would've made you mad. Every situation is different. I just try to keep myself and everyone else, including you, alive. You're worth it, for sure."

"No truer words," Henry said aloud. "I'm worth it." Inspired and resolute, confident he'd be exonerated through DNA testing, if nothing else, he applied to BC Supreme Court for an order compelling production of medical evidence—"donor deposit (blood type)"—and for a mandamus order requiring the doctors to specify the blood type apparently found.

At night, he dreamed about his story finally being heard. If Truscott, sentenced to die at fourteen, could get his wrongful conviction reversed and go public, so could he. Rubin ("Hurricane") Carter, an American boxer, also wrongfully convicted of murder and ultimately freed, told Truscott: "You're stepping into the public spotlight for the same reason I did. I refuse to be condemned by history."[2]

Damn right, thought Ivan William Mervin Henry. *I.W.M.H. I will make history.*

• • •

IN 2001, DUE to overcrowding, Henry was forced, again, to double-bunk—this time with a bug named Weird Ricci. His snores were loud enough to wake the dead. Because CSC didn't stock earplugs in its canteens, Henry took to stomping on his arms to wake him. By day, Weird

Ricci barraged him with stories about how he'd bilked seniors from coast to coast out of their money.

Waking one morning with fever and nausea, Henry begged for relief—an Aspirin, the nurse, anything. Weird Ricci gave him a pill "guaranteed to cure everything," and Henry popped it. A few minutes later, he was hurtling through the galaxy on a flying saucer, his legs amputated and then reattached, white, bloodless—one busted limb atop the other. In and out of consciousness, afraid he was dying, Henry screamed for help. Somewhere, always just out of sight, Ricci was laughing his head off.

When Henry came down, he grabbed Ricci by the throat and demanded an explanation. "Special K, man," Ricci said, his eyeballs bugging out. "K-k-k-ketamine. I thought you'd get off on it."

"It's a fuckin' horse tranquilizer, you moron. Listen up and listen good. If you ever do that again, I'll sic Manfred on you."

Weird Ricci went grey, and that was the end of it. A few weeks later, he was gone. Prison's like that—cons transferred, consigned to the hole, the infirmary, the psych unit, then released. No one asks; no one tells. One day, the cell next door is empty; the next, a stranger moves in.

• • •

HENRY'S NEW CELLMATE was an older, church-going Métis man from the Prairies. On September 11, 2001, the two of them were riveted, along with everyone else, by the collapse of the Twin Towers of the World Trade Center. Massive clouds of billowing smoke enveloped lower Manhattan—emergency vehicles, sirens screaming, rushed to the scene. It was chaos.

Henry watched as office personnel, desperate to escape the flames and poison gases, plunged to their death. It was horrific, but the horror was tinged with envy: tragic as it was, there was something to be said for certain, sudden death. What if he was destined to endure the slow-motion death of life behind bars, futilely proclaiming his innocence to the end?

Once again, though, he found cause for hope when a drug trafficker who'd been transferred back to Canada from the United States told him about Marvin Lamont Anderson. Convicted of robbery, forcible sodomy, abduction, and two counts of rape in 1982, the eighteen-year-old

Anderson had been sentenced to 210 years' imprisonment in the Virginia State Penitentiary. With the aid of an organization in New York, the Innocence Project, he'd become the ninety-ninth person in the United States to be exonerated due to post-conviction DNA testing. After nineteen years of imprisonment, he was a free man.

Always, Henry reminded himself, even in the darkest moments, there is hope.

CHAPTER 30

NO JOKE

The injustice done to Henry made him sensitive to issues of fairness and equality in prison, and he took pride in doing what he believed was right. "In the butcher shop," he told me, "I began increasing the amount of meat I was allowed so as to ensure sufficient for those too timid to voice that they weren't getting enough. I protected the ones most hated as best I could. When the night came, these 'bad' inmates could be killed outright. Once, during a power outage, we were forced into Unit 13—no lights at all. To create light, we soaked cotton batten in candles and baby oil or shoe polish. In my attempts to stop violence, I'd ask the men, 'Do you really want another lockdown?'

"If someone offered me more for something than it was worth, I'd say that's too much and let him off with half. I did this not to get brownie points, but because I believed in fairness and equal opportunity."

Late at night, though, despair was sometimes hard to keep at bay. "Don't think I didn't cry at chosen moments," he told me. "I was human and very vulnerable. Being alone most of the time, I did have friends, but very few on the list I could talk to or personally associate with. The guards loved telling me about my failures. That's why, when I got an official-looking letter, I always left it unopened until the next day. Failures disturbed me, and I didn't want to get eaten up.

"My darkest moments were usually just before or after New Year's—another year starting off with the same question: why am I still here? It never really sank in until 2002. I'd been in for twenty years. I was turning into an old man. It was no joke."

•••

ON FEBRUARY 22, 2002, newspapers across the country featured the same story on page one. Robert William Pickton, a pig farmer in the Vancouver suburb of Port Coquitlam, had been charged with the first of dozens of counts of first-degree murder involving some of Vancouver's most destitute women, most of them drug-addicted sex workers.

· Revolting as Pickton's crimes were, it was VPD member Kim Rossmo who caught Henry's attention. In the months leading up to Pickton's arrest, Rossmo, a Ph.D. candidate in the new science of geographical profiling—an investigative methodology used to analyze the locations of a connected series of crimes to determine the most probable area of offender residence—had concluded that a serial killer was at work in the Downtown Eastside.

For years, Henry had been compiling accounts of rapists in and around Vancouver. Applying Rossmo's methodology to his research, he began to develop a profile of the likely culprit of the assaults for which he'd been convicted. Meanwhile, he paid close attention to other wrongful conviction cases. In November 2003, James Driskell, having spent thirteen years in jail for a murder in Manitoba, was released on bail after applying for ministerial review of his conviction. Evidence that had recently come to light pointed to secret payments and immunity from prosecution provided to Crown witnesses. What's more, DNA tests excluded the three hairs used to convict him.

Reading about the case in the newspaper, Henry cheered Driskell and cursed the gods for the institutional deafness with which his own pleas for mercy were being met.

•••

LATE ONE NIGHT in 2004, long after lock-up and last count, Henry's cellie was fast asleep behind the drawn curtain. Before long, Henry's fingers were flying solo. A bright flash of light through the security window, and he reached for his blanket. Blushing, he covered himself and sat up. There she was—hatchet-faced Flannigan, pointing and staring. Worse yet, a newbie officer, also female, was at her side.

Flannigan was the worst guard to have witnessed him doing the dirty. Weeks earlier, he'd brought a halt to her little work-to-rule campaign. While the guards marched up and down the grounds, demanding "danger pay" for having to deal with such savage offenders, he'd found a commissioner's directive saying that inmates must be fed within a fourteen-hour period. They'd eaten supper at 5:00 p.m., which meant they had to be fed again by 7:00 a.m. That brought an end to the guards' wildcat strike, but not to Flannigan's enmity.

"What the hell just happened?" whispered Sammy, after Flannigan left.

"Can't say," said Henry. "But with a battle-axe like her, you better believe she'll come up with something."

And she did. Accusing him of "self-abuse" in her presence—his "clear intention" being to harass her and her partner—she also claimed that he'd stolen her work schedule. How else would he have known the exact time of her rounds?

"Just let them try charging me with public indecency," he told Sammy. "No cases directly on point, as the lawyers like to say, but I'll argue that a locked jail cell is hardly a public place."

"No way would someone like you, claiming innocence and all, risk a charge like that," said Sammy, who volunteered to testify on his behalf. Henry said no thanks; they'd never accept the word of a con over a guard.

Not long afterwards, guards barged in and trashed his cell. On the excuse that he must've hidden the work schedule, they confiscated his locker boxes, which contained his most recent research, privileged documents, and discs. They held them for nine days while the correctional investigator dealt with his complaint—days Henry spent worrying. Would files be deleted, and incriminating items like pornography planted? What if he never saw his belongings again?

Eventually, the boxes were returned intact, and he heard nothing more of the allegations. But this didn't stop Flannigan from exacting her revenge. For weeks afterwards, her sidekicks took turns activating a battery-operated mechanism outside his cell. Like a Chatty Cathy doll, the thing intoned, "Fuck you, fuck you, fuck you," at all hours of the day and night.

CHAPTER 31

A RAY OF HOPE

No Catholic was happier than Ivan Henry when, on April 19, 2005, Pope Benedict XVI succeeded Pope John Paul II. *At last, he thought, they've elected a pope prepared to adhere to fundamental Christian values.* Not that he attended chapel as regularly as he should. He was too busy working on the most comprehensive petition he'd ever written.

To pay for stamps, paper, and filing and photocopying costs, he was charging other inmates twenty dollars a pop to help with their submissions. He was also gambling on just about every sport—football, hockey, basketball—and winning more often than not. "You're a lucky bastard," one loser told him. "It's a necessity," Henry shrugged. "The University of British Columbia Law Library charges sixty dollars to photocopy five cases. You get a discount if you do it in person. Fat chance of that, huh?"

"Thank God," he later told me, "that both Lee Atkinson, the forensic photographer, and Gary McDaniels of Precept Investigation Services, the South Florida firm I hired to try to track down Miss Kavanagh, cut me some slack. Neither one charged me for the full extent of their endeavours. I am in their debt."

Undeterred by his lack of funds, he "studied the *Criminal Code* going back a hundred years, and discovered that the Crown and court had literally shit on me. By 2005 or thereabouts, I'd pieced it together. I tried to understand the true meaning of each section—case law showing all propositions and how to reuse a statute that wasn't used. The study for knowledge was horrifying because one case law would sanctify what was done, while another would prevent this procedure completely.

"Without the *Charter*, the law way back then was functional and worked well. But as the generations took over, it became apparent that legal-aid appointees were watering it down. Where proof was necessary, it was being tainted by stupidity. Over the years, the law weakened, meaning a witness could say anything.

"Teaching oneself the law while one's fighting the law is hard. The Crown could rest easy with judges like Bouck because they knew the system and had answers to any count."

By December 2005, Henry was putting the final touches on his petition, complete with multiple attachments and iterations—including close-ups and enlargements—of the lineup photo.

• • •

A FEW MONTHS after Henry had applied to add the Vancouver office of the BC Attorney General to his list of approved phone numbers, he was granted permission. "Yes," said the receptionist when he called, "of course you can have our address. Send us a copy of your petition when it's in final form." By early January 2006, he'd sent it off. Maybe this time somebody would actually listen.

Meanwhile, the media was full of news about the notorious child killer Paul Bernardo. He'd just confessed to the 1987 sexual assault of a fifteen-year-old girl in Toronto, supplying details known only to the perpetrator. The twist: a man named Anthony Hanemaayer had already pleaded guilty to the crime in return for a (provincial) sentence of two years less a day. Released in June 1990, Hanemaayer had served sixteen months in prison, including eight months in pretrial detention.

Asked why he'd pleaded guilty to a crime he did not commit, Hanemaayer said, "Back then, I was 19, I was scared. Because of the charge, I didn't want to go to a federal prison. So in other words, I had to take the deal. I didn't want to do 10 years. With two years less a day, given the time I'd already spent inside, I figured I'd just do another eight months and get out, get it over and done with."[1]

Then, in April 2006, the Attorney General of Ontario ordered that the body of Lynne Harper, Steven Truscott's alleged victim, be exhumed to be tested for DNA evidence. When it was determined that, after forty-seven years' interment, no usable DNA could be recovered from the remains, Truscott was devastated. He was out of prison, and he had his life back, but he knew that a finding of absolute innocence would forever elude him.

•••

EACH TIME HENRY phoned the BC Attorney General's office—and there were many calls in 2006—the receptionist, polite and friendly, gave the same answer: "We're reviewing your petition, Mr. Henry. Thank you for your patience." When he called on November 15, he said, as firmly as possible, "No disrespect, ma'am, but can I please speak to [then-Deputy Attorney General] Robert Gillen?"

"He's in a meeting, sir."

"It's Ivan Henry."

"My goodness, sir, they're talking about you at this very moment."

Finally! Surely his time had come. It wasn't until the inmate behind him coughed loudly that he came to his senses. Fumbling the receiver, he replaced it and got the hell out of there. He would keep his joy to himself, for now. In the joint, seeming happy can have unhappy consequences. Men had been killed for whistling cheerfully in their cells.

CHAPTER 32

MISSING EVIDENCE

Although the trip from Mountain Institution to Vancouver usually took two hours or so, on this day in early 2007, it seemed to take five. Was it Henry's imagination, or were the sheriffs jerking him around by lingering at every pit stop along the way? When they finally arrived at the courthouse, Henry was escorted along the same hidden hallway he'd first walked twenty-four years earlier, en route to his Supreme Court trial, and then a year later, to his Court of Appeal hearing.

In the courtroom, a buttoned-down, suited man about his height and age waited as Henry's handcuffs were removed. After introducing himself as Special Prosecutor Leonard Doust, the man said, in a voice quiet and formal, "I appreciate that you don't trust anyone, but I've been appointed to look into whether a miscarriage of justice occurred in your case."

"Yeah, sure," said Henry.

But then, despite his misgivings, he nodded and shook the man's outstretched hand.

A few weeks later, Doust suggested that Henry retain Peter Wilson, Q.C., to handle his case. "Peter Wilson is a highly regarded criminal lawyer," Doust told him. "Among his many other distinctions, he acted as counsel for Tom Sophonow in Winnipeg. He's prepared to handle your case on a pro bono basis."

Henry's daughters, however, convinced him that activist lawyer Cameron Ward, whose children they used to babysit, would be a better bet. After being retained, Ward enlisted Marilyn Sandford and David Layton to work with him on the case.

In his letter to the special prosecutor, Ward asked for information on the "as yet unidentified individual" that Doust had mentioned to a reporter. In his letter to Doust (provided to me by Henry), he wrote that the physical evidence seized by the police—including clothing, bedding, and bodily fluids—had apparently been analyzed by a Mr. Beaton, City analyst. "It is surprising," he said, "that this evidence was not tendered by the Crown at trial. Given the serious and high-profile nature of the case, it is inconceivable that the physical evidence and analyst's reports would be destroyed. Have you obtained this evidence yet?"

All well and good, thought Henry, *but why wasn't anybody talking about the lineup photo?*

Peter Ryan had mysteriously withdrawn from the Law Society of British Columbia and seemingly vanished off the face of the earth. (His mother, whom I contacted in London, England, said that the last she'd heard, he was "at sea" and not expected back any time soon.) Too bad; Ryan had been the one lawyer prepared to take up the matter of the doctored photo. What he wouldn't give now to have him in his corner.

Henry fired off his own missive to the special prosecutor, urging him to make the lineup photo part of his investigation and enclosing several copies, as well as close-ups of particular parts of the photo. Hearing nothing in reply, he assumed that the special prosecutor was part of the conspiracy against him. In 2013, when I questioned Doust about this, he said that if Cameron Ward had asked him to make the photo part of his inquiry, he would have done so.

• • •

IN DECEMBER 2007, Henry learned that his beloved mother had passed on. It's true she had whaled on the boys when they were young, but life hadn't been easy for her and they'd usually deserved it. Had he been allowed to attend her funeral, he would have eulogized her as a proud woman who did not let anyone demean or disrespect her. "She stood completely independent," he would have said, "even prior to leaving Vukusha. She wasn't a bigot; she had a way about her that never showed fear, nor did she ever act like she was better than anyone. Walking into a room with her, I felt an odd sort of confidence. She was only five feet four, but she was bigger than life. She carried her purse like she had a million dollars in it. She taught me the strengths needed as a jailbird. I'm sorry, my dear mother, for hurting you, but it was my cycle of life. Nobody is perfect, but nobody should be convicted of something they didn't do."

Darwyn, Henry's brother, later told him that when their mother was leaving Mountain the last time she went to see him, they'd confiscated her extra chocolate bar. "Some horrible woman strip-searched her twice," Darwyn said, "both going in and leaving."

"Mother never said a word," Henry told me. "When I asked who was on duty, she said something about some lady guard being rude to her. That was it. After all the cancer surgery she'd undergone, I hated to think of her humiliation at being forced to expose her body to strangers."

"Trust Mom to keep it from you," said Darwyn. "She always said you had more than enough on your mind."

CHAPTER 33

FREE AT LAST

On the night of March 29, 2008, a full-scale riot broke out at Mountain Institution. Disgruntled by measures taken to curtail the drug trade, and by a new rule restricting the number of visitors allowed at any one time from 250 to 50, inmates suspended negotiations with the warden and went on a rampage.

The riot erupted so suddenly in the gym and spread so quickly to the living areas and health-care unit that more than twenty officers abandoned their posts and fled to the roof without ensuring that security cameras—which would have caught the inmates' activities—were turned on. Several hours passed before officers from nearby Kent Institution and an emergency-response team arrived with shotguns.

In the meantime, prisoners broke through two heavy metal doors of the health-care unit and grabbed medicine off the shelves, including as many as eighty bottles of methadone from the drug-addiction treatment program. In their living areas, roving inmates smashed computers and the panel that controlled cell locks. Roaming through the cells, they bashed toilets and sinks. Through it all, Henry stayed locked in his cell—out of reach of the skinner-haters. Two deaths happened that night: one was a methadone overdose; the other was the beating death of a convicted child pornographer.

While most of the guards got to the roof, slamming the console door behind them, one was not so lucky. Hiding in the classification office, unable to shut out the nightmare noises of the diddler being clubbed to death, she prayed for survival. Two and a half hours later, in shock, almost comatose, she was carried out on a shield. It was the reviled Miss Flannigan.

Although he tried to follow the path of righteousness, Henry took a certain satisfaction from her trauma. Maybe it was karma. Most of the female staff were impeccable. Not Flannigan, though. One day she said to him, referring to the big key used to lock up a steel door in the kitchen, "It's as old as you are." Disrespect, plain and simple. Anyone who treated inmates that way was lucky to survive to old age.

• • •

ON MARCH 31, 2008, two days after the riot at Mountain Institution, the report of the special prosecutor looking into Ivan Henry's case was released. Although its contents are confidential,[1] the following recommendations were made public:

1. The Crown make full disclosure to Henry of something called "Project Smallman," described as "relevant and potentially exculpatory to his case";

2. The Crown make full disclosure of evidence in its possession and ensure that Henry has the benefit of any potentially exculpatory evidence that may not have been previously available to him;

3. The Crown provide counsel with a copy of his report and disclose to Henry documents and information collected by him;

4. The Attorney General appoint a special prosecutor independent of the office of Crown counsel to represent the Crown; and

5. The Crown not oppose any application brought by Henry to reopen his appeal.

Attached to the report was the Project Smallman file. At three thousand pages, it was as thick as the *Oxford English Dictionary*. In it, Special Prosecutor Doust named Donald James McRae as the possible perpetrator of the crimes of which Henry had been convicted.

With Mountain still in lockdown, legal-aid lawyer Cameron Ward received permission to visit Henry. "Big news, Ivan," he said, producing a photo of McRae, who looked startlingly like Henry. (See insert 7).

"According to the authorities, this is the real perpetrator. He's the Smallman in Project Smallman."

Never having come across the name before, Henry was confused. Based on his extensive research, he was convinced that the real perpetrator was Terry Driver, convicted in 1998 of the attempted murder of fifteen-year-old Misty Cockerill and the rape and murder of her friend, sixteen-year-old Tanya Smith. For months, Driver had taunted the RCMP, admitting to the crimes, daring them to find him. In calls to police and emergency services, he had identified himself as the killer and threatened more violence. Driver, whose father was a former VPD detective, used a police scanner to monitor responses to his calls. On his three-by-two-foot geographical profile, Henry had plotted Driver's places of employment, addresses of relatives, everything he could think of. Every point connected, in some way or other, with one of the crimes for which Henry had been convicted.

"Ivan became obsessed with Driver," Bill Black, Henry's old friend, told me. "He profiled him extensively. It may be that he can prove that some of the crimes were Driver's or other serial rapists in that area. If the cops were as clever as they say they are, they'd pay out old Ivan and get him on their payroll. Ivan has investigated many other offenders secretly, and he has a wealth of knowledge and information to share."

And now here was Cameron Ward suggesting McRae was the real perpetrator? *No more blind alleys, please God.* As Henry had instructed Richard Peck twenty-five years earlier, he urged Cameron Ward to "go after Luchenko, White, the cops—everyone involved in the state corruption. There were no rapes. This photo? It's nothing but a head on a body."

CHAPTER 34

LIMBO

On January 13, 2009, the Court of Appeal agreed with Henry's application, uncontested by the Crown, that his 1984 appeal should be reopened—primarily, it said, because of the Smallman reinvestigation "involving approximately 25 unsolved serious sexual assaults in Vancouver in the mid to late 1980s, at a time when Mr. Henry was in prison." (After Miss Kavanagh's assault on June 8, 1982, the next one bearing the same MO occurred on March 17, 1983, shortly after Henry's conviction.) Six months later, in June 2009, Henry was finally released from custody.

For years he'd dreamt of the day he would walk out of Mountain a free man. He had lived every moment in his mind: sitting on a patio chair, wriggling his toes, and soaking up the sun; grabbing a smoke or an ice-cold brew whenever he felt like it; choosing what he ate and when; watching his daughters leaning into each other, giggling and whispering; and best of all, inhaling the God-given air of freedom.

As it turned out, however, life on the outside wasn't nearly so glorious. Before his release, he had electronic monitors strapped to his ankles and was given detailed instructions about curfews and reporting—where and when and to whom. He was not to venture unaccompanied beyond Tanya's tiny backyard in North Vancouver, and the dark basement room where he slept was not much bigger than a prison cell.

Freedom, so ardently longed for, turned out to be dicey. At first, Henry was afraid to go outdoors. The pace of life, the traffic, the commotion, the technology—everything sent his heart racing. When his daughter asked him to mow the lawn, he was terrified; the task seemed

186

monumental. When someone posted his address in a nearby shopping mall, he got death threats. Anxious and paranoid, struggling to cope, he thought his best option might be to return to prison. "One day you're in this shithole that's your life," he explained. "The next day you're out, trying to make sense of it all."

On June 21 and 22, 2010, Henry's lawyers argued that his convictions should be overturned. Hour after hour, Henry sat, jaw clenched, as the lawyers—his and the Crown's—discussed and debated and made nice in that way he hated: "my friend" this and "my friend" that. Memories of the preliminary hearing almost three decades earlier moved through him, wave after nauseating wave.

Still out on bail, anxiously awaiting the court's decision, Henry was more paranoid than ever. Convinced that police were watching him 24/7, he was certain that women were being placed in his path to entice him into sexual overtures. Not a day went by that he didn't suffer the pain of those decades of being deprived of his liberty, the humiliation and disgrace of prison. Looking ahead, he saw dim prospects for work, physical and mental health, romance, and social relations generally.

Henry resented his lawyers for the way they treated him, for refusing to take up the fake-photo issue Whenever he asked them why not, they changed the subject. He still hadn't seen the report of the special prosecutor; when he asked for it, they blew him off. At sixty-three, he was too young for old-age pension, and he had not a nickel to show for the decades he'd spent working in prison kitchens and laundries, sewing shops and warehouses. He wasn't entitled to compensation for the money he'd spent getting his convictions overturned or for the rent money CSC had made him pay for his cell. He had no résumé, no modern skills, and little understanding of the high-tech world into which he'd been sprung. When he was convicted, in 1983, Mark Zuckerberg had not yet been born.

Henry would have been better off if he'd been paroled after serving a sentence for murder—at least he'd have gotten free room and board, counselling, job-placement assistance, and a gradual return to society via a halfway house. As someone wrongfully convicted and then imprisoned for almost half his life, he was entitled to nothing but the right to sue state entities that had vast resources and no reason to hurry.

And as a man who'd had guilty verdicts changed to not guilty ones, he was widely assumed to be a criminal who—rather than being factually innocent—had gotten off on a technicality.

In 2011, Henry's lawyers launched a lawsuit in BC Supreme Court, seeking damages from the provincial attorney general, the federal minister of justice, the City of Vancouver, and three members of the VPD. "As a result of the wrongful acts and omissions of the defendants," reads his statement of claim, "the plaintiff was charged, detained in custody, wrongfully convicted and imprisoned, and his wrongful convictions were not set aside until 2010. He has consequently suffered, is suffering, and will continue to suffer, loss and damage."

Further, reads the statement of claim, Henry lost his "liberty, reputation, and privacy, and suffered humiliation, disgrace, and pain" and was denied "the enjoyment of life, everyday experiences, and income, as well as benefits and a pension." The suit also seeks compensation for his two daughters, who were "effectively deprived of a father and of the benefits of a father's love, guidance and affection."

This is all true, of course, and if the stars align, he stands to one day receive a major settlement. Sophonow, who spent four years in prison convicted of a murder he did not commit, got $2.7 million. Milgaard, who spent twenty-three years in prison for a rape and murder he did not commit, got a tax-free compensation package worth $10 million.

Exactly when the defendants will compensate Henry is far from uncertain. To date, the defendants have been dragging their heels. And so Ivan Henry does what he's been doing for three decades now.

He waits.

PART THREE

THE CASE FOR INNOCENCE

"We must believe in the gods no longer
if injustice is to prevail over justice."

— EURIPIDES, *ELECTRA* —

The role of the prosecutor—
to ensure that justice is done—
excludes any notion of winning
or losing. Michael Luchenko,
lead prosecutor in the Henry
trial, seemed determined from
the outset to convict him.

COURTESY OF *THE ADVOCATE,*
VANCOUVER BAR ASSOCIATION

Ivan Henry's former wife
moved into this home,
directly across the street
from Donald McRae, in
March 1982. An addict,
she later confessed to her
daughters that she had
fingered Henry in return
for $1,000 from the
VPD's "fink fund."

PHOTO BY JOAN McEWEN

Early in the trial, the prosecutor substituted the 8 × 10 inch photo for this 5 × 7. The photo Henry viewed throughout the trial was different from the one everyone else in court was viewing. Forensic experts say this 5 × 7 photo was also doctored.

Calling the police lineup a "farce," the 2010 Court of Appeal said it should never have been conducted. Henry says he was never even in a lineup, handcuffed. Forensic experts confirm that this 8 x 10 inch photo was doctored. PHOTO BY JOAN McEWEN, FROM THE IVAN HENRY FILE IN THE BC COURT OF APPEAL REGISTRY [THIS PHOTO HAS NOT BEEN ALTERED BY THE PUBLISHER IN ANY WAY.]

1982
MAY 12
PC 388

Calling the July 27, 1982, photo array "biased," the 2010 Court of Appeal pointed out that Henry is the only person shown in front of a jail cell, and with a VPD officer's arm in the foreground: "The photograph of [Henry] stands out unfairly and would have focused the viewer of the array on him."

PHOTO BY JOAN McEWEN, FROM THE IVAN HENRY FILE IN THE BC COURT OF APPEAL REGISTRY

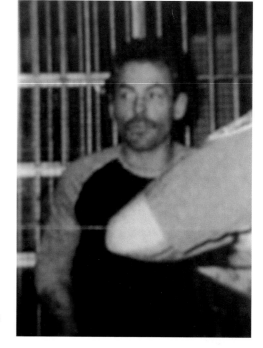

Not only is this photo biased; Henry points out that his hair was not curly at the time, he had no moustache, and the only VPD officer in the room was the one taking his picture.

PHOTO BY JOAN McEWEN, BASED ON MATERIAL OBTAINED FROM THE BC COURT OF APPEAL PUBLIC DOCUMENTS

Although Ivan Henry doesn't even appear in this 1981 lineup, one of the Henry complainants identified #12 as her attacker—a man who looked nothing like Henry and whose identity remains unknown. PHOTO BY JOAN McEWEN, FROM THE IVAN HENRY FILE IN THE BC COURT OF APPEAL REGISTRY

This photo array (Donald James McRae is No. 2) is properly done—black and white, neutral background, no props—and underscores how biased the Henry array was.
PHOTO BY JOAN McEWEN, FROM THE IVAN HENRY FILE IN THE BC COURT OF APPEAL REGISTRY

In 1982, Henry had just completed mandatory supervision after an attempted-rape conviction in Winnipeg. Meanwhile, a rapist was terrifying women in Vancouver, and Henry, who'd moved to the West Coast, seemed a promising suspect. COURTESY OF IVAN HENRY

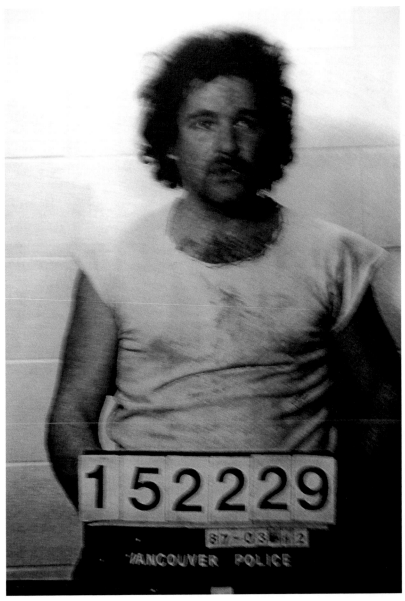

Donald James McRae, who had an extensive record for break and enters, "night-prowling," and "peeping Tom" activities, bore a remarkable resemblance to Henry and is likely the perpetrator of the Henry crimes. PHOTO BY JOAN McEWEN, FROM THE IVAN HENRY FILE IN THE BC COURT OF APPEAL REGISTRY

David Milgaard (*left*) was exonerated in 1997 after DNA retained from 1969 excluded him. Though semen samples were collected in the Henry case, the Crown refused to produce medical evidence at his trial. The VPD advised, decades later, that the samples had gone missing.

PHOTO BY JOAN McEWEN

In 1985, Rubin "Hurricane" Carter, who was freed from jail after serving almost twenty years for a murder he did not commit, vowed: "I refuse to be condemned by history."

PHOTO BY JOAN McEWEN

INSERT 8

Thomas Sophonow (*left*), convicted of the 1981 murder of a doughnut-shop clerk in Winnipeg, was exonerated thanks to DNA testing after serving over four years. Sophonow is shown here with Henry and the author.

COURTESY OF JOAN McEWEN

CHAPTER 35

THE FINK FUND

We now know that Ivan Henry's arrest on May 12, 1982, was triggered by statements his drug-addicted wife, Jessie, made to the police. As stated in an undisclosed document entitled *VPD Surveillance Project MCS, #82-04,*

> (Henry's) divorced wife was interviewed by Detective Bruce Campbell on 82.05.02 at 1400 hrs. She gave him considerable insight into Henry's activities both in Winnipeg prior to his problems, as well as his current activities.
>
> She says there are similarities, and she is concerned about it. She called the police department prior to this interview. She also provided photographs of Henry.

Although Detective Campbell painted a picture at the trial of only fleeting contact between Henry and Jessie—they met on a street corner, he said, and she gave him the striated photo—Henry knew better. When Jessie told him about the two police constables entering their home, he was outraged. How dare the police frighten his kids, coerce his wife into handing over clothing and photographs, manipulate her answers, and threaten her?

Police interview notes, suppressed at the time, record Jessie as telling them that Henry had grown a moustache to hide his loose front tooth, had worn a gold chain around his neck since Christmas, smoked cigars, and used the term "rip-off" regularly. She is also quoted as saying that Henry went out frequently at night, that his wardrobe changed frequently, that he owned a green velour shirt and wore a watch, and that he is circumcised.

Henry has always denied that he went out late at night. He maintains that he never wore a gold chain; he's never smoked cigars; and he's never owned a green velour shirt. The last time he wore a watch was in 1960. When I asked him about the disparities, he said, "If they'd written down what Jessie actually said, it would have been more accurate and true. It's obvious the police were inventing things to put me in jail."

During the trial, Campbell rejected the suggestion that Jessie was an informant, but a letter dated January 30, 2008, from Henry's older daughter, Tanya, to the special prosecutor paints an entirely different picture:

Two months before my mother's death in October 1990, we had a lengthy "heart-to-heart" discussion about several important family issues. She was not under the influence of drugs or alcohol, nor was I. Although she had told me before that my father was innocent, this was the first and only time she discussed the situation in depth with me.

My mother's first words to me were, "Your father didn't do it. I know he is innocent because I'm the reason the police started investigating him."

She told me she was in a horrible state in her life, heavily into the use of illegal drugs, when she read an article in a newspaper about a series of rapes. Thinking the description of the predator sounded like my father, she contacted the police. They'd been fighting, she thought he had a "lady friend," and reporting him would be a "way of getting back at him."

She said she met a police officer downtown near a pay phone, and he gave her $1,000 for her information.

Asked whether Henry owned a black turtleneck, my mother said no, but gave them hers, which they took away. She said she provided untrue statements about her suspicions to the police, partly because she was upset with him, partly because of the money they gave her, and partly because of the threats the police made to her. The police said they'd take Kari and me away from her because of her drug addiction if she didn't give them the information they wanted.

After she told me these things, I asked her why she didn't do something about it. She said, "Who would believe me now?

I can't now, it's too late, it's done. I am an ex-addict living on welfare, and nobody will believe me."

She said she was guilt-ridden about it, and that she would be until the day she died.

Campbell downplayed the extent of Jessie's involvement, but the statement of defence filed by the City in Henry's civil suit makes clear that she provided the police with extensive information.

• • •

WHEN MY ATTEMPTS to interview Bob Stewart as well as the current VPD chief, Jim Chu, proved unsuccessful, I looked for other sources to comment on this case. Through friends of friends, I was able to find and interview three retired Vancouver police officers. To protect their identities, I'll call them Constable Janet Almgren, a beat cop in the early '80s; Detective Fred Montgomery, who was familiar with the Henry lineup; and Detective Joseph Witt, who was familiar with both the Henry and McRae investigations.

That these three officers agreed to talk to me—even on condition of anonymity—is a minor miracle. Although Detective Campbell testified that he'd never heard the term "blue curtain," even lay people understand that terms such as "blue shield," "blue wall," and "blue code of silence" symbolize the view that at least some police are honour-bound not to report a colleague's errors, misconducts, or crimes, even if they are questioned under oath.

When I asked Detective Witt about the VPD's use of informants in the 1980s, he described something called a "fink fund":

Money was put into it every year. Though the name could be a code name, all payments had to be recorded, as well as the nature of the information given. For substantial payments, let's say anything over $1,000, you needed approval from the higher-ups. The rule was that such large amounts could only be paid out if the informant had given credible information in the past.

Until the early to mid-'80s, the administration of this fund was pretty loosey-goosey, less than professional, veiled in mystery. Just as the courts were demanding more professionalism in the area of suspect identification by victims via photo and physical lineup presentations, so was the area of informant control, registration, and compensation under the microscope.

Those in power were coming to see the writing on the wall, and the whole "informant control" issue had to be overhauled and given some semblance of legitimacy. This was somewhat accomplished by establishing a registry, handlers, control mechanisms, and an air of transparency. It took the whole operation out of the Dark Ages. For the first time, it was accountable.

First asked about Tanya's account of her mother's confession, Detective Montgomery said: "You mean she gave a death-bed confession? There's no proof she was telling the truth then, or that the daughter is now."

"Money aside," I said, "Detective Campbell testified that he and two constables had had dealings with Jessie prior to Henry's arrest during which he says she gave them two photos. He never owned a black shirt with grey sleeves, nor did he wear one in any photos taken of him. How is it, then, that they have him wearing one in the May 12 and May 13 photos?"

"More importantly," I continued, "Given that Jessie was interviewed at length and that, in addition to information leading to Henry's arrest, she gave the police various articles of clothing, shouldn't she have been called as a witness by the Crown?"

"Absolutely. I've never heard of an informant not being called. Obviously, she had relevant information."

"What if she'd refused to come?"

"She'd have been subpoenaed and, if necessary, declared a hostile witness. Either way, she'd have been forced to say what she knew, and what she told the police."

Because of the Crown suppression of key evidence, Judge Bouck was not privy to the full extent of Jessie's involvement leading up to Henry's arrest. Nevertheless, he had no business chiding Henry for not calling her as his witness. Even knowing as little as he did—that Jessie had co-operated with the police—Bouck should have instructed the jury that they could infer, by the *Crown's* failure to call her, that she would have given evidence harmful to its case. Had Jessie testified, her status as a paid informant would almost certainly have come out, as would the fact that the money she received went, almost certainly, into her veins.

CHAPTER 36

DETAINED FOR QUESTIONING

When Henry asked Sergeant Edward McClellan, the officer who processed his release from jail on May 13, 1982, why he'd been "detained for questioning," McClellan answered: "Based on the document I read, a burglary charge." Henry knew better. In the course of being interrogated by Detectives Sims and Campbell regarding a whole raft of sexual assaults, they'd made it clear that he was under investigation for being the "rip-off rapist."

After Ivan Henry called Detective Campbell as his own witness—a move that served only to dig Henry a deeper hole—Luchenko used the opportunity to "cross-examine" him. It was not cross-examination in the classic sense, with adversaries going toe to toe, but more like spoon-feeding desirable answers to an ally in the middle of pitched battle. For instance, Campbell agreed with Crown suggestions that the only photos available to the police were not of acceptable photo-lineup quality, that the police were intent on doing everything possible to try to curb or stop the sexual assaults, and that a physical lineup was the only method of obtaining an identification.

Detective Witt disagreed that the VPD had no choice but to hold such an unfair lineup. Yes, he said, it would have been difficult to assemble a lineup on short notice. "Sometimes members of the jail staff would be sent to skid row drinking holes with a handful of cash. For five or ten dollars, men similar in appearance to the suspect would do their thing."

Detective Dan Montgomery said that the police could have readily found alternatives to the physical lineup. "We'd try to find people who were similar," he said. "I must say that, in my own experience,

I never felt it necessary to convene a physical lineup. Usually, we put together photo arrays." Asked whether, in such a photo array, the police could have used Henry's mug shots from Winnipeg five years earlier, Montgomery said yes, they would have sufficed. "Even the striated photo would have been better than the sight of Henry being held by the police in a chokehold."

Henry was interrogated for who knows how long. The only record of what was said are police notes in summary form. Towards the end of the initial interrogation, Detective Sims threw in, almost as an after-thought, "I'm assuming you know that anything you say here may be given as evidence. You are welcome to call a lawyer." Too little, too late. The right to counsel is triggered before a lineup is held. Section 10 of the *Charter* states: "Everyone has the right on arrest or detention . . . to retain and instruct counsel without delay and to be informed of that right." As the US Supreme Court said in 1967:

> The trial that really determines the accused's fate may not be in the courtroom, but "at the pretrial confrontation"—where "the state is aligned against the accused, the sole jury is the witness, and the accused has little or no effective appeal from the judgment there rendered by the witness—'That's the man.'"[1]

When Campbell and Sims asked Henry whether he would take a polygraph on the "three who'd identified him by voice."

"You bet," he said, "bring it on. I'll take a lie detector test, anything." No polygraph test was ever administered.

• • •

IN THE MONTHS prior to Henry's arrest in May 1982, the ongoing disappearance of young people had alarmed the entire Lower Mainland. While the VPD and RCMP squabbled over jurisdiction, Clifford Olson—their number-one suspect—was released from custody four times. By the time the government accepted Olson's bodies-for-cash offer—anything to bring closure to the families—he'd racked up eleven murders. "I'll give you eleven bodies for $100,000," he said. "The first one will be a freebie."[2]

In its rush to judgment in the Henry case, on the heels of the botched Olson investigation, was the VPD driven by a desire to bag someone—anyone? On the other hand, if they were in such a rush, why did they wait ten weeks after Henry's release from jail to arrest him? This despite the fact that two more sexual assaults had occurred, each of them involving the same "rip-off rapist" MO.

Among the documents disclosed to the special prosecutor was an inter-office memo dated August 8, 1982—a week after Henry's arrest in 100 Mile House—from Crown counsel Sandy Cunningham to her colleague Michael Luchenko. The memo reads as follows: "The lineup photo is disastrous . . . The accused is obvious. It is pathetic. But that's the way it is! Detective Harkema can help you with this! . . . The file is 'hot.' There's an incredible amount of pressure to keep him in custody."

If the file was so hot, why did the subsequent trial garner relatively little publicity? As Henry recalls, apart from a young woman who wandered into the courtroom one day, not a single member of the public was in sight—not even a *Vancouver Sun* reporter. When I asked then-courthouse-beat reporter Neal Hall what he recalled about the trial, he could offer up little. In the local newspaper archives, I found only fleeting mention of the arrest, a few brief snippets about the trial, and a short article announcing the convictions.

Did the state—given the shaky foundations of its identification evidence, the biased lineup and lineup photo, the May 13 photo of Henry, and the photo array—do what it could to keep the trial out of the public eye? Although no one can control who walks into an open courtroom or what the media decides to cover, the silence that hung over the trial remains a mystery.

CHAPTER 37

LINEUP IDENTIFICATION

When Henry asked at trial why the police had released him on May 13, 1982, Detective Campbell testified, "I had a discussion with my partner, Detective Sims, and my superiors, and also with Crown counsel. As a result, you were released pending further investigation." Sims testified that Henry was released due to "questionable" lineup identification—a claim supported by Detectives Michael Barnard and Lars Gronmyr in the recently disclosed *VPD Surveillance Project MCS, #82-04*:

> HENRY was arrested on 82.05.12 and was placed in a physical lineup at 312 Main Street. He was tentatively identified by three victims.
>
> Because he was forced physically to go into a lineup, the quality of lineup (identification) is not of strong evidentiary value.

Sometime after May 13, then, and before mid-June (when Harkema took over as lead detective), Detectives Sims and Campbell concluded, in consultation with the Crown and their superiors, that the lineup identification was insufficient to warrant the laying of charges. The 2010 Court of Appeal concurred, calling the "pre-court" lineup identification "fraught with problems":

> There is no telling what influence the prominent display of the appellant by the police officers during that event ultimately had on the six complainants when they were asked in court if they could identify the assailant.

Police investigators should have prepared a proper and fair photographic lineup instead of forcing the appellant to participate in the physical lineup.

In other words, the impugned lineup identification was incapable of rehabilitation. How, then, did it come to be resurrected? Given the conclusion of Detectives Campbell and Sims that it was too tainted to be of any use, on what basis did Luchenko approve, first, the swearing of the multi-count information in late July and, second, Harkema's "re-interviews" three to four months later?

• • •

IN A DISCUSSION paper written in 2006, the former VPD chief Bob Stewart reflected on his commitment to upholding the highest of moral standards during his ten-year stint as chief, from 1981 to 1991:

> My father was a police officer. Two of my sons and a daughter-in-law serve with pride. My career and, arguably, my life have been devoted to Canadian justice and police issues. I could not possibly be more proud of both our national and local police forces; they are second to none in this world.
>
> I had the privilege of being Vancouver's Chief Constable for 10 years, longer than anyone else in the now 120-year history of the force. When I would occasionally hear that someone with a complaint was too distrustful of police to bring it to me, it always hurt.[1]

I left phone messages for Chief Stewart—a thirty-five-year VPD veteran, a Parole Board of Canada member from 1996 until 2005, and now a member of the Variety Club of BC. I wanted to ask whether he was involved in the decision to resuscitate the lineup identification. As well, I wanted to know why he'd written Henry the letter on behalf of the Solicitor General of Canada:

> My inquiry reveals it was you who introduced this photo into Court, and also provided an expert witness in an attempt to prove that the picture had been altered. The expert witness said, in fact, that the picture had not been altered. The photo was taken after the lineup had been completed, and was part of

the usual procedure of photographing the lineup for the purpose of record and scrutiny by interested parties at subsequent proceedings.

Chief Stewart did not return my calls.

CHAPTER 38

TEN WEEKS

About twelve hours after Henry was released from jail after the May 13 lineup, Miss Fields was raped. The unnamed author(s) of the VPD's May 14, 1982, *Investigation Report (Case #82-30158)*, written the day of that rape, state that the "suspect used the same MO as the 'rip-off-rapist.'" On June 8, three and a half weeks after Miss Fields's assault, Miss Kavanagh was attacked.

In a heavily redacted report, withheld until recently, the unnamed author(s) write that Henry was under surveillance from May 13 onward. (Redacted portions are indicated by the symbol "< >.")

```
These notes have had some information removed
that could harm the effectiveness of surveillance
technique.
     This subject was placed under surveillance <   >.
     A rape occurred on May 14th, which is almost
certainly his doing. Surveillance was resumed <   >
for several weeks. A meeting was held on June 7,
which consisted of all of the rest of the
surveillance people.
     <   >
     A rape attributable to our subject was committed
on June 8.
     Surveillance was again established by these
people until June 21, when a surveillance group was
established by Sergeant Howland to take over the
problem.
     As of June 23rd, the Vice-Section took over
surveillance.
```

< >
```
    This subject was placed under surveillance
shortly after he was released from the city jail. The
surveillance was not immediately placed on him, and a
rape occurred on 82.05.14, which is almost certainly
his doing.
    A meeting was held on 82.06.07 which consisted of
all the surveillance people discussing their problems
and no surveillance maintained throughout the night.
This was because of a change of shifts, etc., being
involved. A rape attributable to our subject was
committed in the early morning of 82.06.08.
```

Incredibly, the only two times surveillance was lifted between May 13 and Henry's arrest at the end of July were the times two more women, Miss Fields and Miss Kavanagh, were assaulted. Although surveillance began upon Henry's release on May 13, 1982, it was lifted roughly twelve hours later, just before Miss Fields's attack at 1:00 a.m. on May 14. The reimposed surveillance was lifted on June 7, just before Miss Kavanagh was assaulted in the early morning of June 8.

When asked about this, Detective Witt, familiar with the Strike Force that tracked Henry between May 14 and July 29, 1982, said that surveillance was expensive—lots of overtime. "Typically," he said, "after a suspect is released, we'd establish one full, ten-hour shift of surveillance to suss out such things as address, car make, possible associates, etcetera. It is entirely possible that, after that first block of ten hours, the police went back to the drawing board to assess long-term surveillance strategy.

"Further," he said, "it appears that surveillance was suspended as a result of the June 7 meeting—likely, again, for budgetary reasons. When a woman was raped that very night, it was resumed.

"It should be noted that effective surveillance was difficult to maintain on Henry—his erratic driving and paranoid personality lent itself to extremely difficult problems encountered in following and observing him."

For seventy-seven days after Miss Fields's assault, and fifty-two days after Miss Kavanagh's, the police did nothing. Only when Miss Kavanagh told them, "I'm leaving the country in a few days. If you want my help, this is your last chance" did Detective Harkema, the lead detective as of mid-June, spring into action.

Asked at trial to explain the delay, Harkema said, "There were a whole lot of other things I was involved with before I went to see her."

Was the real reason that the police did nothing that they knew Henry was not their man?

• • •

RIGHT AFTER HER attack, Miss Kavanagh described the intruder as being in his mid-twenties (Henry was then thirty-five), with "light brown, possibly curly" hair. Police notes taken eighteen hours after the attack record her as saying she "might be subconsciously blocking out some of the suspect's description . . . She stared at him, but had difficulty describing him."

According to a later-disclosed document—an excerpt purporting to be from Miss Kavanagh's hypnosis session—"hypno-investigator" Detective Michael Barnard constantly reassured her that an image of her attacker existed in her mind's eye, "like a camera will zoom in and freeze it like a photograph." The details of the hypnosis session are not known—whether, for instance, any photos were produced and discussed.

After being hypnotized, Miss Kavanagh described her attacker as "in his 20s or early 30s," his hair "brown with red and gold highlights" and not so much "curly" as "closer to being frizzy than ringlets." These descriptions were recorded in Harkema's notes.

Prior to producing the photo array, Harkema had warned Kavanagh not to expect any "typical black-and-white mug shots. We do them a little differently," he said. "We take them in different places, we do them in colour. When you look at the array, don't worry about what the photographs look like. All you're looking at is the faces, and all you're thinking about are your reactions to them."

Not so, according to Constable Almgren. Even back in the '80s, she said, a photo array consisted of a photo of the suspect and a half-dozen or so closely matched stock photos. These stock photos were kept in the third-floor Identification Room of VPD headquarters and categorized by the subjects' age, ethnicity, height, weight, length and style of hair, facial hair, etcetera. Given the unusual colour of Henry's hair, Almgren said, the array should have been in black and white.

Detective Montgomery agreed, calling the photo-array picture of Henry unfair. "Pictures should be taken against the neutral background in the Identification Room," he said. "Plus, his is in front of cell bars."

The photo array itself? "Absolutely unfair," he said. "The backgrounds should all be the same."

Although Harkema interviewed Miss Kavanagh for two and a half hours on July 27, 1982, and for three hours and forty minutes the next day, his notes are a mere two and a half pages. They include her reaction to the photo array and, specifically, the image of Henry:

> When I had calmed down a bit, I started to study his face. He had changed his appearance by cutting his hair, by growing hair on his face. When I covered the part of his face that was covered by hair, I looked at just the upper face. My brain started working on this. My conscious impression started to agree with my first reaction of recognition. I hadn't talked about this with [name of girlfriend]. I had a shock reaction in the afternoon and was sick—the same reaction I had on June 8.
>
> I thought it might be possible to see a full front photo of him before I left the country, so I decided to wait and see if another photo would be available, one of the same guy without the changes he'd made in his appearance.
>
> This wasn't because I wasn't sure of him, but I wanted to confront as much evidence as was available. I knew last night I was definitely going to be calling Detective Harkema to tell him I was positive of the ID.

Whether the Crown played a role in Miss Kavanagh's decision not to fly back to Vancouver for the trial is not known. What is known is that although her friend testified that Kavanagh's father had recently died—the inference being that this was reason she didn't attend the trial—an investigator hired years later by Ivan Henry reported that her father was still alive.

• • •

AS RETIRED SUPREME Court of Canada justice Ian Binnie said, writing for himself and the three other dissenting justices in the *R. v. Gerald Regan* case,[1]

> The police investigate. Their task is to assemble evidence and, assessing it as dispassionately as they can, determine whether in their

view it provides reasonable and probable grounds to lay charges. The prosecutors provide the initial checks and balances to the power of the police. As the late Mr. Justice Arthur Martin observed in his Report of the Attorney General's Advisory Committee on Charge Screening, Disclosure, and Resolution Discussions (1993) ("Martin Report"), at p. 117, "[a]s ministers of justice, their ultimate task is to see that the public interest is served, in so far as it can be, through the use, *or non-use*, of the criminal courts" [ITALICS ADDED FOR EMPHASIS.] Further (at pp. 117–18):

> Discharging these responsibilities, therefore, inevitably requires Crown counsel to take into account many factors, discussed above, that may not necessarily have to be considered by even the most conscientious and responsible police officer preparing to swear an information charging someone with a criminal offence.

The Crown prosecutor thus stands as a buffer between the police and the citizen. As the Martin Report emphasized, at p. 39:

> Separating the investigative and prosecutorial powers of the state is an important safeguard against the misuse of both. Such separation of power, by *inserting a level of independent review between the investigation and any prosecution that may ensue*, also helps to ensure that both investigations and prosecutions are conducted more thoroughly, and thus more fairly. [ITALICS ADDED FOR EMPHASIS.]

Consistent with that "separation of power, in British Columbia no criminal charges may be laid without Crown approval. "Though the VPD work 'very closely' with prosecutors," said Detective Montgomery, "the Crown approves the charges before the information is sworn, and then they assign you tasks that need doing. Both Michael Luchenko and Judith Milliken were especially thorough in reviewing our investigation summaries in what are called Reports to Crown."

Asked to describe what would have occurred before Sergeant Howland swore the information against Ivan Henry, Montgomery replied, "Bill [Harkema] would've presented Mike [Luchenko] with a

Report to Crown. Gord [Howland], being senior to Bill, would have been at the same meeting. If Mike agreed with the contents of the report, he'd have given them the green light to proceed."

Hence, when Howland swore on July 29, 1982, that he had "reasonable and probable cause" to suspect that Henry had committed seventeen sexual assaults, he would have done so only after Luchenko had authorized the laying of charges. Asked whether he'd be surprised to know that no Report to Crown has ever been disclosed in this case, Montgomery said, "I'd be very surprised." Both Almgren and Witt said they would be surprised, too.

In its October 12, 2011, response to Henry's civil claim, the defendant City of Vancouver said:

25. *The May Lineup Photograph was not used by the Vancouver Police in its investigation of the Sexual Assaults.*

31. *The interviews conducted by Detective Harkema were made under the direction of a senior Crown prosecutor.*

32. In or around July 1982, Detective Harkema prepared a photographic lineup chosen from a selection of photographs kept by the Identification Section of the Vancouver Police Department (the "July Photographic Lineup").

33. *After preparing the July Photographic Lineup, Detective Harkema obtained senior Crown prosecutor approval for its use when re-interviewing victims of the Sexual Assaults.*

Once the criminal sexual assault charges were laid against the Plaintiff, the Crown became responsible and remained responsible, at all times, for the prosecution of the charges.

[ITALICS ADDED FOR EMPHASIS.]

In an amended response dated January 28, 2014, paragraph 33 has been deleted—the key role played by Luchenko is no longer flagged, and the erroneous claim that it was the "July Photographic Lineup" that was shown to the re-interviewees has been removed.

The false statement in paragraph 25 remains: "The May Lineup Photograph was not used by the Vancouver Police in its investigation of the Sexual Assaults."

So much for efforts by police and Crown to distance themselves from the bogus lineup photo and to downplay the extent of memory contamination that occurred. All along, they've blamed Henry for introducing the photo into evidence. As will be seen, the 2010 Court of Appeal made short work of that argument.

As their responses to his civil claim show, they continue to scorn his use of the photo at trial and to breathe new life into their claim that only a guilty man would resist so violently when asked to participate in a lineup.

CHAPTER 39

TATTERED SCARECROW

I n August 2011, I researched Wallace Craig, the judge in Henry's preliminary hearing. Reading the handful of commentaries on his 2003 self-published memoir, *Short Pants to Striped Trousers: The Life and Times of a Judge in Skid Road Vancouver,* I quickly got a sense of the man—born in southeast Vancouver in 1931, brought up and educated in the bleak days of the Great Depression, followed by the uncertainty of the Second World War. The images of him portrayed an imposing figure with perfectly parted, slicked-back hair and a no-nonsense manner—the quintessential law-and-order man.

As he wrote in the preface, "During my twenty-six years in court, I sensed that the criminal justice system, and particularly the judiciary, was dispensing justice without any real sense of law and order, leaving our fair city at risk of being Canada's drug capital, a place where property crime is rampant, and perpetrators of violence receive only notional punishment."[1]

"If the reality in Vancouver is that crime pays and is without punishment, and I believe it is," one online reviewer quoted him as saying, "then the criminal justice system is truly a tattered scarecrow"—a reference to one of his favourite Shakespeare quotations:

We must not make a scarecrow of the law,
Setting it up to fear the birds of prey,
And let it keep one shape, till custom make it
Their perch and not their terror—[2]

I called the bookseller mentioned in the article and was told that "His Honour" was retired and living in North Vancouver. "Yes," said the woman, "I have his number." Judge Craig answered on the first ring.

"I'm a lawyer writing a book about Ivan Henry," I said. "I'd love to get your impressions of the preliminary hearing."

I expected a quick demurral—no judge was likely to discuss a case with a stranger. Instead, he started chatting.

"I remember the case well," he said. "The bastard represented himself. He was always yelling at the witnesses."

"No, he had a lawyer, John White," I said, taking notes. "Do you remember him?"

"If you say so."

"Are you aware that Henry was exonerated by the BC Court of Appeal last October?"

"Not exonerated. No one ever said he was innocent. This innocence business is nonsense. More like the Scottish system—'guilt not proven.'"

"My book is intended to explore that very issue—factual versus legal innocence. But given that the police lost the semen samples, how could Henry demonstrate actual innocence?"

"Semen samples would have done no good back then."

"Serology testing was available. And DNA testing was just around the corner. Many men convicted back then have since been exonerated on that basis."

"In all my years on the bench, I've never experienced a man being wrongfully convicted," said Craig. "There are fewer of them than you'd imagine. We judges like to call the *Charter* the 'Criminal Charter.' As we like to say, a narcotics case without the *Charter* is a guilty plea. All the *Charter* does is gum up the works—slow things down."

"I'm interested in meeting with you to talk about the case."

"Sure, call me in mid-September and we'll set something up. I'm busy right now."

"What keeps you so busy?"

"I'm a part-time member of the Canadian Human Rights Commission."

I was taken aback. "That must be interesting work."

"While the preliminary hearing was taking place," Craig recalled, "a girl who lived next door to my wife and me in Kitsilano came running to our door, said there was a man in the back alley. I ran out, but he'd fled by then. I was sure it was Henry."

I knew (but did not say) that, by then, Henry had long been behind bars.

"Given that at least half the complainants either weren't asked to ID Henry or, if asked, said they couldn't, why did you commit him to trial on all seventeen counts? Isn't the test for committal whether there is sufficient evidence upon which a reasonable jury, properly instructed, could return a verdict of guilty?"[3]

Speaking carefully, he said, "The decision to commit involves a very low threshold. The test is whether it's possible that a jury could convict."

"But isn't it whether there's sufficient evidence on which a jury, properly instructed, could convict? Not that I'm a criminal lawyer, of course."

"At any time during the preliminary hearing," said Judge Craig, "Henry could've re-elected to be tried by a Provincial Court judge alone."

"Would you have been the judge?" I asked.

When he said yes, I again asked why he'd committed Henry on counts for which there was no identification evidence.

"I never took notes at preliminary hearings," he said, his voice suddenly clipped. "The minute the first woman identified Henry, I'd have stopped listening. That would be that. Let the jury sort it out at trial."

"Fair enough," I said. "I may call you for a face-to-face interview in September?"

Although he said yes, the many voicemail messages I left thereafter went unanswered.

• • •

CONSTABLE ALMGREN SHARES Judge Craig's sentiment about the rarity of innocent people being convicted. Even after I'd pointed out some of the worst injustices done to Henry, she said, "Assuming you're right, the question is whether they got the right guy in the end." She added, with obvious pride, "Back then, I viewed myself as a garbage collector, keeping the streets of Vancouver free from detritus."

When I asked Almgren to describe her job with the VPD, the pride wasn't so evident. "As a woman," she said, "my career path stalled at the Parole Division. In the '80s, women went nowhere."

CHAPTER 40

WHITEWASH

Ineffective assistance of counsel (IAC) is a significant cause of wrongful convictions. A recent study in the United States found that IAC was the primary error in 21 percent of cases of reversal.[1] Commentators in Canada have identified it as a factor that contributes to wrongful convictions; so have appellate courts and commissions of inquiry.[2]

As noted, prosecutor Michael Luchenko had the May 13 lineup photo as early as August 8, 1982—a little over a week after Henry's arrest. Yet in the weeks and months that followed, requests from Henry's lawyers for lineup photos went unanswered.

On October 29, 1982, day two of the preliminary hearing, John White, Henry's legal-aid lawyer, sought disclosure of "any lineup photos that might exist." Luchenko said, untruthfully, "To the best of my knowledge, Your Honour, I'm aware of no such photo."

Frustrated by the Crown's equivocation, Judge Craig adjourned the proceedings to give Luchenko time to look into it. When Luchenko returned with a blurred black-and-white photo and White said it was indecipherable, Judge Craig asked, "Will the original be forthcoming at some point?" Luchenko replied, "It's not immediately available. It will be entered at some point down the line."

When Judge Craig asked where it was, Luchenko said, "The police station, across the street." Then he added, "There's only the one copy that I'm aware of. I haven't seen the original copy myself."

"It should be made available. Your friend needs it for cross-examination."

After more back and forth, Judge Craig ordered Luchenko to produce it, adding, "I'll wait for as long as it takes."

After Luchenko returned and handed the five-by-seven-inch colour photo to White, the complainant Miss Simpson identified Henry as #12 in the photo, and it was marked "Exhibit One."

Although Ivan Henry continues to believe that John White was part of a conspiracy against him, it is more likely that White's casual attitude was ill suited to this case.

At first sight of the lineup photo at the preliminary hearing, Ivan Henry became apoplectic, insisting there was no way it was him in the photo; the thing was a farce. Yet White didn't say a word—not then, not later. I had to know why.

When I contacted White by phone in 2011, he said he had no memory of Henry's preliminary hearing. "We do so many of them," he said. "After a while they all run into each other."

"But surely the Ivan Henry matter wasn't your typical case?"

"I can't remember a thing."

In 2013, I called him again. "I'd like to take another crack at refreshing your memory," I said. "I'll be discussing your involvement in the book, and your perspective is important."

"Try me," he said.

"When you asked if there were any lineup photos, Michael Luchenko hemmed and hawed. First, he said the photo was not immediately available, that it would be entered at some later point. It was only after being pressed by Judge Craig that he produced a blurry, black-and-white rendition. Does that help twig your memory?"

"Not really."

"Okay, try this. Luchenko made the nonsensical suggestion that *you* could ask the police for it—as though the police would co-operate with defence counsel. That's when Judge Craig jumped in and said, 'Mr. Luchenko, produce it. I'll wait for as long as it's necessary for it to be produced.' Finally, Luchenko offered up the actual photo. Is it coming back to you now?"

There was muttering over the phone. Maybe he remembered; maybe he didn't.

"Why didn't you raise a ruckus when you saw it?" I asked. "Henry's hectoring would have strained the patience of Job, I know, but even if you didn't agree it was fake, you must've recognized how bizarre and highly prejudicial it was?"

Chuckling, White spoke with a sudden bounce in his voice. "At least I had the good sense to demand that it be produced! I'd forgotten that part. Good for me. That was a very smart thing for me to do."

"But why not at least flag the photo as outlandish? Twenty-eight years later, the Court of Appeal described it as 'biased and farcical.' Why not move at once to have it thrown out?"

"I left it to the trial judge to sort out," White said, sighing as though at my ignorance of criminal law practice. "I did my job, getting it produced. It's the job of the trial judge—his and the jury's—to determine its validity."

"Are you saying that a preliminary-hearing judge's powers are limited to rubber-stamping the charges?"

"Bingo," he said. "Almost every preliminary hearing involving a serious crime goes to trial. Check out the stats; you'll see that I'm right."

"Maybe, but why not, at the very least, build a record—make your views known? According to the transcript, you didn't say boo."

"These are things to be dealt with by the trial judge," White said, "not at the prelim." Then he hung up.

• • •

A SENIOR CRIMINAL lawyer I'll call Francis Lévesque agreed to weigh in on White's representation—"on condition of anonymity," he said, eyes twinkling. "Professional courtesy, you understand.

"At the time of Henry's preliminary hearing," he said, "the *Charter* had just been enacted. Still in its infancy. No one knew if it would have teeth. Given that Judge Craig had no jurisdiction to deal with alleged *Charter* breaches, the best that defence counsel could do is build a record—flush out possible holes in the Crown's case such as the lineup photo, the photo array, etcetera. That way, when the trial began, defence counsel could apply for a judicial stay.[3] If successful, the counts flowing from the flawed lineup identification may well have been stayed."

"Are you saying," I asked, not quite believing my ears, that had White objected to the lineup photo, the counts regarding those who had viewed the lineup might have been thrown out?"

"Yes."

"What about the woman assaulted after the lineup—[Miss Kavanagh] the woman who was shown the equally bizarre photo array?"

"Same answer. Not that it was a gimme, but a good lawyer would have had a real shot at it."

"What are your views about Judge Craig?"

"A bad draw. Any number of other judges would've ripped a hole through the lineup photo."

CHAPTER 41

CONTAMINATION

C linical studies demonstrate how powerful eyewitness testimony is and how readily memories can be contaminated. As the renowned memory expert Elizabeth Loftus, a professor at the University of California, Irvine, has said,

> A pointing finger of blame has a powerful hold on even the most informed and intelligent of juries . . . The danger of eyewitness testimony is clear: Anyone in the world can be convicted of a crime he or she did not commit . . . based solely on the evidence of a witness who convinces a jury that his memory about what he saw is correct.
>
> Why is eyewitness testimony so powerful and convincing? Because people in general, and jurors in particular, believe that our memories stamp the facts of our experiences on a permanent, non-erasable tape, like a computer disclosure or videotape that is write-protected.[1]

"Memories don't just fade," Loftus said at a May 2012 lecture sponsored by Simon Fraser University in Vancouver, "they also grow. What fades is the initial perception, the actual experience of the events. But every time we recall an event, we must reconstruct the memory, and with each recollection the memory may be changed—coloured by succeeding events, other people's recollections or suggestions, increased understanding, or a new context."

Loftus breaks down the process of remembering into three stages—acquisition, retention, and retrieval. At each stage, she says, information offered as "memory" can be distorted, contaminated, even falsely imagined:

The witness does not perceive all that a videotape would disclose, but rather, getting the gist of things, constructs a "memory" on "bits of information . . . and what seems plausible.

The witness does not encode all the information that a videotape does. Instead, memory rapidly and continuously decays. Retained memory can be unknowingly contaminated by post-event information, and the witness's retrieval of stored "memory" can be impaired and distorted by a variety of factors, including suggestive interviewing and identification procedures conducted by the enforcement personnel.[2]

● ● ●

AFTER HENRY'S ARREST at the end of July 1982, Detective Harkema conducted what he called "re-interviews" of the lineup attendees, each one lasting two to three hours. Hidden from Henry at trial was, first, that Harkema also re-interviewed Miss Ramirez, who had not been at the lineup; and, second, that he had shown the interviewees the lineup photo.

In addition to those re-interviews, the suppressed document enti-tled *VPD Surveillance Project MCS #82/04* lists other steps taken to facilitate positive identification:

Every witness and victim identified as having any part in each (of 21 rapes) has been interviewed personally by the original-assigned detective team.

They have also been exposed to photo lineups, physical lineups, and so-called "brainstorming" sessions.

The RCMP witness-viewing system of rape or indecent assault suspects has been utilized extensively as have sev-eral police "artists" for the purposes of drawing a composite of this person. Every conceivable similarity in the victims' backgrounds has been followed up with nothing conclusive to report.

Every rape has been detailed on an MO chart with the similar facts compared. There is strength in this comparison because, on close examination of these charts, it is very clear that the same person is responsible for these assaults.

It's clear, then, that the complainants were exposed to a veritable petri dish for the cultivation of memory distortion—both complainant-to-complainant and police/state contamination. No wonder the differing descriptions of the attacker first given by the six lineup attendees evolved, over time, into similar descriptions.

Initial descriptions of the attacker's hair colour morphed from very "dark," "black," "dark brown," "coppery-tinged," "coarse brown," and "blonde to light brown"—into "brown with reddish highlights." The assailant's voice, once variously described as sounding American, having a slight French accent, having a slur/accent, whispering and sounding nervous, came to be described by everyone as low and gruff.

In 2010, the Court of Appeal concluded that this pretrial process of identification was so "polluted" as to render in-court identification highly questionable and unreliable. All ten verdicts, said the court, were unsafe—they were not verdicts that a properly instructed jury, acting judicially, could reasonably have reached.

• • •

IN 2001, HARKEMA wrote a report for Inspector Barbara Morris. The small excerpt to which I am privy makes for riveting reading. Harkema writes that the (August/September 1982) re-interviews were required "because the initial response of the quite intelligent women was one of total disgust at the unfairness of the lineup"—that being the reason they failed to "conclusively pick someone out."

Nothing in any transcript so much as hints at the fact that the lineup attendees were disgusted with the "unfairness of the lineup." (And so much for the evidence of Acting Sergeant David Baker that the lineup was perfectly "fair.") Farther on in the report, Harkema writes: "They were all questioned in detail at a later date after Henry had been charged with the [Kavanagh] attack. They were shown the lineup photo again, and were able to add some of their comments to their earlier apprehension. They all said they were 95% sure it was him."

And then the last sentence: "They all said that the voice was his, and that they recognized the voice as belonging to their attacker."

This is all well and good, but for one thing: none of the lineup attendees heard Henry speak between May 12 and the preliminary hearing at the end of October. What then caused them suddenly to be sure—months after the lineup and months before the preliminary hearing—that Henry's voice was that of their attacker?

At the lineup, Miss Larson and Miss Horvath left their ballots blank. Miss Browning identified #18, who was a foil. Miss Jacobsen noted "12/18" on her ballot. Asked at the preliminary hearing how, having left her ballot blank, she could now identify Henry, Horvath replied, "Because, for the first time, I can see his face full on." Not a word about his voice.

Asked the same question, Miss Larson agreed that she couldn't recognize her attacker by voice at the lineup: "It didn't seem the same, but then I thought I should probably ignore it because he's got someone's arm around his neck."

At trial, Miss Simpson testified that when Henry made his outburst at the end of her preliminary hearing evidence, she first "became sure it was him." Both Miss Horvath and Miss Jacobsen testified that they knew, when they heard Henry's voice at the voir dire in late February or early March 1983, that Henry was their attacker. Miss Larson said, based on the accused's voice at the preliminary hearing and at the voir dire, she was able to identify him as her attacker. In other words, not a single complainant testified that the turning point in their voice identification came, as Harkema said in his report, during or prior to the re-interviews.

Morris asked Harkema to provide her with this report. Had I been able to talk to her, I would have asked her whether she had knowledge of the Smallman investigation then underway and, if so, whether she felt obliged to alert the Attorney General.

In 2006, Crown prosecutor Jean Connor made the connection between the Henry crimes and the Smallman crimes. Had she kept silent—as so many others did over the years—Henry would doubtless still be rotting in jail.

CHAPTER 42

MEMORY IMPLANTATION

In 1992, Robert Baltovich of Toronto was convicted of killing his girlfriend. In September 2004, the Ontario Court of Appeal granted a new trial stating that the trial judge did not give the jury the proper directives. The testimony of two important Crown witnesses was obtained by hypnosis. (After eight years in jail, Baltovich was freed in 2008 after eighteen minutes of deliberation. His current lawsuit against the police and Crown for $13 million is inextricably connected to Henry's Supreme Court of Canada proceeding [discussed below], set for November 2014.)[1]

In 1985, the American Medical Association Council on Scientific Affairs reported that, "due to evidence that hypnosis can create false or inaccurate memories, some courts bar all testimony by hypnotized witnesses at trial. Other courts admit the evidence, but only if experts can testify as to the dangers of such techniques."[2]

In 2007, the Supreme Court of Canada held that even "the most stringent guidelines afford no protection against external sources of influence or against the other problems associated with hypnosis, such as the creation of hallucinated or false memories (confabulation), an increase in detail without sufficient assurances that this new information will be accurate, and memory hardening. Given these problems, the danger that the accused will be denied a fair hearing is obvious."[3]

Foremost among those stringent guidelines, said the court, is that a qualified professional—an individual independent of the party requiring his services—must conduct the session. Detective Barnard, Miss Kavanagh's so-called hypno-investigator, hardly fits that description.

Acting as a lineup participant on May 12, and as a lead detective on both the Henry crimes and those committed after his conviction, Detective Barnard was anything but independent.

Despite the many problems associated with hypnosis, Judge Bouck made no mention of them in his jury charge. That fact, plus the tediousness of the "reading into evidence" of Miss Kavanagh's preliminary-hearing evidence, doubtless explains why the two jurors with whom I spoke[4] have no memory of any reference to hypnosis. Each said, in separate interviews, that if they had realized Miss Kavanagh had been hypnotized, they would have have discounted her evidence entirely.

• • •

THE SIX LINEUP attendees whose complaints went to trial all testified that the lineup photo was accurate. Assuming that the photo doesn't accurately depict what they saw, and that they did not knowingly give false testimony, how could they all be wrong? How can six witnesses "remember" something that never happened?

Elizabeth Loftus puts it this way: into waters of memory, originally empty, are planted fish. "These fish," she says, "begin wriggling around when the investigating detective starts asking questions and, as the detective continues throwing out the hooks—frothing the water, trying to get a bite—the fish leap up and swallow the hook. Once the memory is hooked, it becomes real. In my studies, a subject's reported confidence for suggested or imagined memories is often as great as that reported for memories based on actual perceptions."[5] This is all the more so, Loftus says, when visual images are used to reinforce the bogus memory.

In June 2010, *Slate Magazine* published an article about an experiment in which photos were fabricated to depict events that never happened: Vice President Dick Cheney rebuking Senator John Edwards for mentioning Cheney's lesbian daughter (in fact, Cheney thanked him), and President Obama shaking hands with Iranian president Mahmoud Ahmadinejad (it never happened). Mixed in with these fake incidents were three real ones: the Florida recount in the 2000 US presidential election, Colin Powell's prewar assessment of Iraq's weapons of mass destruction, and the 2005 congressional vote to intervene in the Terri Schiavo case.

Each participant looked at photos of the true incidents and a randomly selected fake one. They were asked, picture by picture, whether they remembered each event. At the end, they were informed that one of the incidents was fake and asked to guess which one.

Although the true incidents outscored the false ones, the fake images were effective. Twenty-six percent of participants remembered seeing Obama meeting Ahmadinejad, while 42 percent remembered the Edwards–Cheney confrontation. As the authors of the study said:

> These figures match previous findings. In memory-implanting experiments, the average rate of false memories is about 30%. *But when visual images are used to substantiate the bogus memory, the number can increase. Several years ago, researchers using doctored photos persuaded 10 of 20 college students that they had gone up in hot-air balloons as children. Seeing is believing, even when what you're seeing is fabricated.*[5]
> [ITALICS ADDED FOR EMPHASIS.]

I asked Loftus how six women could honestly believe they'd seen something that isn't real. She said it happens regularly: "To speculate, perhaps they had no preconceptions of what typical lineups look like and were exposed to a lot of suggestion in the many hours of interviewing."

CHAPTER 43

I WAS WRONG

Misidentification is widely recognized as the single greatest cause of wrongful convictions. In his study of the first 250 DNA exoneration cases in the United States,[1] Professor Brandon Garrett found eyewitness misidentification in 190 of them. In at least a third of the convictions obtained with eyewitness testimony, lineups were either biased or stacked to make the suspect stand out. If some of the foils in a lineup look nothing like the description of the suspect, Garrett concludes, then the lineup is not a sound test of the eyewitness's memory.

In 1983, Mr. Justice John Bouck had been on the bench ten years. He had co-authored publications on criminal law practice, was an acknowledged expert on jury trials, and boasted a razor-sharp grasp of criminal law jurisprudence. Despite that, he made a number of major legal blunders during the Henry trial—most notably, his failure to reject the identification evidence of each and every complainant.

In 2010, the BC Court of Appeal found that the "critical element of identification," the singular basis upon which Ivan Henry was convicted, "was not sufficient to sustain a conviction on any of the counts in the indictment." The court said that concerns about the reasonableness of such verdicts are particularly high when, as here, "the person identified is a stranger to the witness, the circumstances of the identification are not conducive to an accurate identification, pre-trial identification processes are flawed and where there is no other evidence tending to confirm or support the identification evidence."

Emphasizing that honest eyewitnesses can be mistaken, the court referred to a decision predating Henry's 1984 appeal:

The authorities have long recognized that the danger of mistaken visual identification lies in the fact that the identification comes from witnesses who are honest and convinced, absolutely sure of their identification and getting surer with time, but nonetheless mistaken. Because they are honest and convinced, they are convincing, and have been responsible for many cases of miscarriages of justice through mistaken identity.

The accuracy of this type of evidence cannot be determined by the usual tests of credibility of witnesses, but must be tested by a close scrutiny of other evidence. In cases where the criminal act is not contested and the identity of the accused as the perpetrator the only issue, identification is determinative of guilt or innocence; its accuracy becomes the focal issue at trial and must itself be put on trial, so to speak.

Honesty is determined by observing and hearing the witness, but correctness of identification must be found from evidence of circumstances in which it has been made or in other supporting evidence.[2]

Calling the identification so "polluted" as to "render in-court identification of [Henry] on each count highly questionable and unreliable," the 2010 Court of Appeal said that it resulted in verdicts that must be considered unsafe. "On each count," it said, "the intruder was a stranger to the complainant; the encounter was in poor lighting, the circumstances were extremely stressful, the intruder took steps to obscure his visage and two of the complainants were without their eyewear; the pre-trial identification procedures were seriously flawed and unfair; and there was no evidence independent of the complainant capable of confirming or supporting the identification made in court. In addition, pre-court and in-court identifications were made by the complainants often months after the traumatic event."

Citing an Ontario Court of Appeal decision, the court went on to say:

The weight of evidence of identification of an accused person varies according to many circumstances.

(I)f the means employed to obtain evidence of identification involve any acts which might reasonably prejudice the accused, the value of the evidence may be partially or wholly destroyed. Anything which tends to convey to a witness that a person is suspected by the authorities, or is charged with an offence, is obviously prejudicial and wrongful. Submitting a prisoner alone for scrutiny after arrest is unfair and unjust. Likewise, permitting a witness to see a single photograph of a suspected person or of a prisoner, after arrest and before scrutiny, can have no other effect, in my opinion, than one of prejudice to such a person.[3]

The pre-court identification of the complainants was invalid because, in each case, the accused had been made to stand out: in the lineup, he was the only one of the attendees who was in a chokehold; in the photo array viewed by Miss Kavanagh, he was the only man standing in front of bars and behind a police elbow; and in the case of Miss Ramirez, her one and only identification took place in court.

The physical lineup should not, the Court of Appeal said, have been conducted because "it became a farce" and because the impact of "the prominent display of the appellant by the police officers" on the complainants cannot be known.

As for Miss Kavanagh's identification of Henry, the court called the photographic lineup (array) unfair. "In particular, the photograph of [Mr. Henry], from the waist up, shows him standing in front of a jail cell with the arm of a uniformed police officer in the foreground. None of the foils is shown in this manner. The backgrounds in the other photographs are either blank or otherwise neutral. In addition, each of the six foils is, by appearance, at least ten years younger than [Mr. Henry]. [Mr. Henry] is the only one with a full moustache, and [Mr. Henry] is the only one with curly hair. In addition, the foils all have hair length that is at least to the collar and over the ears, by a substantial amount with respect to three or four of them. [Mr. Henry]'s hair is cut back and higher on the forehead." In summary, "the photograph of [Mr. Henry] stands out unfairly and would have focused the viewer of the array on him."

A full thirteen months passed after her attack before Miss Ramirez made her first identification of Henry at the preliminary hearing. (As noted, the Crown kept hidden the fact that she was among the women re-interviewed by Harkema.) Not only was the lapse of time substantial, but the identification occurred in the courtroom. Given that the accused is typically seated beside his lawyer, courts view in-dock (in-court) identification as unreliable. As stated in the 2012 Report of the FPT Heads of Prosecutions Committee:

> A first time in-dock identification, though admissible, has little weight and has particular frailties over and above the normal frailties associated with identification evidence. It is therefore considered undesirable and unsatisfactory.
>
> A specific warning should be given to a jury when considering the impact of this form of evidence. If an eyewitness's evidence becomes stronger with the passage of time as the matter proceeds through the court, this may imply that the identification is in fact "post-event reconstruction," which undermines its reliability.[4]

Henry's trial judge gave no such warning. In his charge, he said this: "On January 26, 1982, Miss Ramirez saw the accused in a Supermarket at 19th and Cambie . . . She didn't call the police. She'd called them a couple of times before about something bothering her, and the police said it was all in her head." The 2010 Court of Appeal described her identification evidence as "wholly unreliable."

In short, the court said, "the evidence against [Henry] on the critical element of identification was not sufficient on appellate review to sustain a conviction on any of the counts in the indictment."

• • •

A FEW MONTHS after meeting Ivan Henry, I hired a skip-tracing firm to obtain the complainants' contact information. I wrote each of the eight women whose addresses were found the following letter:

> Earlier this year, I began writing a book about Ivan Henry's wrongful conviction case. As part of my research, I hired a private firm to help me obtain contact information for the complainants. The company I retained came up with your name, among others. First, let me give you a little background.

What first piqued my interest regarding the "Henry" case was what it would be like to spend 27 years in jail as a sex offender . . .

I would be grateful if we could chat—not regarding the particulars surrounding the sexual assault itself but, rather, any insights you might have regarding how the criminal justice system played out, or did not play out, in your particular case.

Only four of the eight responded. Miss Fields and Miss O'Reilly, two of the seven whose charges did not proceed to trial, agreed to talk to me. The other two—both trial complainants—expressed grave concern at the fact that Henry, by protesting his innocence, was making them relive, again and again, the horror of their experience. It was bad enough, they said, that they had been forced to endure aggressive cross-examination by the man they were convinced had sexually assaulted them; they were now being forced not only to endure every tortuous step in his action for compensation, but also, now, this call from an utter stranger suggesting that their assailant just might be innocent.

After sincerely apologizing for intruding upon their lives, I determined to make no further attempts to reach out to any of the complainants. On May 19, 2011, I received a letter from the Victim Court Support Program, BC Ministry of Public Safety and Solicitor General:

> Many of the complainants in this matter have advised that they do not want you to contact them or anyone related to them with regard to Ivan Henry or your writing project. This includes any form of contact, by way of example but not limited to mail, phone, email, in person, through another party. In case you are not aware, there is a ban on disclosure of the identity of the complainants.
>
> I trust you will respect the wishes of the complainants and we ask that you make no future attempts to contact them.

• • •

ELIZABETH LOFTUS AND Katherine Ketcham write,

> Eyewitness identification is the most damning of all evidence that can be used against a defendant. When an eyewitness points a finger at a defendant and says, "I saw him do it," the

case is "cast-iron, brass-bound, copper-riveted, and airtight," as one prosecutor proclaimed. For how can we disbelieve the sworn testimony of eyewitnesses to a crime when the witnesses are absolutely convinced that they are telling the truth? Why, after all, would they lie?

Ah, there's the word—*lie*. That's the word that gets us off the track. You see, eyewitnesses who point their finger at innocent people are not liars, for they genuinely believe in the truth of their testimony. The face they see before them is the face of their attacker. The face of innocence has become the face of guilt. That's the frightening part—the truly horrifying idea that our memories can be changed, inextricably altered, and that what we think we know, what we believe with all our hearts, is not necessarily the truth.[5]

As horrific as it must be to be sexually assaulted, I can't imagine the layers of added emotion, stress, and trauma when one's attacker's is released from prison—worse yet, his claim of innocence.

In June 2000, an American rape victim named Jennifer Thompson published a *New York Times* op-ed piece entitled "I Was Certain, but I Was Wrong." Having just discovered that her actual attacker, a man identified through DNA testing, was not Ronald Cotton, the man she'd identified years earlier, she wrote about how she had "studied every single detail on the rapist's face. I looked at his hairline; I looked for scars, for tattoos, for anything that would help me identify him. When and if I survived the attack, I was going to make sure that he was put in prison and he was going to rot . . . I knew this was the man. I was completely confident. I was sure."[6]

Not only was Cotton, ten years into a life sentence, found to be innocent, but the man guilty of the rape was one of his fellow inmates. Indeed, he was a man whom, ten years earlier, Thompson had sworn she had never seen before.

"I felt like my whole world had been turned upside down, like I had betrayed everybody, including myself," Thompson said at the 2013 Innocence Network Conference in Charlotte, North Carolina, which I attended. "For years after," she said, "I beat myself up, over and over again."

Cotton isn't angry. He and Thompson, now friends, make joint presentations on misidentification. "You can't forget, but you can forgive," Cotton says. But he also counts his blessings every day. And he thanks God for DNA. "If it weren't for that, I wouldn't be where I am today."

Thompson, who says she went from victim to offender in an instant, finds it nowhere near as easy to forgive herself. "Ten years in prison for something that horrific? You never get back that part of your life."

At the 2014 Innocence Network Conference in Portland, Oregon, the over five hundred attendees—including over a hundred exonerees and members of their families—gave Jennifer Thompson a standing ovation as she received the annual "Champion of Justice" award for 2013.

CHAPTER 44

BLUE 3

I t is not easy to be a prosecutor," wrote Daniel A. Bellemare, longest-serving head of the Federal Prosecution Service in Canadian history and recipient of the Governor General's Meritorious Service Medal in 2003. "It is often a lonely journey. It tests character. It requires inner strength and self-confidence. It requires personal integrity and a solid moral compass. It requires humility and willingness, where appropriate, to recognize mistakes and take appropriate steps to correct them. Prosecutors must be passionate about the issues, but compassionate in their approach, always guided by fairness and common sense."

In 1838, the British House of Lords emphasized that a prosecutor's job is not to win but to see that justice is done[1]—a sentiment echoed by the Supreme Court of Canada in 1955:

> It cannot be over-emphasized that the purpose of a criminal prosecution is not to obtain a conviction. It is to lay before a jury what the Crown considers to be credible evidence relevant to what is alleged to be a crime. Counsel have a duty to see that all available legal proof of the facts is presented: it should be done so firmly and pressed to its legitimate strength, but it must also be done fairly.
>
> The role of the prosecutor excludes any notion of winning or losing; his function is a matter of public duty than which in civil life there can be none charged with greater responsibility. It is to be efficiently performed with an ingrained sense of the dignity, the seriousness, and the justness of judicial proceedings.[2]

Michael Luchenko—"Blue 3," who passed away in 2013—viewed his role as prosecutor the same way a high-performance athlete views a competition. He was a man whose very DNA did not, at least in the Ivan Henry case, include the "notion of losing."

In support of his 2010 appeal, Henry raised several instances of alleged Crown misconduct. Yet the court's sole reference to Luchenko is complimentary. While discussing how Henry's appeal came to be reopened, the court said: "About this time, two senior prosecutors in the Vancouver Regional office, *including lead counsel at the appellant's 1982 trial*, became aware of certain similarities between the case against the appellant and information generated by Project Smallman. *In the best traditions of prosecutorial fairness*, they brought their concerns to the attention of the Criminal Justice Branch of the provincial Ministry of the Attorney General. [ITALICS ADDED FOR EMPHASIS.]"

That is not exactly what happened. As reporter *Vancouver Sun* Neal Hall wrote shortly after the court's 2009 decision to reopen Henry's appeal, if it weren't for "the investigation of pig farm murderer Robert Pickton, Ivan Henry's case might never have been reopened. In 2006, then-administrative Crown counsel Jean Connor was reading a memo about an accused serial rapist, in the context of cold sex cases, when she made the connection between the Smallman and Henry crimes—the MOs were identical! Remarkably, when Connor compared the cases of Donald McRae and Ivan Henry, neither man's name appeared in the other man's file.

"Marching down the hall to her colleague, Michael Luchenko, Connor read out details of the Smallman crimes. Oddly, she noted, the Ivan Henry trial transcript was still in Luchenko's office, more than twenty years later. Soon thereafter, Connor brought the matter to the attention of Wally Oppal, who was then Attorney General of BC."[3]

Having read Hall's piece, I was none the wiser about whether Luchenko had, as the Court of Appeal suggested and as I doubted, co-operated in Connor's efforts to take the first step in reopening the Ivan Henry debacle. When I learned that Jean Connor had retired and that her health was failing, I contacted her sister, defence lawyer Patricia Connor, a law school colleague of mine.

According to Patricia, Luchenko was unhappy with Jean's decision to report the matter to the Attorney General. "Though Jeannie might have been accompanied by someone," Patricia said, "it certainly wasn't by Michael."

...

IN HIS 2013 book, *The Innocent and the Criminal Justice System: A Sociological Analysis of Miscarriages of Justice*, Dr. Michael Naughton, founder and director of the United Kingdom's Innocence Network, wrote that there are "miscarriages of justice," and then there are "abortions of justice."[4] Asked why he used a word so politically charged as "abortion"—a word that, to many women, is the ultimate symbol of freedom of choice—in the context of wrongful convictions, he explained. "Mistaken eye-witness identification is a miscarriage of justice," he told attendees at the 2014 Innocence Network Conference, "and, by that, I mean unintentional. However, in some cases—the most insidious cases of them all—wilful breaches of due process occur. What better term to describe those most severe cases of ill intent than 'abortions of justice'?"

What better term to describe what happened to Ivan Henry?

•••

FROM AS EARLY as August 12, 1982—two weeks after Henry was charged with fifteen sex crimes—defence counsel repeatedly sought full disclosure from the Crown, including "copies of all medical or technical reports (serology, alcohol, hair, and fibre, etc.)." On November 10, soon after the preliminary hearing ended, Henry wrote Crown counsel requesting disclosure of various materials including "copies of all medical and technical reports—(hair, serology, fibres, etc.)." Over and over again—before and during his trial—Henry made similar requests. All such entreaties were met with silence.

Towards the end of the Crown's case at trial, Henry said that, given the lack of disclosure, he couldn't defend himself and would, therefore, not be calling evidence.

In response, Luchenko said, "I am concerned with that comment. Mr. Henry has not requested anything further that has not been provided to him. If Mr. Henry wishes more, I would ask him to say so now so that the Crown can take whatever steps it wants." In response to this, Judge Bouck said, "Given that no coherent statement can be expected from the accused, it's best to just carry on."

Luchenko's comment was disinguous. In truth, as we've seen, the Crown had done nothing but stonewall Henry's numerous and entirely legitimate disclosure requests from the outset.

Among the items the Crown failed to disclose are the following:

- approximately thirty statements of the eight trial complainants—documents replete with inconsistencies between one interview and the next;

- Harkema's re-interview notes regarding Miss Ramirez (fifty minutes) and Miss Larson (over three hours);

- information that, at the outset of those re-interviews, the lineup attendees expressed "disgust" with the lineup, but, in the end, identified Henry by voice;

- information that, during the re-interviews, the lineup attendees had been shown the May 12 lineup photo;

- forensic reports, including medical reports, fingerprint analyses, etcetera—including documents listing physical evidence seized, obtained, and/or collected from the victims;

- police "report(s) to Crown";

- particulars regarding police contacts with Jessie Henry, including the amount of money, if any, she was paid and the circumstances thereof;

- particulars regarding continuity of evidence in respect of the photographs;

- police reports showing that Donald McRae was a suspect in the Henry crimes and that he had been arrested in 1982 for late-night predatory behaviour in two of the neighbourhoods where the sexual offences were occurring; and

- particulars regarding other suspects, including information regarding past lineups, composite sketches, etcetera.

Two days after the preliminary hearing, Luchenko wrote in an internal memo, "I am holding all police reports and notes (two large volumes) at this time." Who knows how many of those documents— mislaid or destroyed—went missing in the years that followed?

In a 1991 decision,[5] the Supreme Court of Canada commented on the Crown's duty to make full disclosure:

It is difficult to justify the position which clings to the notion that the Crown has no legal duty to disclose all relevant information. The arguments against the existence of such a duty are groundless while those in favour, are, in my view, overwhelming.

I would add that the fruits of the investigation which are in the possession of counsel for the Crown are not the property of the Crown for use in securing a conviction but the property of the public to be used to ensure that justice is done.

The right to make full answer and defence is one of the pillars of criminal justice on which we heavily depend to ensure that the innocent are not convicted. Recent events have demonstrated that the erosion of this right due to non-disclosure was an important factor in the conviction and incarceration of an innocent person.

In the *Royal Commission on the Donald Marshall, Jr., Prosecution,* the Commissioners found that prior inconsistent statements were not disclosed to the defence. This was an important contributing factor in the miscarriage of justice which occurred and led the Commission to state that *"anything less than complete disclosure by the Crown falls short of decency and fair play."*

[ITALICS ADDED FOR EMPHASIS.]

The *Crown Counsel Handbook* in effect in British Columbia in the 1980s expressly states that, where evidence is relevant, it must be made available to the defence:

Crown counsel is an officer of the Court and must conduct himself at all times as such. A criminal prosecution in our law is not a contest between individuals, nor is it a contest between the Crown and an accused endeavoring to be acquitted.

Crown counsel is present in Court to present the case for the Crown and has a discretion to do so as he sees fit. This discretion must be exercised with a feeling of responsibility to assist the judge in fairly putting the case before a jury. He also has a discretion to decide what witnesses shall be called and what evidence is relevant, credible, and material, and his discretion will not be interfered with unless it is exercised with some oblique motive.

But he does have a duty to offer all the relevant evidence or make it available to the defence.

[ITALICS ADDED FOR EMPHASIS.]

In short, while disclosure standards might have been more lax in the early *Charter* days, they were not so lax as to permit the Crown to withhold relevant—what could be more relevant than exculpatory?—material or information.

• • •

MISS SIMPSON TESTIFIED in direct examination that she saw, two days after her attack in May 1981, "248 East 17th" on the envelope of a man on the bus Henry put to her in cross-examination, "The coincidence of it all, ma'am, is that I never lived at that address in 1981, so whoever you got—"

Chided by Judge Bouck for giving evidence from the well of the court, Henry said to the witness, "But you stated it was 248 East—?" To which Miss Simpson replied, "Well, the reason I brought that back up again was I heard on the television at the time you were arrested, they gave your age and ad—"

At this point, Luchenko—who had no business doing so—bounded to his feet and said, "My Lord, I question whether this sort of evidence, which is hearsay and probably not admissible, should be in front of the jury."

Although Miss Simpson's account was not hearsay—information gained or acquired from another and not part of one's direct knowledge—the interruption had its intended effect: Henry, thrown off track, never returned to the subject. Instead of upbraiding Luchenko for his improper, tactical interruption, Judge Bouck commiserated with him.

Had Henry continued this line of cross-examination, he might well have highlighted a critical point for the defence: Miss Simpson's evidence was deceitful at worst, unreliable at best. If she'd learned of Henry's address only when he was arrested at the end of July 1982, how could she possibly remembered seeing that address on an envelope ten months earlier?

Henry asked Miss Simpson whether the man on the bus was him. She said no. Missing the crucial import of that answer, Henry asked whether it was "somebody like me." Miss Simpson replied, "Somebody, at the time that—he resembled very closely the man who attacked me, which is why I think it was him."

"You saw some guy similar to me getting on the bus, is that right?"

"I saw a guy who struck me as so much like my attacker. He had dark curly hair, a beard, a leather jacket, and jeans. Quite short— five-foot-seven or five-foot-eight—the same build—not quite as broad as you are, I think . . . Naturally, I told the police."

Thanks to one of many documents disclosed, for the first time, during the special prosecutor's investigation, we now know that before Miss Simpson took the stand at trial, the Crown caused her to swear an affidavit stating that she'd "had the opportunity to hear Ivan Henry's voice during my cross-examination [at the preliminary hearing], and I am now satisfied and prepared to swear that his voice is the voice of the man who indecently assaulted me on May 5, 1981." As the Crown surely knew, this oath-binding—the swearing of affidavits in advance of testifying— is, in circumstances such as these, antithetical to the interests of the criminal justice system and society:

> Binding a witness to a statement made before trial by having
> it sworn compromises this interest by setting up serious con-
> sequences for a witness who wishes to testify truthfully, when
> the truth is in conflict with the statement. The threat to the fact-
> finding process is the more insidious when it is understood that,
> if the testimony at trial is consistent with the sworn statement,
> the Court may never learn of the existence of the statement.[6]

If not for the special prosecutor's investigation, Miss Simpson's affidavit would never have come to light.

CHAPTER 45

THE TROPHY

What kind of judge displays the primary exhibit in a trial he's conducting as if it were a hunting trophy? Yet that's exactly what Supreme Court Justice John Bouck, who passed away in 2010, did. He hung the lineup photo in the one place in the Law Courts building where the most judges would see it—the judges' coffee lounge.

"Back then," a retired judge told me, "the lounge was shared by both Supreme and Appeal Court judges. Virtually daily, John regaled anyone who cared to listen with anecdotes from the trial—in particular, the 'openly hostile' accused. The rest of us kept our heads down and tried to ignore him. John's ego knew no bounds. It irritated the heck out of us. In retrospect, I should have taken it down. It just seemed easier to ignore him than make an issue of it."

Soon after the Court of Appeal's January 2009 reopening decision, then-retired Judge Bouck posted a blog from his home in Victoria on Vancouver Island. Although he removed it shortly thereafter, Canwest News Service reporter Ian Mulgrew had already read it and had this to say about it in the *National Post*:

> Retired B.C. Supreme Court Justice John Bouck says he did every-thing possible to ensure Henry got a fair trial and he continues to believe justice was done in spite of last week's announcement that another man may be responsible for Henry's crimes.
>
> *"I am handicapped with respect to some of the particulars since I do not have a copy of the trial transcript or the investigator's report,"* he began on his Sunday posting.

"Before the 1983 trial commenced, Mr. Henry's lawyer advised me that Mr. Henry did not want his representation. He wanted to defend himself. In open court and in the absence of the jury, Mr. Henry confirmed his position. I urged him not to proceed without legal advice. He insisted that he wanted to go ahead without a lawyer."

In its unprecedented ruling, the Court of Appeal cited the Special Prosecutor's concerns that Justice Bouck had failed to give Henry as much aid during the trial as he should have.

"I did my best to help him but with little success. The gist of the prosecution's case was Mr. Henry's alleged modus operandi.

"All of the rapes occurred near his residence.

"The Crown alleged that, around 2:00 a.m. to 4:00 a.m., he jimmied open ground floor sliding glass doors where the single women complainants lived and sexually assaulted them. When the time came for his defence, he did not call any witnesses and declined to take the stand in his own defence."

Justice Bouck said also that Henry put into evidence a picture of his police lineup that put him in a bad light even though he was told not to do so.

"Henry was on parole for two earlier rapes he'd committed in Saskatchewan at the time he committed the 1983 offences."

Justice Bouck today asks why Henry's wife, who is now dead, didn't testify on his behalf at the trial.

"The Attorney-General criticized my handling of the case. I admit that Mr. Henry did not get a perfect trial or a perfect dangerous offender hearing. Nobody does. Trials are conducted and decided by imperfect human beings applying imperfect laws. The most the criminal justice system can offer is a fair trial. Mr. Henry got both a fair trial and a fair dangerous offender hearing."

Justice Bouck insists that, if Henry did not receive a fair trial, it is his own fault.

"According to media reports, Mr. Henry asked for legal help in pursuing his appeals but never got it. If that is true, it is a condemnation of the Attorney-General's Legal Aid system which lawyers and judges constantly criticize.

"The Attorney-General's investigators did not bother to interview me before they condemned me publicly, nor did they send me a copy of their report."[1]

Judge Bouck's commentary is riddled with errors. Only two of the eight trial complainants—Miss Browning and Miss Kavanagh—were attacked anywhere near where Henry was living. Henry called many witnesses and testified at length on his own behalf.

Not only is there nothing in the transcript to support the judge's assertion that he warned Henry against introducing the photo, but the 2010 Court of Appeal faulted him for blaming Henry for putting the lineup photo into evidence.

No lawyer for Henry appeared before Judge Bouck, and and nothing in either the transcript or the trial record supports his assertion that he urged the accused not to proceed without representation.

Henry's parole ended six months before his arrest. Rather than having committed two rapes, as claimed by Judge Bouck, he had pleaded guilty in 1977 for a single attempted-rape charge. The offence occurred in Winnipeg, Manitoba, not in Saskatchewan.

As noted, given that it was Mrs. Henry's information that led to Henry's arrest, it behooved the Crown, not the accused, to call her as a witness.

CHAPTER 46

TUNNEL VISION

The concept of tunnel vision was first discussed in Canada in the public inquiry into the wrongful conviction of Guy Paul Morin. In concluding that tunnel vision had affected both the investigators and the prosecution, Commissioner Kaufman defined the term as "the single-minded and overly narrow focus on a particular investigative or prosecutorial theory, so as to unreasonably colour the evaluation of information received and one's conduct in response to that information."

In the *Inquiry into the Wrongful Conviction of Thomas Sophonow*, former Supreme Court of Canada justice Peter Cory emphasized the harmful impact of tunnel vision:

Tunnel vision is insidious. It can affect an officer or, indeed, anyone involved in the administration of justice with sometimes tragic results. It results in the officer becoming so focused upon an individual or incident that no other person or incident registers in the officer's thoughts. Thus, tunnel vision can result in the elimination of other suspects who should be investigated. Equally, events which could lead to other suspects are eliminated from the officer's thinking. Anyone, police officer, counsel *or judge* can become infected by this virus.[1]

[ITALICS ADDED FOR EMPHASIS.]

Tunnel vision or otherwise, the police and Crown relentlessly pursued, to the point of conviction and beyond, a man they very likely knew to be innocent.

Not only that; early in the trial Judge Bouck apparently formed a dislike of, and indeed intolerance for, Ivan Henry—an attitude that permeated both his conduct of the trial and his jury charge.

Henry called as his witnesses three of the investigating officers: Detectives Sims, Campbell, and Harkema. Although the judge at times intervened to stop him from asking "leading questions"—questions suggestive of the answer—he allowed Luchenko to, in effect, channel the Crown's case in the course of cross-examination.

For instance, before Campbell could respond to Luchenko's question—"Why not construct a photo array using the striated photo?"—Luchenko answered it for him: "Would you agree with me, sir, that that particular photograph is not of a quality that you would ordinarily use in a photograph plan?"

Luchenko asked Detective Campbell, "Is 248 East 17th situated basically in the heart of the area where these incidents were occurring?" Campbell answered yes, but what was left unsaid was that most of the assaults occurred before Jessie moved to that address. Instead of setting the record straight in his jury charge, Judge Bouck parroted the misleading impression left by the Crown.

Using leading questions, the Crown elicited from Detective Sims that because Henry struggled from start to finish of the lineup, the women could not get a good look at his face. In other words, it was his fault—not that of the police who, having forced him to participate, put him in a chokehold—that identification was so difficult.

Leading questions are generally prohibited in direct examination but allowed in cross-examination. Because the witness is presumed to be biased against the questioner's position, the risk of eliciting unreliable evidence is reduced. However, where a witness is unsympathetic to the calling party or is partisan to the cross-examiner's position, a trial judge may reverse the usual rules in the interests of justice.[2] Judge Bouck's failure to put a halt to the Crown's shaping of police evidence was, in the context of an unrepresented accused, unconscionable.

The Crown should not object to cross-examination properly directed at testing the reliability of a witness's identification evidence.[3] Yet that is precisely what Luchenko did during Henry's cross-examination of Miss Simpson. In the course of exploring her clearly unreliable assertion that she had seen his address on an envelope ten months before he had moved there, Henry was interrupted by Luchenko, who called the evidence hearsay. First, as we've seen, the Crown's hearsay objection was meritless. Whereas hearsay is an out-of-court statement led for its truth,[4] Henry was simply trying to show that Miss Simpson received information about his address after his arrest. Instead of reproving Luchenko for the interruption, the trial judge said, "He's got the right to pursue his own cross-examination. If it's against him, that's his burden he has to carry. I can't interrupt his cross-examination."

The judge's acerbic remark—signalling as it did to the jury that the cross-examination was irrelevant or worse—had a predictably chilling effect on Henry. Once the flow of his cross-examination was disrupted, he abandoned the point.

At another critical point, during Henry's direct examination of Colin Bradbury, Luchenko again interrupted, saying, "I appreciate my friend isn't quite up on what he's doing, but perhaps he could describe to the jury, rather than explain to the witness, these points. I think it's being lost on them." When the judge agreed, Luchenko said, "I certainly can't follow what's going on."

But for that improper exchange, Henry would almost certainly have compared the photo in his hand with that in Bradbury's.

When Luchenko told Henry, just before the trial, that the Crown would be proceeding on all counts, he was being duplicitous. According to both Miss O'Reilly and Miss Fields, they had been advised, soon after the preliminary hearing, that the Crown wouldn't be needing them because they couldn't identify the accused. On day one of the trial, following a discussion between Luchenko and the judge—a discussion Henry was not privy to, and of which was never produced—the indictment was reduced from seventeen to ten counts.

However, instead of dropping the other seven, Luchenko played coy. So confused was Henry as to their status—were the counts stayed, withdrawn, held in abeyance?—that he conducted his defence as though all seventeen were before the jury. His repeated references to these "off-indictment" crimes alerted the jurors to facts that should not have been before them—for instance, that at least four non-trial complainants had viewed the May 12 lineup; that Henry had originally been charged with seventeen or more offences and was a suspect in assaults going back to

November 1980; and that a rape had occurred on May 14, 1982, a date not listed in the trial indictment.

The trial judge did nothing to prevent the jury from hearing evidence of this kind. He erred in failing to instruct the jury not to use such information to assess Henry's guilt. The jury may well have concluded that the accused committed not only the crimes before them but other crimes as well.[5]

In his jury charge, Judge Bouck allotted—despite Miss Simpson's evidence that the man on the bus with the envelope was *not* Henry—a single, incorrect, sentence to her evidence: "Two days after the incident, she saw a man on a bus who looked like the accused, and she told the police." That was a wholly inaccurate summary. Judge Bouck also conflated, not for the first time, the words "accused" and "attacker."

In summary, the trial judge made evident his personal views about Henry throughout the trial. While it is human for judges to form visceral opinions about those appearing before them, they are not only required to be fair and impartial; they must also satisfy the appearance of justice. A judge's appearance and behaviour must not indicate to the jury that he believes the defendant is guilty.

The courts, legal scholars, practitioners, and social scientists recognize that a judge's verbal and non-verbal behaviour may have important effects on trial processes and outcomes.[6]

"Written trial transcripts cannot possibly detect or illuminate the subtleties of courtroom dynamics," says MaDonna Maidment, a professor at the University of Guelph. "The courtroom is a living space where body language, gestures, interactions, and off-the-record comments make irreversible impressions on juries."[7] In inquiring into the wrongful convictions of Gregory Parsons, Randy Drukens, and Ronald Dalton,[8] Commissioner (and Supreme Court of Canada justice) Antonio Lamer commented as follows:

> I wrote a report back in 1975 when I was on the Law Reform Commission of Canada suggesting that charges by a judge to a jury should be taped and filmed. Body language, you know, [is communication] but Parliament, as usual, didn't do anything about it.[9]

CHAPTER 47

ELSEWHERE

P ressed by Luchenko after the preliminary hearing to produce his alibi statement, Ivan Henry met the deadline. It was no easy task behind bars at Oakalla, but he got addresses and phone numbers for over a dozen people and businesses. Because Luchenko had indicated that the Crown would be proceeding on every count, Henry had provided alibis or explanations for as many as he could.

Calling Henry's alibi defence "worthy of consideration," Judge Bouck pointed out that "the Crown must prove that Henry was at the various addresses mentioned in the Indictment." Worthy of consideration, indeed. If true, he was living and working at locations far removed from the crime scenes. But the judge then said, "However, there doesn't seem to be any evidence that I can find that, with respect to any of these counts, the accused can say exactly where he was on the dates in question." Talk about a mixed message. Was the onus on the Crown to prove the accused was at the crime scenes, or on Henry to prove he was not?

The Ontario Court of Appeal has said that evidence must be presented in a logical manner. "It is always the responsibility of the trial judge," said the court, "to ferret out the important pieces of evidence and present them in a logical manner so that the jury will be equipped to reach a judicial decision on each issue."[1] Instead, Henry's trial judge delivered a confusing, often incoherent, summary. The following, from his jury charge, illustrates the point:

> He says he purchased the AMC on December 15. At one time he
> had a blue Chevette. He also had a 1980 Acadian. He didn't have
> a car for the whole month of January, until January 26. Exhibit 7

was taken between January 5 and 6. Around the 12th, he took the Acadian back. He believes the AMC Spirit was given to him on February 2 or 3.

He says he was in a lineup, but never a lineup handcuffed to anyone. He said they dragged him in, but it wasn't a forcible lineup.

He said Exhibit Five was a picture taken of him on May 13. He said Exhibit One might be his head, but not his body. He said that, in May '81, he'd been living part-time in West Vancouver. Bradbury was also living there.

Starting June 1, he was at the Woodbine, driving back and forth to Chilliwack. No-one at the Woodbine could say where he was. On June 10, he would have been with his girl on her birthday. On May 5, he would have been at the Woodbine. He may also have been with his wife—either place. Then he said he started living with Mr. Bradbury the first 8 or 10 days of June. This lasted to August. Mr. Bradbury was living there by himself.

It was against the law as the house was under construction. He was on one side, Mr. Bradbury on the other. There was a telephone there. Mrs. Bradbury and her children moved in the first part of July or the 15 of August. He stayed in West Van for 28 to 35 days. Some parts of June he was with his wife, and some parts at other places.

And so it was that Henry's carefully prepared alibi statement, followed by his concordant evidence at trial, came to naught. Because of Judge Bouck's mangling of his alibi defence, jurors were left scratching their heads.

I asked juror A.L. whether she remembered the accused's alibi evidence. "No," she replied, "it meant nothing to me. If he'd produced proof of where he was, maybe that would've made a difference." Asked whether it had occurred to her that the Crown bore the onus of proof, she replied, "Definitely not."

Although Henry filed his alibi statement in the court registry, when he asked Madam Clerk to produce it at the outset of his case, Luchenko said, "I am not familiar with that alibi as such." After Henry had testified, Madam Registrar found it—in the registry file, exactly where it had been all along. When Judge Bouck asked Luchenko if he had a copy of it, he said yes. In the meantime, the trial judge, having cast a fleeting glance over it, said it would not be "admissible into evidence in that form."

As noted, the defence of alibi—a Latin word meaning "somewhere else"—is based on the premise that the accused is truly innocent. While the privilege against self-incrimination usually protects an accused from being required to furnish information to the prosecution, this case is an exception because the defence involved evidence of innocence rather than reliance on the Crown's failure to prove guilt.

Alibi statements are required to be filed in a timely way, and with sufficient particularization, to allow for meaningful investigation. Failing that, the judge can rule that an accused's alibi evidence is inadmissible.[2] Had Luchenko believed that Henry's alibi statement was vulnerable to attack, surely he would have instructed the VPD to run it to ground.

Having said that, Henry failed, without question, to present the kind of iron-clad alibi that would have proven, beyond a reasonable doubt, that he did not commit the crimes in question. Who recalls past events with such clarity, or records them faithfully in a diary? What Henry did do, though, is demonstrate that he was nowhere near the majority of the crime scenes. His testimony to that effect was not impeached by the Crown.

When Miss Simpson was attacked on May 5, 1981, in Mount Pleasant, Henry was living in Burnaby on Canada Way and working in Chilliwack—ninety-three kilometres away. The Parole Board of Canada had issued Henry a travel permit, valid from April 24 to May 24, 1981, to work on a construction project in Chilliwack.

When Miss Horvath was attacked on June 18, 1981, in Mount Pleasant, and when Miss Jacobsen was assaulted in Marpole on August 5, 1981, Henry was living in Burnaby and working on Colin Bradbury's home in the Caulfeild area of West Vancouver. As Henry testified, "From early June 'til the end of that summer, I worked for Bradbury in West Vancouver. On the few occasions I didn't stay there overnight, Bradbury drove me home to Burnaby and picked me up, as prearranged, on the corner of East Hastings and Cassiar." As for the Horvath attack, he said, "In the early morning of June 16 or 17, my wife phoned me [at Colin's house] to say our house had been broken into. Colin woke me up to take her call." Henry provided the Crown with autobody-shop receipts to back up his claim—his "smashed-up car" was out of service from May 31 to September 3. For much of that time, there was a transit strike in Vancouver.

When Miss Ramirez's was attacked on October 17, 1981, in Mount Pleasant, Henry was living at the Station Hotel on Main Street. While he could have travelled thirty or so blocks to assault her, how likely is it that he did? Not only that, but Miss Ramirez attested to numerous subsequent sightings of her assailant—in the same area.

When Miss Larson was attacked in Kitsilano on February 22, 1982, Henry was living with a friend in Fraserview and working for a contractor in the area. Although he admitted that he couldn't account for February 22 itself—an admission clearly underscoring his credibility— he did recall being "picked up on a traffic ticket on the 16th" and being held at the police station overnight.

Around the times of Miss Browning's assault in Mount Pleasant (March 8, 1982) and Miss Cardozo's attack in Marpole (March 19), Jessie had just moved into the house on East 17th (in Mount Pleasant). Henry testified that at some point that same month—he could not recall the exact date—he checked Jessie into a detox centre in Burnaby and cared for his daughters for the entire two weeks of her absence. Miss Browning, remember, is the complainant who picked an innocent foil (#18) at the lineup after having told herself to memorize her attacker's face. The case of Miss Cardozo was lumped together with other rapes committed, after Henry's incarceration, by "the Marpole Rapist."

As for Miss Kavanagh, although her attack (June 8, 1982) occurred relatively near where Henry's wife was living, the fact that the case lay dormant for the next ten weeks illustrates, in my view, that the police did not believe he was the culprit. Remember that Detective Harkema did not take over as lead detective until mid-June and had other priorities after that.

Rather than challenging the specifics of each of Henry's explanations, the Crown, endorsed by the judge in his jury charge, flipped the onus of proof on its head. Unless Henry could prove he had been elsewhere at the precise time of each crime—they typically occurred between 1:00 a.m. and 5:00 a.m.—he must be guilty.

The judge should have dealt with the defence crime by crime, clearly delineating Henry's explanation in each case and questioning whether it raised a reasonable doubt as to whether he was the culprit. It was not up to Ivan Henry to prove he was elsewhere; it was up to the Crown to prove his guilt beyond a reasonable doubt.

CHAPTER 48

MEDICAL EVIDENCE

Henry repeatedly sought disclosure of medical reports, reasoning that if the medical evidence excluded him on a given charge, "then I wouldn't have to deal with one extra charge."

Despite the Crown's duty to disclose relevant materials—including anything pointing to innocence—Judge Bouck refused to order disclosure. Instead, he accepted the argument that because the Crown wasn't relying on medical evidence in its case, such reports need not be disclosed. As he said in his jury charge:

> The Crown is not obliged to call every witness involved with the investigation of a crime. All it need do is present sufficient evidence so as to prove its case beyond a reasonable doubt.
>
> If there are other witnesses who might give relevant evidence, the Crown is required to give up their names to the accused upon request, then it is up to the accused to decide whether or not to call them in support of his defence.
>
> Sometimes an inference can be drawn against a party, Crown or accused, if they do not call relevant evidence, but this is not an instance where you should draw an unfavorable inference against the Crown.

We now know that the Crown withheld the names of the doctors who compiled rape kits on four of the "rip-off rapist" victims. Judge Bouck should have compelled disclosure of the requested reports. At a minimum, he should have told the jury that the Crown, by not disclosing them, was likely hiding something that would hurt its case. The jury should have been instructed to draw an "adverse inference" against the Crown for its failure to disclose.

We also now know that the City Analyst's Laboratory in Vancouver had in its possession recovered spermatozoa from those same four women. In its defence to Henry's civil claim, the City of Vancouver states that forensic testing of perpetrator spermatozoa was not the practice in British Columbia in 1982 and 1983.

True, DNA testing had not yet been perfected, but serology testing—using either ABO blood grouping or enzyme testing—was being widely used by police. As early as 1963, the laboratory at New Scotland Yard in London, England, was conducting ABO grouping on semen stains. As Justice Edward MacCallum, the commissioner in the inquiry into the David Milgaard case, said: "In 1967 and 1970, the science of serology, including blood typing, could lead to the exclusion of a suspected donor of a biological substance, but not to his positive identification. It had value as an investigative tool because of its ability to reduce the pool of potential suspects by reference to their serological profile."[1]

Brian Wraxall, executive director and chief forensic serologist of the Serological Research Institute (SERI), in Richmond, California, swore an affidavit in Henry's 2010 appeal saying that serology testing could have been used to include or exclude Henry as a potential suspect in the recovered spermatozoa cases. Noting that criminalist Paul Norvell of the City Analyst's Laboratory in Vancouver had thrice attended training courses in forensic serology at SERI between 1980 and 1987, Wraxall said:

Both ABO and enzyme testing could have been conducted on (the four stains), and that such testing would have shown whether Henry had blood and enzyme types or sub-types consistent with those derived from testing the semen stains. If either his blood or enzyme type or sub-type was inconsistent with those obtained from the stains, the testing would have excluded him as the semen donor.

I have no personal knowledge as to whether the Vancouver City Laboratory was conducting ABO and enzyme tests at the time these four offences occurred. However, if they were not, I know of no reason why the physical evidence could not have been outsourced for testing, whether to the RCMP (as the Milgaard Report indicates was done by the Saskatoon Police) or a private laboratory like SERI.

Recently disclosed records make clear that the VPD, in the course of investigating sexual assaults that occurred soon after Henry's conviction, used serology testing to rule out suspects. In an undated 1983 report regarding the "Marpole Rapist," lead detective Michael Barnard wrote that "< >, having been found to have blood type 'B,' was eliminated as a suspect." And in the VPD 'Confidential Bulletin' Re Marpole Sexual Assault Update, dated December 23, 1983, Barnard wrote that "suspect < >, having been found to have blood type 'O,' was eliminated as a suspect."

The VPD's decision not to conduct serology testing in the Henry case is suspect, as is its failure to retain the semen samples from the attacks. Such samples retained in 1984 led to the exoneration of Guy Paul Morin in 1995. Semen samples retained in 1969 led to the exoneration of David Milgaard in 1997. And samples retained in 1981 led to the exoneration of Thomas Sophonow in 2000.

Before the special prosecutor's investigation from 2006 to 2008, the defence had no idea that the City Analyst's Laboratory had recovered spermatozoa from four women in the Henry case. At the same time as that fact was brought to light, the VPD was advising the special prosecutor that all such samples had gone missing or been destroyed.

Had Henry known at trial that such samples had been collected, he could have asked the Crown to conduct serology testing. If the Crown refused, he could have sought an order from the judge to have such tests performed or, alternatively, asked the jury to draw an adverse inference from the Crown's failure to do so.

CHAPTER 49

MORE JUDICIAL ERRORS

The Supreme Court of Canada has said that evidence of a criminal record may not indicate bad character or propensity to commit crimes.[1] An individual is to be tried not for who he might be, but for the offence he may have committed. Juries are inclined to convict an accused with a criminal record, which is why such protection is vital.

Having correctly told the jury that evidence of Henry's criminal record was led purely to test his credibility[2]—and that his truthfulness reflected "favourably on one aspect of his credibility"—the trial judge then, inexplicably, told the jurors that they may decide not to believe him.

Further, a trial judge has the discretion to prohibit the Crown from cross-examining the accused on a prior conviction where the prejudicial impact of disclosing the conviction outweighs its probative value on the issue of credibility.[3] Had Judge Bouck applied the relevant criteria, he almost certainly would have edited out Henry's attempted-rape conviction. This is an important point. Evidence of that prior conviction presented the jurors with a powerful temptation to conclude that Henry arrived in Vancouver after his release on that charge and shortly thereafter embarked on a string of sexual assaults.

• • •

AS NOTED, JUDGE BOUCK devoted a single sentence to the need for jurors not to import evidence of one crime into all the others: "Members of the jury, it is necessary that you consider each count separately." After this, he proceeded, in his charge, to treat all the counts interchangeably.

In its 2010 judgment, the Court of Appeal said that where there is no compelling reason for having a joint trial, multiple counts of sexual offences must, absent extenuating circumstances, be severed. "By failing to declare a mistrial when the Crown withdrew its similar fact evidence application," the court said, "there was a high risk of count-to-count prohibited reasoning by the jury resulting in prejudice to the appellant and rendering the trial unfair. Accordingly, I would also give effect to this ground of appeal."

Furthermore, Luchenko said, in his opening statement at the criminal trial, "the man who stealthily came into these various premises and who perpetrated these crimes must be the same man, and that man was Ivan Henry." It was inevitable, from that point on, that the jurors would treat evidence relevant to one crime as relevant to them all.

• • •

A KEY PART of the Crown's case was that, if Henry were innocent, he would not have resisted participating in the lineup. The suggestion was that Henry's "demeanor evidence"—his resistance—pointed to his guilt. In resisting the lineup, Henry cited *Marcoux*, a 1976 decision of the Supreme Court of Canada.[4] Not only was he correct, but the Crown and the trial judge would most certainly have known about that case.

In its 2010 decision, the Court of Appeal ruled that Judge Bouck's instruction regarding "consciousness of guilt"—a guilty mind inferred from the act of resistance—was wrong in law. After agreeing that *Marcoux*—the same case cited by Henry twenty-eight years earlier—stood for the proposition that suspects are not obliged to participate in lineups, the court added that without the subject instruction to the jury, conviction would have been unlikely.

Ruling that Henry's denial of culpability withstood cross-examination, the court said that the trial judge should have pointed out that the Crown did not challenge Henry about the reasons he gave for his resistance to the lineup—key among them that he was the only redhead:

> The jury could not have properly considered the inference sought by the Crown without being reminded of the explanations given by the appellant. If jurors concluded that the appellant's reasons for resistance might have been legitimate,

they would have had to reject the inference and consider the balance of the evidence on the element of identification.

In that event, the Crown's case against the appellant would have been back on its shaky foundation.

Just as jurors have a hard time believing someone would confess to a crime they did not commit, they have a hard time imagining why an innocent man would object to participating in a lineup. All the more so when a Supreme Court justice tells them they are entitled to infer that resistance equals guilt.

Jurors A.L. and P.D. said as much. Asked whether she knew that suspects have the right to refuse to participate in lineups, A.L. said, "No, but if you're innocent, why would you care?" P.D., citing Henry's resistance as key to his finding of guilt, said, "Why keep trying to hide his head? If you have nothing to hide, why not go into the lineup willingly?"

In January 2010, when Commissioner Kaufman released his inquiry report on the wrongful conviction of Guy Paul Morin, he urged (among many recommendations) the "placing of limits on the use of 'consciousness of guilt' evidence—evidence in which the mere attitude of the suspect is used to implicate him or her."

Speaking of the Henry lineup and the photo, Judge Bouck said this to the jury: "Presumably, the accused wanted you to draw the inference that any identification of him is a farce, since he's the only one being restrained by three police officers. On the other hand, the Crown suggests his obvious reluctance to participate leads to an inference of consciousness of guilt on his part. *It is for you to draw the proper inference upon considering all the evidence.* [ITALICS ADDED FOR EMPHASIS.]"

The Court of Appeal characterized that "dismissive comment" as "a faint presentation of a strong point for the defence—namely that the pre-trial identification process was flawed and seriously called into question the reliability of all other identification evidence." Instead of giving Henry's point the consideration it deserved, said the court, the trial judge appeared to treat it "quizzically." Because Henry had the right not to participate in the lineup, no "consciousness of guilt" could be inferred.

CHAPTER 50

FRIEND OF THE COURT

I n 2010, Henry's lawyers argued before the Court of Appeal that Judge Bouck had breached his duty of fairness by, among other things, failing to give Henry the most basic assistance and failing to appoint an amicus curiae—a friend of the court—to represent his interests. In his written argument, counsel for the Crown acknowledged Henry's need for assistance:

> Mr. Henry qualified for legal aid, but he refused counsel. The Court cannot force counsel upon the accused.
>
> (In retrospect, however,) it is apparent that Mr. Henry required legal counsel to advocate legal positions on his behalf, to examine witnesses, and to fully bring out to the court the basis for viable defences, unencumbered by Mr. Henry's theories and tactics.

Despite the two sides' agreement on this point, the Court of Appeal disposed of the duty-of-fairness argument in two sentences:

> These circumstances imposed a duty on the trial judge to fully inform the appellant of his rights and his options, and to instruct the jury correctly and completely, particularly with respect to the law that applied to the element of identification and the evidence that related to that issue.
>
> It is my view that Judge Bouck did render adequate assistance in explaining to the appellant the trial process and what options were available to him from time to time.

As I wrote in the Vancouver Bar Association's publication, *The Advocate*, in 2012,[1] the conclusion that the trial judge rendered adequate assistance is unfounded. Rarely did Judge Bouck offer assistance, and when he did, he was disdainful. When Henry finally said that he needed the aid of a lawyer, the judge responded with ill-disguised contempt. And, finally, the many errors of law made by the judge provided the jurors with a virtual road map along the path to conviction.

In response to Henry's civil suit, the state claims that because Henry chose not to be represented by counsel, he is responsible for his own wrongful conviction. Based on the preliminary hearing, Henry had good reason to be skeptical of lawyers—indeed, of the entire criminal justice system. He believed that White failed to represent his best interests, that Luchenko falsely presented as "the lineup photo" a doctored mash-up, and that the complainants were lying.

When an accused represents himself, the playing field of "advocacy" is uneven. The transcript of Henry's trial is replete with illustrations. When Henry told the trial judge he would testify on his own behalf—waiving his "right to remain silent"[2]—Judge Bouck's sole response was this:

You are perfectly entitled to, but you will be subject to cross-examination. The Crown only has to . . . Let me put it another way. The burden of proof is on the Crown to prove its case beyond a reasonable doubt. You do not have to take the stand unless you want to.

Given the lack of clarity in Judge Bouck's response, it is no wonder Henry failed to grasp the significance of subjecting himself to cross-examination.

Research suggests that when a defendant remains silent, he has less chance of being found guilty than when he takes the stand to proclaim his innocence.[3] (It also suggests, paradoxically, that if jurors feel they are being denied access to important information about the accused, they may place greater weight on the information not provided.)

If an accused makes a poor witness, jurors tend to view the accused's testimony as self-serving. When an accused testifies, which entitles the Crown to question him about a criminal record, a guilty verdict becomes more likely, regardless of the care taken by the court in instructing the jury. Finally, a jury told at the outset about the presumption of innocence and the burden of proof may well undergo an "unconscious burden shift" if the accused takes the stand.[4]

It is clear, based on my interviews with the two jurors in the Henry case, that all four factors played a role in their negative view of Henry.

Lacking expert guidance on whether to testify—possibly the riskiest decision facing any accused—an unrepresented accused will soon feel out of his depth. A self-represented accused dealing with an oppositional prosecutor and an unhelpful, at times hostile, judge must feel doubly disoriented. Many times, Henry missed conversations between prosecutor and judge; often, they discussed legal matters that eluded him.

In a 2011 report entitled *Foundation for Change*, Leonard Doust, Q.C., the lawyer who served as special prosecutor in the Henry case, discussed the impact of British Columbia's legal aid crisis on criminal law:

> The criminal justice system cannot work without effective Crown and defense counsel—both are equally necessary to a properly functioning system. Submissions made by Crown counsel emphasized the impact of inadequate legal aid on the ability to do their jobs. They cannot engage in any of the discussions such as possible admissions, pleas, and joint sentence submissions that make the criminal justice system work.
>
> In addition, an unrepresented accused makes it difficult for complainants in sexual assault cases since they will be cross-examined by the individual accused of the sexual assault. One Crown Counsel related how unrepresented accused will often ignore the disclosure package provided by the Crown (containing important information including witness statements and indications about sentencing).
>
> Time and time again when individuals stand up to speak to sentence the pages are in pristine condition. These accused usually aren't pristine people . . . These are people who are either so resigned or are so out of their depth when it comes to representing themselves that there's really not a level playing field.[5]

As Canadian courts have long made clear, judges owe unrepresented accused a duty of fairness. And, where the prosecution relies primarily on identification evidence, both the trial judge and Crown counsel have a special duty to ensure a fair trial.[6]

In a 2012 case involving an accused even less sophisticated than Henry, the Newfoundland and Labrador Court of Appeal said that even though judges must avoid becoming "an advocate for the accused, thereby compromising judicial impartiality," the trial judge's "fundamental duty is to see that an accused receives a fair trial":

> Every case depends on its unique facts. The need for guidance varies depending on the crime, the facts, the defences raised and the accused's sophistication. The judge's advice must be interactive, tailored to the circumstances of the offence and the offender, with appropriate instruction at each stage of a trial.[7]

Not only did the accused in that case refuse a legal-aid lawyer, he also repeatedly resisted the trial judge's suggestions that she declare a mistrial, given his apparent difficulties—"including," the judge wrote, "the unique obstacles posed by virtue of his being incarcerated."

Judge Bouck's assistance to Henry was woefully inadequate. Towards the end of the trial, Henry advised the court that he was out of his depth, having in his possession only an out-of-date copy of the *Criminal Code*. In response, Judge Bouck noted that a lawyer could do him no good and then asked Luchenko to provide him with an excerpt from a textbook on identification evidence, effectively washing his hands of the problem.

While mistakes are endemic to cases involving what Professor Brandon Garrett has called "the typically weak defence of innocence,"[8] most of them fall into the category of what Michael Naughton has called "miscarriages [unintentional or systemic breaches] of justice."[9] First, Garrett says, defendants have little ability to collect evidence of their innocence. The primary investigators of crimes are the police; they work for the prosecution, and their work may be underway or completed by the time people even become suspects. Second, it is inherently difficult to prove that one did not commit a crime. It's not easy to remember what one was doing on an unremarkable evening many months ago; indeed, it might be suspicious if one did have a vivid recollection. Third, defence lawyers often do not effectively challenge the prosecution case. "In the cases studied," Garrett said, "the defence called, on average, less than half as many witnesses . . . and retained fewer experts. Many of these innocent people could not afford an attorney, much less expert witnesses . . . And while we do not know how often this occurred, in some exonerees' cases, police or prosecutors concealed evidence of innocence from the defence lawyers."[9]

Such cases have exposed patterns of incompetence, abuse, and error, as well as evidence corrupted by suggestive eyewitness procedures, coercive interrogations, unsound and unreliable forensics, shoddy investigative practices, cognitive bias, and poor lawyering. The cost to defendants is catastrophic: not only are they convicted of crimes they did not commit, but those acquitted as a result of procedural error are viewed, by most people, as offenders who got off on a technicality.

Although Judge Bouck, in his blog post, criticized Ivan Henry for not retaining a lawyer (as do the defendants in Henry's current civil case), the judge should have appointed an amicus curiae the minute it became obvious that Henry needed help in mounting an effective defence. Henry, facing a plethora of major crime charges, was owed the assistance of someone who, though not a party to the case, could make legal arguments and point out legal pitfalls and opportunities. Had an amicus curiae been present to protect Henry's interests, the judge would not have gotten away with conducting such a travesty of a trial.

CHAPTER 51

SLEIGHT OF HAND

Months after meeting Ivan Henry in February 2011, I set out to meet Madam Court Clerk, the long-retired Sarah Miller. I hoped she might provide me with a little background colour about the trial. She welcomed me warmly into her West Vancouver apartment. I was offered tea and Timbits and a tour of her tiny living room, which featured embroidered cushions and porcelain ornaments, glass cabinets crammed with family photos, and a card table with four bridge hands laid out.

Once seated, Miller pointed, with excitement and pride, to a thick binder lying open on the coffee table. After flipping through page after page of courthouse memorabilia—birthday celebrations, special occasions, Friday lunches with "the Chief" (Chief Justice Allan McEachern)—she stopped. And there, in front of us, was an eight-by-ten-inch colour copy of the lineup photo. "My most prized souvenir," she said. "A retirement gift from a colleague who knew I kept a scrapbook."

While I leaned in for a closer look, she said, "Ivan Henry is a horrible, horrible man. Everyone was so patient with him. Too patient. That lovely judge especially. And the prosecutor, too. Like a dog with a bone, that Michael Luchenko. What a lovely man. He worked like crazy to ensure the bad guys got their due. No one worked harder."

"As for Henry," she said, "how stupid of him to put the photo into evidence. Did he not know what the jurors would think?"

I was riveted by the photo—the enlarged version Luchenko had refused to give Henry at trial. "Would you mind if I made a copy?"

"Not at all," she said. "Just bring it back quickly. I hate having it out of my sight."

When I told Henry what I had, he insisted we meet immediately.

"Only if you bring your copy," I said. He'd emailed me a copy but, to date, had refused to let me see the original. (Henry's trust level was low. At times, he viewed me as credible and sincere; at others, as someone in pursuit of his "pending fortune" or an undercover agent sent to inveigle him into sexually predatory behaviour.)

After studying the photo Miller had given me, Henry proffered his own, deeply creased, copy. Placing it carefully on the table, he said, "Finally, you get to see it. You should be grateful." He added: "What the guards wouldn't have done to destroy this. Dozens of copies I made over the years. In a single heist alone, they stole thirty-three of them."

Side by side, the differences between the photos popped out. The pants were darker in the eight-by-ten, and the light colours were much lighter. The bottom of Henry's vest/shirt was obscured in the eight-by-ten, but it stood out, in its oddity, in the five-by-seven. If the eight-by-ten in Madam Clerk's possession was a copy of Trial Exhibit One, what was the five-by-seven print Henry had clung to all those years?

• • •

ON JANUARY 3, 2012, the BC Court of Appeal granted me access to review all "Henry records, except specified psychological reports, and subject to publication bans." After poring through boxes of documents under the watchful eye of court registry staff, I found what I'd been half expecting: Supreme Court Exhibit One in the Henry Appeal Books (filed in the 2010 reopening proceedings) was the same photo as the one in Court Clerk Miller's possession. This meant the larger version of the lineup photo had suddenly become Exhibit One in the trial.

But how could that be? Hadn't Henry's five-by-seven been marked Exhibit One? Although I'd read the documents in my possession many times—including the preliminary hearing and trial transcripts—I now approached them with a specific purpose: namely, to solve the mystery of Exhibit One.

As noted, before the preliminary hearing, Michael Luchenko was asked more than once to produce "any lineup photos that might exist," but he turned a deaf ear to this request.

When Henry's lawyer, John White, repeated that request at the preliminary hearing, Luchenko said, "To the best of my knowledge, Your Honour, I'm aware of no such photo." In fact, Luchenko had the photo in his possession as early as August 8, 1982, a little over a week after Henry's arrest.

In fact, as we've seen, it was only after further obfuscation and foot-dragging that Luchenko finally returned to the courthouse with the five-by-seven colour print. It was marked "Preliminary Hearing Exhibit One," and David Baker, acting jail sergeant as of May 12, 1982, attested to its accuracy.

• • •

REMARKABLY, AT SOME point during the roughly three and a half months between the end of the preliminary hearing and the start of the trial, Luchenko had the lineup photo sent to Henry in Oakalla. Henry recalls it arriving in January 1983, along with the preliminary-hearing transcripts; yet a recently disclosed letter to Henry dated February 23, 1983, marked "hand-delivered by Sheriff" and signed by Luchenko, states: "Enclosed please find a copy of the photographic lineup."

Whatever the correct date, the point is that, inexplicably—between the preliminary hearing and the trial—Crown counsel sent the accused a copy of the lineup photo, Exhibit One. No other exhibits—just that one. Why would Luchenko have done such a thing?

On day two of the trial, as noted, Henry began his cross-examination of Miss Simpson, the first of the lineup attendees to testify. Producing the five-by-seven photo from his muddle of files, he asked Simpson whether he was "anywhere in that picture." When she said yes, the photo was marked Trial Exhibit One.

As the jurors passed it around, Henry said, "If you people hold that up to the light, you'll see a shirt's been placed on top of the picture." Rebuked by Judge Bouck for giving evidence rather than asking questions, Henry abandoned the point, and Exhibit One was returned to Madam Clerk.

The next day, March 4, 1983, soon after Luchenko began his direct examination of Miss Larson, the second lineup attendee, he asked Madam Clerk for Exhibit One. After passing it to Henry, Luchenko said, "I have additional copies of the exhibit that Mr. Henry has introduced into evidence. I am prepared to give these to the jurors for their records." The transcript continues:

> **THE COURT**: Fine. Have you got one for me?
>
> **MR. LUCHENKO**: I believe I have an additional one for the Court as well. I am handing up copies of the lineup to the Court, my Lord, one for each two jury members and one for the Court.
>
> **THE COURT**: Thank you.
>
> **THE ACCUSED**: I have one, yeah.
>
> **MR. LUCHENKO**: I have given an additional one as well to Mr. Henry. *His is actually the exhibit.*
>
> [ITALICS ADDED FOR EMPHASIS.]

Henry was in possession of the photo marked Exhibit One. Luchenko, having distributed to everyone else the copies he'd brought with him, asked that the witness be shown Exhibit One. However, instead of showing her the photo he'd returned to Henry—the actual Exhibit One—he showed her the larger version. Henry, thinking a bigger size would better reveal the photo's fakery, asked for a copy. In response, Luchenko said Henry did not need one as he had his own copy.

Thus, Henry never came into possession of the eight-by-ten photo—until over a quarter-century later.

• • •

AT A SECOND meeting with Madam Court Clerk, I raised the possibility that Luchenko had substituted one photo for another. She bristled at the suggestion. "No way," she said. "Exhibits are official court documents. As such, they are jealously guarded."

Explaining that exhibits can include everything from illicit drugs to laundered money to photos of defaced gravestones, she said that strict protocol and tight security attend their transfer from Provincial Court to Supreme Court. "Our practice, once they arrived," Miller said, "was to review them with the exhibits clerk. Together, we meticulously listed all of them."

I asked if prosecutors had access to the exhibits. "Of course," she said. "Their role is to sort out which ones they want to go to trial and which ones they won't be needing. The Exhibits Room was available to them at a time or times of their choosing."

Did she recall seeing the lineup photo before the trial began? After pausing for the longest time, Miller said, "No, now that you mention it, I don't. The first time I saw the lineup photo was in the courtroom. Who could forget that moment? I was stunned that Mr. Henry—that awful man—would want the jury to see such a thing. It did him no good—no good whatsoever."

"If you'd seen it before the trial, is it something you would have remembered?"

"Definitely!" she said, "We all talked about it—how, had the Crown introduced it, there would have been a mistrial for sure. You have to be so careful with exhibits."

• • •

SEVERAL MONTHS LATER, I noticed something I'd missed before. Although the lineup ballots included in the 2010 appeal books contain an exhibit tag marked with both a "Provincial Court" and "Supreme Court" exhibit number, the lineup photo contains only one number—the Supreme Court exhibit number.

In other words, the appeal books make no mention of the five-by-seven photo—either as a preliminary hearing or a trial exhibit the photo initially marked Exhibit One.

Who better to ask about this than Madam Clerk, the person responsible for filling out the exhibit tags? When I called to ask if she would agree to meet me a final time, she initially agreed—"in the interests of accuracy."

A few days later, she called to say that she felt terrible about talking to me at all and wanted no further involvement in this book.

CHAPTER 52

CUT AND PASTE

U nbeknownst to anyone but the Crown, as we've seen, Ivan
Henry had in his hand during his trial a photo different from
the one everyone else was looking at. One can only imagine the
impression he left with the jury when he badgered a witness about why
he or she denied seeing the "floating vest." It was apparent in his photo
but not in theirs.

When the complainants finished testifying, Henry resolved to
enlist the expertise of his old buddy, Colin Bradbury, a man who occasionally got paid to take wedding pictures. "Please don't subpoena me,"
Bradbury said. "You say you're innocent, but how do I know? Doctored
photos? You've got to be kidding."

"Not to worry," said Henry, "the fakery's as plain as the nose on
your face. One look at it, you'll know what I mean."

Escorted into the courtroom, Bradbury avoided eye contact. Given
that the Crown was making all the arrangements for the calling of his
witnesses, Henry had no opportunity to prepare anyone before they
testified. Instead of sitting down with him and reviewing the evidence—
the normal course of events—Henry was forced to act on the fly.

"Is the lineup photo a phony?" Henry asked Bradbury.

"No, I wouldn't think for a moment," Bradbury said.

Surprised, Henry asked, "So there's no way I could cut the negative out and put a head in there, and do it that way?" When Bradbury
said, "That hasn't been done," Henry said, "What about that little chest
protector thing he's wearing? You know, like the kind umpires wear so
that they don't get hit with a baseball?"

Incredulous that Bradbury couldn't see the "floating vest," he moved towards the witness box. Once there, he'd point out the obvious and that would be that. But for Luchenko's strategic interruption—"I appreciate my friend isn't quite up on what he's doing"—Henry might well have noticed the discrepancy. Had he done so, the Crown's substitution of exhibits would have come to light.

• • •

IN HIS JURY charge, Judge Bouck said that Henry's own "expert" had put the lie to his tampering claim. "Mr. Bradbury is," he said, "a professional photographer. He said that nobody had doctored Exhibit One and he doubts if it was retouched." Given that Bradbury had not been qualified as an expert in forensic photography, one would have expected the Crown to object to his providing evidence. Luchenko's failure to object suggests he had spoken to Bradbury and knew what his evidence would be.

Opinion evidence is allowed when the opinion furnishes the court with scientific information likely to be outside the experience and knowledge of a judge or jury. If on the proven facts a judge or jury can form their own conclusions without help, then an expert opinion is unnecessary. However, given the weight that jurors place on forensic expert evidence, it is incumbent on judges to closely regulate what expert evidence gets admitted and what does not.[1]

When I asked juror A.L., twenty-eight years after the fact, what credence she had put on Henry's claim that the lineup photo had been tampered with, she said, "That photo looms large in my memory. Who could forget it? He thought it was his ticket to freedom. The man's a goof. When he kept going on about it being doctored, it was obvious he was clutching at straws."

For years, various courts and government officials confronted with Henry's fabrication allegation rebuffed him because his own "expert" opined that the photo was real. As Federal Court Justice Reed wrote in 1992: "Mr. Henry's main complaint in this case is that the Minister of Justice has failed to review 'new evidence' of a fabricated lineup. The photo wasn't a crucial piece of evidence at trial. Henry himself called an expert who said it wasn't doctored. There is no doubt the photo looks bizarre, but it can be explained. Mr. Henry has never been able to produce any expert opinion that the photo was fabricated, then or now. After reviewing the evidence—noting that the photo wasn't a crucial piece of evidence at trial, that Henry's own expert said it wasn't doctored—I must dismiss the action."

Despite Henry's countless applications over the years, no court has ruled on the authenticity of the lineup photo. In 1997, the Court of Appeal dealt with a reopening application—complete with the photo and, for the first time, the 1992 affidavit of Lee Atkinson. The court made no reference to either document in its decision.

In late 2011, I asked Atkinson to elaborate on his 1992 opinion, and to comment on the eight-by-ten-inch photo introduced at trial. Atkinson, a member of the City Council of Prince Albert and the Saskatchewan Penitentiary Citizens Advisory Board, had business in Saskatoon, so we arranged to meet at the Bessborough Hotel, a grand old chateau built by the CNR in the early 1930s. It was a bone-chilling day. A rather short, ordinary-looking man walked through the door dressed in a shell jacket and a pair of thin mittens.

"Why do you care enough to meet with me?" I asked, after the niceties.

"Anything I can do to help out an innocent man who's been convicted," he said. "Though I never knew the ins and outs of his case, I always admired his tenacity. Ivan and me, we've kept in touch over the years. Every time he turned around, he was asking me to make him more copies—some of them pretty big. Sometimes he paid me, mostly not."

Atkinson graduated from Ryerson Polytechnical Institute's department of photography in 1987. His four-year certificate program in materials and processes included courses in photography-related materials, different kinds of film, the development of emulsions, paper-printing processes, dye transfer, graphics in the print-copy media, photography chemicals, the design and operation of photography machines, and the combining and manipulation of images.

He spent seven years with the Canadian Centre for Remote Sensing (CCRS), Energy, Mines and Resources, in the Prince Albert Satellite Station. As section head, he provided remote-sensing geographical information to decision makers, related industries, and the general public; acted as technical advisor to the federal government regarding specifications for material processes and processing equipment; consulted on the development of remote-sensing technology and applications in other countries; and introduced manipulation techniques to improve the quality of the data.

In January 2012, Atkinson provided me with an opinion letter describing photo one, Henry's five-by-seven, as a "composite of images." (See insert 2.) He said Henry and the three officers had been cut and pasted in. "The outlines of #12's black shirt are very straight and regular," he said, "consistent with cut-lines, not with the folds of fabric. The cut-line dividing the dark, shirt-like object and the waist is disjointed. The lines of the black object around the upper area are also too square, appearing to have been cut in the area around the right arm.

"As for the larger grouping of four, many areas appear to be circumscribed by straight cut-lines. For example, the back of #17's hand appears to be exacto-edge flat, as do the heads of the three uniformed officers. The alignment of the handcuffs 'joining' numbers 17 and 12, and 12 and 1, appears unnatural. In addition, given the obvious struggle being depicted, the positioning of #1's left arm—hanging loosely at his side—appears anomalous.

"The photo contains other anomalies," he continued. "For example, #18's thumb appears disjointed, unnaturally elongated. The handcuff appears to be unnaturally cutting into his right wrist, yet he shows no signs of distress.[2]

"In addition, #12's torso doesn't line up with the legs. Following the natural outline of #12's right leg contour, it does not appear to connect to anything, suggesting a portion of his upper body is missing." The photo, Atkinson said, was created by means of a photo-mechanical process. "Just as Aunt Jean can be added to a family photo, Henry and the officers appear to have been added to the lineup photo."

Regarding photo two, the eight-by-ten distributed by Luchenko at trial (see insert 3), Atkinson wrote that it "contains a much higher index of contrasts, namely more darks and lights, as opposed to in-between colours. This higher contrast image could have been produced in a number of ways, including: 'burning' and/or 'dodging,' a process in which light is added to or taken away from a print; a process wherein the same negative is subjected to a series of longer developing (exposure) times, until the right contrasts are achieved; and a process wherein the film is developed in a warmer developing solution, causing the middle tones to be depressed and creating a higher contrast index.

"The outcome," Atkinson said, "is that the dark colours, found mostly below the waist, became even darker; the light colours—T-shirts, etc.—became even lighter. In particular, the cut-lines surrounding the black object have been rendered virtually invisible." In short, according to Atkinson, photo number two is a redoctored version of the photo originally marked Trial Exhibit One before being returned to Henry.

In early 2014, I sought a second opinion. Gregg M. Stutchman is a forensic analyst and expert witness in imaging forensics and forensic photography. Based in Napa, California, he has worked on cases in both the US and Canada. Of the five-by-seven-inch photo, he said:

> The person #12 (Mr. Henry) appears to have a dark floating vest/shield object in front of his torso.
>
> The legs of the jeans which are supposed to be Mr. Henry are straight up, with no leaning at all. His torso isn't visible, because it is covered by the dark vest/shield object, but the position of his head and shoulders in relationship to his legs and hip, gives the appearance that the upper body is not connected to his lower body and legs.
>
> The vest/shield object has clear, straight sharp edges, suggesting that it was cut and pasted after the fact.
>
> Markers #17, #1 & #15 are washed out, whereas the other markers are crisp and clear. Given the straight-on flash, if any number marker would be washed out, it should be #12. This is not the case, however. I also note that markers #10, #21 and #18 are also dark and clearly visible. The washed out numbers are indicative of post processing.
>
> There are conflicting issues with the shadows behind the people in the lineup. #10 has no shadow. #17 has a shadow of his head and left shoulder which are significantly above his head and shoulders. #21 has a shadow of his head, which can be seen on the wall behind him, but which is lower than his head.
>
> There is a hot spot above the middle of the lineup, which indicates the use of a straight-on flash. There is also a shadow

behind the head of the red-haired officer who has Mr. Henry in a chokehold.

Regarding the second (eight-by-ten-inch) photo, he writes:

> This is another version of the lineup photograph in question. This image has obviously been altered when compared with #1 above as described below:
> The back wall on #1 is blue, as compared with the back wall in #2, which appears as dark green or gray.
> The uniform shirts of the officers which are blue in #1, are gray or darker than gray in #2.
> The shadows of the head of #17 is no longer visible. The shadows (the dark tones of an image) had been made even darker, skewing the detail of the floating vest/shield, waist and pants. In fact, the outline and sharp lines of the floating vest/ shield are no longer visible.

In short, Gregg Stutchman, like Lee Atkinson, is satisfied that photo one is a composite of images and that photo two is a manipulated version of photo one.

• • •

I ASKED CONSTABLE Almgren about VPD procedures and photographic evidence. She said after Sergeant Lloyd Foxx took the picture on May 12, 1982, he would "likely have dropped it off at the lab located on the third floor, just opposite the Ident Room. The photo would likely have been developed the next day—either by Foxx himself and/or other Ident people. Or possibly by what we used to call civilian lab rats.

"At the time of Henry's trial, they'd just modernized the equipment," Almgren said. "The lab was quite sophisticated, very high end. Lots of money had been put into it. Because police and other people came and went, because of the number of people through whose hands the photo would pass, a form—called a 'property continuity-of-evidence form'—would have been completed. That form would be entered into court along with the photo." No such form is mentioned in the transcripts, nor has one ever been disclosed.

As we've seen, Henry sometimes testified he was in the lineup; at other times, that he was not. Given the strong-arm treatment of the three VPD officers—to the point where his air supply was cut off—such uncertainty is understandable. What is clear to him, though, is that he was not handcuffed prior to being dragged to the lineup room; he was wearing a blue velour, long-sleeved shirt; he had no moustache; and his hair was neither tang-orange or curly. Taking into account the expert opinions and Henry's testimony, the only conclusion possible is that the lineup photo is a fake.

Asked about this, Constable Almgren said she could imagine the "good ol' boys" engaging in a little hijinks in the photo lab. Assuming the lineup identification was going nowhere, "the boys likely cut and pasted any number of pictures, adding in the handcuffs." Almgren admitted she'd done the same thing with a different lineup gone bad.

"Nothing but boys being boys," agreed Francis Lévesque, the senior criminal lawyer referred to earlier. "Heck," he said, "one of my criminal law buddies—now a judge—hung such a lineup photo in his office. The boys in blue, somewhat into their cups one night, did a little cut-and-paste job on a discarded lineup photo—complete with the actual suspect—just for the hell of it."

Despite all of that, Corporal Baker testified that, as acting jail sergeant, he handcuffed the participants to each other and, after confirming the floodlights were on, led everyone into the lineup room. The scene his evidence conjures up defies belief: The bodies of the six foils plus Henry being torqued and twisted every which way; the three officers squeezing, along with them, through the standard-size doorway shown in the photo. Were such the case, surely the participants wouldn't be looking—a mere three minutes later—calm and relaxed; indeed, downright jovial.

Other parts of Baker's testimony are equally suspect. Asked when the "physical restraint" of Henry began, Baker testified, "Immediately after the lineup itself had concluded. When Foxx asked Henry to smile for the camera, that's when the police people smiled." Yet Detective Sims and many of the complainants testified that they witnessed restraint being applied while the lineup was in progress. Both Baker and Foxx said that the "smiling" began only after the women left. However, Miss Horvath and Miss Larson testified that there was joking and laughing throughout the lineup process.

If the photo is indeed a fake, the officers who testified that it was an accurate depiction of the lineup violated their oath to tell the truth. And the Crown, in implicitly vouching for its authenticity at the preliminary hearing, participated in the kind of conspiracy Henry only dreamed of in his worst nightmares.

• • •

DID THE POLICE, thinking the lineup evidence was going nowhere, create a phony picture for fun? And why, after Harkema had nailed down Miss Kavanagh's identification (with the aid of hypnosis, lengthy interviews, and a biased photo array), did he use that same phony picture to bring the faulty lineup identifications back to life?

But for Judge Craig's badgering, the photo would never have seen the light of day. As it was, Luchenko—knowing full well its unfairness could well torpedo the Crown's case—must have felt compelled to produce it. The identification evidence gleaned from the lineup featured large in its case, and standard operating procedure includes photos of the lineup. After the preliminary hearing, Luchenko pulled it from the exhibits and sent it to Henry in Oakalla. At the very least, when Henry reintroduced it at trial, he would be ready with copies that concealed the most obvious evidence of doctoring: the floating vest.

Doctoring aside, Luchenko needed a strategy for dealing with the photo's unfairness. Thus his spin: the photo didn't document police strong-arm tactics; it represented graphic proof of a guilty mind. Despite the room for error in this game plan—namely, that Judge Bouck would jettison it—his plan went off without a hitch. Indeed, the trial judge's charge to the jury was note perfect:

> Several times, Henry was moving about with his head down and was very uncooperative. When the photographer entered to take a picture of the lineup, one uniformed police officer forced Henry's head up . . . Five of the people (foils) were policemen. Henry was creating such a fuss they had to have other people there for security.

In summary, what might have begun as fun and games between a few officers evolved into something more sinister. That no officer later came forward to reveal the genesis of the fake photo is a disgrace.

CHAPTER 53

THE MAY 13 PHOTO

According to Detectives Montgomery and Witt, Vancouver Police Department rules in 1982 prohibited anyone from taking photos of, or fingerprinting, suspects who were held pending investigation. Sergeant McClellan, who took the photo of Henry that was identified as Exhibit Five during the trial, was, according to them, "not an ID guy." Thus, Staff Sergeant Miles violated police protocol in directing McClellan to take the pictures.

As the Court of Appeal noted in its acquittal decision, the May 13 photo of Henry that was used in the photo array shows jail-cell bars in the background and a VPD elbow jutting out in the foreground, while half the foils in the array look like university students standing in front of bulletin boards. Henry testified that the photo is not only unfair, but also fabricated. Although his face is likely taken from a photo Jessie gave the police, he maintains that on the day in question he was wearing a long-sleeved, blue velour shirt. He'd shaved off his moustache the day before. His hair was wavy, not curly, and definitely not "Tang-orange" in colour. And his sideburns don't grow in a "patchy way."

Lee Atkinson declined to weigh in on the authenticity of this photo because it is "too blurry to be certain . . . In that the only copy I have appears to be several degrees away from first generation," he said, "I am unable to offer an opinion in this regard." He did, however, say that both the bars and the police elbow could readily have been added by way of the same mechanical process as was used in the lineup photo.

Disagreeing with Colin Bradbury's testimony that the blurry nature of the photo makes it more difficult to doctor "because you can't get the out-of-focus consistent," Atkinson said that "the more a picture is out of focus, the easier it is to blend in other elements. The sharper the focus of different images, the harder it is to blend in other elements."

Henry told me that although the bars might have been those of the holding cell opposite the third-floor booking counter of the long-since-abandoned Public Safety Building on Main Street, he'd spent years pondering the significance of the police elbow. First of all, he and McClellan were alone. Second, no officer in his right mind would insert himself between the camera and the suspect, and stick out his elbow. How, then, did the elbow end up in the picture?

After years of researching the point, Henry came across a possible explanation—*The Defense Never Rests*, a book by the famed American lawyer F. Lee Bailey. In a passage about extending the grounds for an insanity defence through the "Irresistible Impulse Doctrine," Bailey writes: "The defendant may have known what he was doing, but nevertheless been physically unable to resist an overwhelming impulse to commit the crime." The idea, Bailey writes, is that some felons are so crazed with the desire to commit crimes they would do so even if a police officer were next to them. One criterion used to prove irresistible impulse is the "policeman-at-the-elbow test."[1]

"That explains it," Henry said one day as we pored over books in the University of British Columbia Law Library. "It was a fuck-you photo op, nothing more. A last hurrah for the boys in blue. They got their rocks off doing me in."

CHAPTER 54

WANT OF PROSECUTION

On January 14, 1984, a month and a half after Henry was designated a dangerous offender, Crown counsel Allan Stewart filed an application to dismiss Henry's appeals from both conviction and sentencing for "want of prosecution." According to then Section 9 (1) of the *Criminal Appeal Rules*, where an appeal is not "diligently pursued," the respondent "may apply to the court for an order dismissing the appeal for want of prosecution."[1]

An incarcerated, self-represented, indigent man had filed two cogent appeal submissions several months earlier. How could it be said that Henry had failed to "diligently" pursue his appeal? The court's reasons for its decision were:

> No appeal books have been filed or ordered. Mr. Henry says if we want to get them he will write some notes in them for us, but that he will not get them, that they are, I think his word was, "garbage," and he would throw them away. He refused legal aid at his trial and he either does not want legal aid now or he cannot get legal aid now, maybe both.
>
> He has expressed an intention not to proceed with these appeals in accordance with the only way in which they can be dealt with.

Although Henry did not have the entire trial transcript at the time of his appeal, he did have the portions pertaining to the complainants' testimony. He wrote in a submission years later:

Missing were the questions I asked so as to interrogate the complainants about specific elements—was I in the lineup? Did they swear their statements under oath? Did they receive a file number and, if so, what was it?

The questions I asked were because I believed this was my whole case and, losing those questions, I felt that the books were garbage because they had lost the strength I sought to adduce. Questions and answers not transcribed, who do I ask to correct them?

I couldn't explain the specifics to the Court because I wasn't skillful in the art of legal submissions when responding to the Court of Appeal. That's why I wanted written argument only. Which I asked for specifically on November 29, 1983—after I'd seen the missing portions of the complainants' transcripts. My letter had been acknowledged.

Although calling the transcripts "garbage" was ill advised, the quality of the transcript eventually produced, eighteen months later, was indeed shoddy. For example, three transcripts exist for the single day of March 14, 1983, the penultimate day of the trial:

1. Two pages, dated March 14 but not signed off on, beginning with "(Proceedings resumed pursuant to adjournment)" and ending with a reference to Henry standing up to address the jury;

2. Eighteen pages, dated March 9 [sic] and entitled "Submission to Jury by the Accused, Ivan Henry," certified by Fraser to be accurate; and

3. Thirty-four pages, undated with no start time and no sign-off page, beginning as follows:

```
(Submission by the accused, Ivan Henry)
(Submission by Mr. Luchenko)

THE COURT: Thank you. Mr. Luchenko. We have still got
a few more minutes to go so I might as well begin,
ladies and gentlemen.
```

The remainder of this portion contains Judge Bouck's jury charge, questions from the jury, the verdicts, and instruction to the jury to return the following Monday.

When I asked Bill Mitchell, the court reporter who had been on duty that day, about the incomplete, confusing nature of the transcript, he kicked me out of his office and told me not to "darken his door" again.

When I asked Kent Edwards, a decidedly more amiable court reporter, about the quality of transcripts in the early 1980s, he said, "Only a few reporters back then had a tape back-up. If something was said too fast, you'd simply drop it. When I joined in 1991, I was told: 'If it's trash, leave a dash. If in doubt, leave it out.' I was appalled. I always use a tape deck."

• • •

THE SUBSTANCE OF the Crown's want-of-prosecution objection was that Henry had failed to produce the appeal books. The appeal books consist mostly of the trial transcript. On November 23, 1983, after declaring Henry a dangerous offender, Judge Bouck ordered Luchenko to send the trial transcript to the Solicitor General of Canada:

> IT IS HEREBY ORDERED, pursuant to Section 695 of the *Criminal Code*, that a copy of all reports and testimony given by the psychiatrists, and the observations of the Court with respect to the reasons for the sentence, together with a transcript of the trial, be forwarded to the Solicitor General of Canada for his information.

Luchenko failed to do as ordered. It was only after being pressured by the trial judge, who had been pressured by the Solicitor General, that he finally sent them—eighteen months later, well over a year after the disposition of Henry's appeal.

In his May 29, 1985, cover letter to the Solicitor General, Luchenko wrote that there had been "a lengthy delay in the production of the transcripts."

Mr. Wilf Roy, then the manager of Official Court Reporters, told me he doubts that explanation. "I have no knowledge of any such delay," he said. "Had Mr. Luchenko raised a concern with me regarding one of our reporters, I'd have dealt with it immediately. As busy as we were, when a judge gave an order, we treated it urgently. It got priority treatment."

Had Luchenko produced the transcript in a timely manner, a want-of-prosecution argument, as far-fetched as it was, could never have been mounted. Hence, Henry's appeal would have been heard on its merits in 1984 rather than in 2010.

I asked whether Henry had other options. "The majority of Crown counsel were generally very good about helping out in such cases," he said. "Plus, had Henry claimed indigent status, I don't know a judge who would have failed to take steps to ensure he got the appeal books he needed."

In short, the want-of-prosecution argument was ill founded, and the 1984 Court of Appeal should have blown it out the door.

• • •

WHEN HENRY FINALLY got his hands on the complete transcript, several key portions were missing. All involve submissions made by the Crown on key matters, including the initial arraignment of Henry on a seventeen-count indictment, the Crown's invitation to the jury to "reason their way to guilt from the appellant's refusal to participate in the lineup," and the Crown's argument regarding "similar fact evidence."

The Crown's submission to the jury is missing entirely. The 2010 Court of Appeal, though commenting on the many missing portions, did not single out that vital omission—not a word about its impact on Henry's ability to formulate an effective appeal. The Crown's jury argument is often the most fertile ground upon which to base an appeal, which means substantive grounds were probably lost to Henry.

Kent Edwards said, "Whoever orders a transcript—it would've been the Crown in the Henry case, as per Judge Bouck's order—must specify what parts, if not all, are wanted. We think of a trial in segments."

In Henry's 2006 petition—the hearing of which was derailed because of the appointment of the special prosecutor in December—he wrote, "Luchenko maliciously avoided complying with the order issued, and therefore criminally disobeyed a lawful order made by a Court. Hence, he is guilty of Section 116 (1) of the *Criminal Code*."

• • •

IN 1984, NOT a single judge—neither Justice Peter Seaton, nor Justice A.B.B. ("Brian") Carrothers, nor Justice Richard ("Dick") Anderson—

considered appointing amicus curiae or asking the Crown to make arrangements on Henry's behalf for the appeal books.

The 1997 Court of Appeal treated Henry no better. Armed with the expert opinion of Lee Atkinson, Henry applied to reopen the 1984 appeal on the basis that the lineup photo had been fabricated (the Atkinson opinion). He also argued that the police witnesses, by testifying otherwise, had perjured themselves. In rejecting his application, Court of Appeal justices Lance Finch, Ian Donald, and John Hall said that, because it raised an issue "not of law but of fact"—namely, an allegation of police perjury—it was a matter for the jury's determination.[2] In other words, because Henry had failed to address the issue of fabricated evidence at trial, he was barred thereafter from doing so.

Not a word was said about an earlier decision of Justice Goldie, in another case, allowing an appeal in nearly identical circumstances;[3] nor about the difficulties Henry faced in representing himself during the trial. Nor was there a single reference to Henry's overarching point—namely that the Crown had obstructed justice by manufacturing evidence.

CHAPTER 55

CONFESS OR FORFEIT

P risoners become effectively invisible after their convictions. Stories about encounters between those claiming innocence and parole boards make for haunting reading. Anecdotal as these instances are, they suggest a pattern: namely, that professing innocence to a parole board can delay or altogether quash a wrongfully convicted inmate's chance at supervised release.

In New York, Dewey Bozella (twenty-six years in prison, released in 2009) refused a plea bargain at trial and steadfastly clung to his innocence claim through four parole hearings in which a show of remorse could have swayed the board to release him. Two years before Nancy Smith was exonerated in 2009 on what turned out to be trumped-up child-molestation charges, she was denied parole because a parole board member "felt she was in denial."

Having practised prison law in British Columbia for over forty years, John Conroy has observed a resurgence in the role of contrition at parole hearings. "The members of the parole board, they're big on that," Conroy told me. "Redemption. My clients must let the board know they've developed insight, that they've understood the various factors as to what made them do it. It's all about not rationalizing, not minimizing, and getting past the board's probing, which is often like retrying the case."

Soon after the January 13, 2009, reopening decision, the Parole Board of Canada released part of Henry's parole records—three "paper reviews" conducted in 2004, 2006, and 2008—to *Vancouver Sun* reporter Kim Bolan. On January 21, 2009, Bolan summarized, without commentary, those paper reviews:

The man a court says may have been wrongfully convicted in a series of rapes has been exposing himself in front of female prison staff members while incarcerated, according to National Parole Board documents.

Ivan Henry even kept track of the work schedule of one woman jail guard and masturbated in front of her, say the documents, dated from 2004 to 2008.

"Specifically, there have been recent incidents of you exposing yourself and masturbating where you could be observed by female staff members," one 2004 board decision says. "The psychologist recommended that you undergo a psychiatric evaluation to explore the issues related to this behaviour. When called on the masturbation incidents, you requested counseling from a female psychologist."

Henry refused to work with his parole officer and prison staff to come up with a plan to reintegrate him into the community, which parole board members said was a major factor in their continual denial of release.

A 2006 parole decision said Henry remained "seriously disturbed" and a danger to reoffend violently and sexually.

"You are keeping track of the schedule of a female staff member in front of which you masturbated before by using numerology to keep track of her schedule and find the number 19 to be important in relation to this."

Last week, the B.C. Court of Appeal reopened Henry's case because of evidence that another man may have been responsible for the Vancouver assaults.

According to the Parole Board, Henry is obsessed with proving his innocence in the Vancouver assaults. "From the time of your arrest and during your incarceration, you have denied responsibility for your offences."[1]

Henry is adamant that never once, during twenty-seven years of incarceration, did he expose himself to any female guard, nor did he ever steal a guard's schedule. The one time Miss Flannigan, the reviled female guard, reported him for performing "self-abuse" within sight of herself and a female newbie, Henry was masturbating in his own cot, long after last count. After guards ransacked his cell and confiscated his belongings, nothing came of that complaint, nor of the complaint that he'd stolen her schedule.

While the parole documents imply that Henry appeared regularly before parole boards and was just as often shot down, he appeared only once—in 1994. When directed to "confess or forfeit any chance of release," he vowed never to go back. From 1996 on, the parole board based its boilerplate rejections on "paper reviews" only—each rejection more dramatic and incriminating than the last.

Speaking in derogatory tones of Henry's "obsession" with proving his innocence, and of his having continually "denied responsibility" for his offences, the board failed to acknowledge his persistent claims of innocence. Instead, it dwelt on his refusal to "work with his parole officer and prison staff to come up with a plan to reintegrate him into the community," calling it "a major factor in the Board's continual denial of release." No mention is made that the "reintegration plan" required Henry to acknowledge his guilt.

In February 2013, I sought access to all of Henry's parole documents. I was advised by Patrick Storey, Regional Manager of Community Relations and Training, as follows: "I regret to inform you that we cannot supply you with the decisions made on Mr. Henry's quashed sentence. This is due to the fact that, based on the Court's findings, the information upon which they were based is no longer considered to be factual, rendering the decisions moot. Sorry about the inconvenience."

CHAPTER 56

WRONGFUL LIBERTY

Professor Frank Baumgartner describes wrongful liberty as the situation where a wrongful conviction occurs, an innocent person is sent to prison, and the real perpetrator remains free to commit more crimes.[1] On May 12, 1982, Ivan Henry told Detectives Sims and Campbell: "Put me in a cell for two months and see if it still goes on and then come back and apologize nicely. Say, 'Ivan, we are sorry.'" Twenty-six years later, the special prosecutor's report indicated that Donald James McRae might well be guilty of the crimes for which Henry was wrongfully convicted.

In 2002, investigating Robert Pickton, the VPD examined some two hundred unsolved sexual-assault files going back as far as the mid-1980s—long after Henry was in jail. By the end of the '80s, the VPD Sex Squad had determined that some fifty such assaults had been committed by an unknown person, dubbed "Smallman." Of those, investigators in 2002 excluded half for one of three reasons: the victim was deceased or could not be located; the victim did not wish to be involved; or there was an "insufficiently strong degree of similarity" to the other offences. The remaining twenty-five sexual assaults spanned five years—beginning on April 12, 1983, a month after Henry's conviction.

A note in a recently disclosed police file says that a woman identified as R.M., who was assaulted on July 3, 1988, represents "the first attack since the Strike Force concluded its (1987) project regarding Donald J. McRae." According to Detective Witt, McRae was a suspect throughout the time that the fifty sexual assaults were being committed. As well, he had been a suspect in the Henry crimes—another crucial fact that had been hidden from Henry.

In 2002, forensic testing confirmed that crime-scene evidence from two of the 1987 offences had yielded a common perpetrator DNA profile. In 2004, a third match was made from a 1985 assault. In June 2004, a DNA sample was secretly obtained from McRae's discarded cigarette butt and coffee cup outside the Main Street courthouse. A DNA match was made for those three assaults.

On May 27, 2005, McRae pleaded guilty to these three crimes.[2] In sentencing him, Provincial Court judge William Kitchen made note of "continuing terror and upset" on the part of the victims. "Without wanting to dishearten the complainants," he said, speaking of the twenty-year-old crimes, "it really has fairly well destroyed their lives."

Describing the offences as "terribly serious," the judge noted three factors mitigating against a longer sentence—the "historical" nature of the offences; "McRae had no similar offences on his record"; and, although McRae had a "very serious record" of post-1988 break and enters, those offences did not match the "turpitude of these three offences," and they occurred after them. Judge Kitchen listed those post-1988 offences as follows:

- **1988**—a conviction for break and enter, and one for attempted break and enter. Sentences were ninety days and nine months;

- **1990**—eight-month sentence for break and enter;

- **1992**—sixteen months for break and enter;

- **1993**—eight months on two charges: break and enter and possession of stolen property;

- **1995**—fifteen months on a break and enter; six months on "lesser property offences"; thirty days for an arson conviction;

- **1996**—one day for a theft, but then another attempt to break and enter on such a six-month sentence was imposed; another break and enter for which a six-month conditional sentence was imposed;

- **1997**—six months for break and enter;

- **1998**—convictions for carrying a concealed weapon and mischief and attempted break and enter: six months concurrent;

- **1999**—possession of stolen property and break and enter: one day concurrent; another break and enter: five months; another break and enter: six months;

- **2000**—a sentence of five months was imposed;
- **2001**—a suspended sentence for a break and enter;
- **2002**—nine months for a break and enter and thirty days concurrent for mischief;
- **2003**—ninety days for possession of break-in instruments.

Counsel for McRae submitted that a 1996 head injury, which resulted in chronic headaches and memory issues, caused McRae to have no recollection of the sexual assaults. Given that Crown counsel Ms. M. Ahrens took no issue with the defence counsel's submission regarding McRae's medical condition, Judge Kitchen accepted that the injury, which occurred in 1989, "obviously makes it difficult for him to deal with daily responsibilities and impossible to resume any sort of occupational responsibilities. It has also caused him, I would note from the record that I have, to have slowed down somewhat in his commission of offences, although I do note that the record is relatively comprehensive right up until recently."

In summary, Judge Kitchen noted:

> The man today is not the same as the man then. He is not of the same mentality and probably of quite a different mindset from the man who committed these terrible offences.
>
> Regarding the brain injury, I am told of his limited ability to comprehend what he has done in the past and his difficulty in recalling these event[s]; that he himself finds the offences reprehensible; that he is remorseful and frustrated that he has done this and that at this stage can't do anything about it.
>
> He is a man who now more understands the damage that was done; a man who needs less emphasis on rehabilitation, less protection of the public, but again a man who must be used as an example to others for the purposes of general deterrence.
>
> McRae recognizes what he has done, and anything at this stage that can be done as far as rehabilitation is concerned has "fairly well been accomplished. He is not likely to be a serious risk to the public at this stage. We would hope that he has learned his lesson from all of this. That appears to be the case."

Accepting counsel's reassurance that McRae had both "insight and remorse," Judge Kitchen sentenced him to six years, minus a one-year credit for time served.

• • •

IN JUNE 2010, McRae's warrant expired and he was (and remains) a free man once again.

A mere four months later, the Court of Appeal, allowing Henry's appeal against conviction, considered whether Smallman had committed the Henry crimes. Saying it would "serve no purpose" to discuss the voluminous detail contained in the Smallman file, the court acknowledged that there are "some geographical . . . similarities between the circumstances of the Smallman assaults and the circumstances of the offences for which the appellant was convicted."

"Some geographical similarities" is an understatement. Although Henry's wife didn't move to Mount Pleasant until March 1982, McRae had lived on the same street all along—in the heart of the city. The Henry and Smallman crimes were committed mostly in the same Kitsilano, Mount Pleasant, and Marpole neighbourhoods. N.C., Miss Ramirez, and Miss Kavanagh were assaulted within a ten-block radius in Mount Pleasant. A.Q. was attacked less than a block away from Miss Browning's attack, and the assaults on L.K. and E.S. occurred within a block of the attacks on Miss Simpson and Miss Horvath.

A number of the Smallman and Henry crimes happened within a few blocks of each other in Marpole. D.S. was assaulted one block from both the L.S. and Miss Jacobsen assaults and two blocks from Miss Cardozo's. E.B. was assaulted within a few blocks of the other three, and P.V. was assaulted in the same vicinity. Ditto E.C., attacked on November 27. On April 9, 1984, shortly after Henry's appeal was dismissed for want of prosecution, A.G. was attacked in the same area.

• • •

THE 2010 COURT of Appeal stated: "There is also some evidence of night prowling by [Smallman] during the time period of some of the subject offences, and nearby some of the locations at which they were committed." In fact, up to 1988, McRae's criminal history includes numerous instances when he was charged with trespassing at night, break and enter, or attempted break and enter, including:

- **August 1973**—arrested for night prowling in Mount Pleasant.

- **August 1974**—convicted of loitering, just blocks from his Mount Pleasant home, and fined $100.

- **September 20, 1977**—charged with trespassing at night. Although he denied having a criminal record when confronted, he had convictions for theft, theft of auto, and a similar trespassing-at-night offence. As well, he was listed on CPIC (Canadian Police Information Centre) as a sex offender.

- **September 15, 1979**—committed to trial on two counts of attempted B and E, with intent to commit an indictable offence, in Kitsilano.

- **December 16, 1981**—convicted on a charge of trespassing at night in Kitsilano; sentenced to a fine of $200 or 20 days in jail. The reportee having provided the police with the licence-plate number, the police stopped the vehicle, which was registered to McRae's stepfather, who was living at the same address as McRae. Appeal against conviction was allowed on the basis that the judge erred in admitting and relied upon hearsay evidence pertaining to the licence-plate number.

- A withheld portion of a memorandum written by Staff Sergeant Miles, some time between July 6 and August 5, 1981, indicates that police were conducting surveillance on suspects "Richards" and "Hobson" (the surname of McRae's stepfather, and a name McRae sometimes used). The surveillance was called off in the second week of June 1981, due to staff shortages, before resuming on June 22–23. Miss Horvath was assaulted during this period of non-surveillance.

- **November 18, 1981**—appeared in court on a loitering-at-night charge.

- **May 17, 1982**—arrested (three days after Miss Fields's rape) after being caught prowling outside a residence in Marpole.

He was charged with trespass by night. (He had a towel in his possession. In two of the three assaults to which McRae pleaded guilty in 2005, he used a towel to cover the victim's face.)

- **July 13, 1982**—arrested, shortly after 3:55 a.m., in Kitsilano and charged with B and E and theft.

- **March 12, 1987**—found in possession of a knife, charged with a B and E in the West End—two blocks from where he sexually assaulted G.J. (June 5, 1985), and two blocks from where he sexually assaulted G.D. and B.W. on August 10 and September 16, 1987, respectively.

- **September 17, 1987**—a woman reported a prowler in Mount Pleasant, in the 1200 block of West 13th Avenue. Fourteen minutes later, a woman reported a possible B and E in progress in her suite in the 1200 block of West 14th Avenue. When McRae was apprehended, he had a buck knife in his possession. The woman on West 13th identified McRae from a photo lineup, and a criminal charge was laid against McRae regarding the West 14th attempted break-in. (On November 15, 1988, he was convicted of attempted break and enter and sentenced to nine months' incarceration.)

- **1987**—the VPD Strike Force surveilled McRae from October 16 to November 6, averaging twelve hours a day. During that time, he was found on four occasions to be looking into ground-level-suite windows in the Mount Pleasant area—spying on women undressing, sleeping, watching TV, etcetera. The surveillance further revealed that he typically stayed up until 5:00 a.m.

- **November 7, 1987**—arrested for B and E with intent. He was charged with possession of a narcotic, four counts of trespassing at night, and attempted B and E; he was given a nine-month prison sentence for the last charge.

- **July 26, 1988**—charged with two B and E offences alleged to have occurred on July 25 in Mount Pleasant. He was acquitted at trial.

- **September 19, 1988**—observed running from an attempted B and E (an alarm had been set off) in the Kerrisdale area of Vancouver.

• • •

THE 2010 COURT of Appeal pointed out: "The Crown says that the commonalities between the Smallman offences are not as strikingly similar as (Mr. Henry) suggests." On the contrary, the commonalities between the Smallman offences and those attributed to Henry could not be more striking. The night-prowling activities of McRae in the 1970s and 1980s were, according to police reports, for a sexual purpose. Moreover, the modus operandi used in both sets of crimes is virtually identical. Whether the term "rip-off" was used or not, the perpetrator often claimed to be looking for someone who owed him money. The perpetrator positioned the victim such that her legs hung over the bed. When he was able to sustain an erection, he ejaculated quickly. The many other commonalities include:

- Ground-floor suites (often unlocked or easily forced open);
- Occurring between 2:00 a.m and 7:00 a.m.;
- Placing a knife against the victim's throat;
- Speaking in a soft, calm voice;
- Having the victim cover her face, usually with a pillow;
- Having vaginal intercourse, or having the victim perform oral sex on him;
- Having the victim count to one hundred after it was over;
- Blaming the victim for not having her doors/windows properly secured;
- Humiliating the victim by saying the police wouldn't believe her, or she would be embarrassed;
- Sometimes taking property.

As noted, so strikingly similar were the two sets of offences that among the crimes listed as being under investigation in the VPD's December 1983 *Marpole Sexual Assault Update* was the March 19, 1982, assault on Miss Cardozo—an assault for which Henry had already been convicted.

The remainder of the Marpole rapes occurred between April and November 1983—all within six blocks of where Miss Cardozo and Miss Jacobsen were attacked; all within seven blocks of where McRae was arrested for sexually predatory behaviour on May 17, 1982; and all with the same commonalities as in the Henry crimes.

Front and centre during the post-Henry sexual assaults was Detective Michael Barnard—the man who had posed as a lineup foil and acted as the hypnotist of Miss Kavanagh. Excerpts from the Marpole Rapist police reports, either written by, or copied to, Barnard, reveal the following:

- Five days after L.R. was assaulted on April 12, 1983—less than a month after the Henry trial ended—Barnard interviewed the victim. The MO used by the offender was the same as Henry's; the victim lived on the same floor of the building as Miss Jacobsen had at the time of her August 1981 assault and a block away from Miss Cardozo's assault of March 1982.

- Five days after D.S.'s assault three months later (July 29, 1983), Barnard interviewed her. On the statement she signed on August 3, 1983, he wrote, "No further information or any other similar acts in the Marpole area. Case inactive awaiting further information."

- In an undated report, Barnard wrote that "<. . .>," having been found to have type-B blood type, was eliminated as a suspect. In a report dated December 23, 1983, he wrote that suspect "<. . .>," having been found to have type-O blood, was eliminated as a suspect.

- An undated memo, *Case Number: 83-77070/ 83-48956*, signed by Detectives Barnard and Gronmyr, reads in part: "As a result of all the publicity concerning the sexual assaults in the Marpole area, an anonymous letter was forwarded to the Department, mentioning that <. . .> was responsible for the attacks." The authors of the memo write that, having obtained a sample of the suspect's blood, they had eliminated him as a suspect.

- On April 9, 1984, Constable J. Howell copied Barnard on a memo regarding A.G.: "0202 hours in Marpole; stolen property; knife; asked for Donna—'Keep quiet and I won't hurt you. Scream, and I'll kill you'—pillow over face; legs swung over side of bed; ejaculation within seconds."

- In an April 24, 1984, memo entitled "Hypnosis of AG," "M. Barnard, Hypno Investigator, member I.L.E.H.I." wrote that A.G. was an "excellent subject and fell into a trance quite quickly."

Although he was unfamiliar with the acronym "I.L.E.H.I.," Detective Witt suggested it might stand for International Law Enforcement Hypno-Investigators.

In a 1985 *Confidential Bulletin*, the police noted that, in each of four break and enters and sexual assaults in August and September 1985, the suspect used a knife, covered the victim's face, threatened to use the knife, and demanded fellatio. In each case, the suspect told the victim to count backwards from one hundred, suggested she lock her doors and windows in the future, and told her she would be too humiliated to call the police—details common to the Henry crimes as well.

• • •

WHEN I TOLD Detective Montgomery about Henry's "obstructionist behaviour" in the lineup, he said it was likely aimed at having the lineup evidence thrown out. "Why else," he asked, "would he kick up such a fuss?"

"Obviously his game plan failed," I said. "The lineup evidence figured large in seven of his ten convictions."

"Surely they had more on him than that," Montgomery said, taken aback.

When I asked him whether he knew that crimes similar to Henry's had continued after his conviction, he said, "Copycat criminals are common. Every detail was reported in the paper."

"Not so," I said. "Virtually no details of the perpetrator's MO were reported."

Asked whether he believed Henry to be guilty of as many as twenty sexual assaults, Montgomery said, "He was probably guilty of most of them. The police likely rolled in another two or so. It happens."

CHAPTER 57

SPECIFIC RUSE

The 2010 Court of Appeal wrote: "Four of the (Henry) complainants testified that the assailant used the term 'ripped off' and a fifth said that the intruder told her that a woman named Valerie had taken money from his boss. This specific ruse does not appear in the particulars of the Smallman offences."

By defining "specific ruse" so narrowly, the court failed to acknowledge that in both sets of crimes, regardless of whether the term "ripped off" was used, the assailant often said he was looking for someone who owed him money. The eight trial complainants testified as follows:

- Miss Larson: Some men had sent him to her apartment to find a woman named Valerie, who owed them money.

- Miss Simpson: Someone living there had ripped him off for a lot of money.

- Miss Horvath: Calling her crude names, he asked where his money was and said, "It's been ripped off."

- Miss Jacobsen: Yolande had ripped him off, and he'd been sent there by his bosses to get money from her.

- Miss Ramirez: He'd come to collect $25,000 that Suzanne owed him.

- Miss Browning: Valerie had taken money from his boss and he'd been sent to get it back.

- Miss Cardozo: No such ruse.

- Miss Kavanagh: Debbie had ripped him off for drugs and he had been told that Debbie lived there.

Police notes—subject as they are to error, omission, and revision, intentional or otherwise—say that eleven of the Smallman complainants reported that the intruder:

- said, "Where's Sherry? She owes me money."
- was looking for Greg who owed him money.
- claimed to be looking for Hickory who owed him and others money that he'd been sent to collect.
- claimed to be looking for Sue, a working girl who owed someone money.
- was looking for someone who owed him money.
- asked her how long she'd lived there as he was looking for someone who owed him money.
- claimed to be looking for someone who owed him money who used to live there.
- was looking for guys who owed him money.
- said, "Are you Suzanne? You'd better not be. She owes us and I've come to collect."
- had come for money and was angry to learn the complainant had none. He was looking for someone named Sue or Suzanne.

Although the Court of Appeal noted that the McRae victims did not use the term "rip-off," the phrase was in common use at that time and simply connotes the unlawful taking of money (or other items) from someone else.

Not only would the police have been motivated to keep the term "rip-off" out of their notes—after all, hadn't they locked up the "rip-off rapist"?—we've seen how well-versed the VPD was at both memory manipulation and writing elliptical and self-serving interview notes. Under the circumstances, it is entirely plausible that McRae used the term "rip-off" during his attacks.

More tellingly, Detective Witt said this to me: "The members of the Strike Force surveilling McRae in 1987 referred to McRae as the 'rip-off rapist.'"

CHAPTER 58

THE GABRIEL REPORT

Identity often cannot be established by *modus operandi*," wrote the Court of Appeal, "because many of the common characteristics relied upon by (Mr. Henry) are common among 'power reassurance' rapists."

As Ronald and Stephen Holmes note in *Profiling Violent Crimes*, unlike the "sadistic-" or "anger retaliation-" rapist types, the power reassurance rapist trolls for his victims close to home or on the job. Even if he has wheels, he mostly seeks his victims in familiar locations:

> Normally looking for a victim in his own age group and of his own race, he is often a nighttime rapist, choosing to attack women between midnight and 5 a.m., while they are asleep in their own homes. Unlocked doors or windows allow him easier entry.
>
> Since this type of rapist typically finds his victims in his own neighborhood—or other nearby neighborhoods—he has the opportunity to watch and learn a female's routines, especially those who live alone. He may attempt to peep in her windows for several nights before attacking, getting a feel for her routine at night and how the home is laid out.
>
> This rapist, like the other types, won't stop raping willingly; they must be apprehended—or fear apprehension—in order to stop them from raping additional women. This rapist's cycle averages one rape every one to two weeks, making his assaults more frequent than other rapists'.

Having sex through rape makes him feel important and significant, something he doesn't experience much in day-to-day life. His low self-esteem drives him to try to control another person physically. But unlike the more aggressive rapist types, this one is less physically dangerous to a victim, since he only uses the amount of force needed to subdue his victim and gain her compliance.[1]

The power reassurance rapist type is often an adult single man living with his mother or parents. He isn't abstaining from sex or relationships with women because he wants to; he is doing it because no one wants to be intimate with him.

At the 2010 hearing, Crown counsel David Crossin, Q.C., argued that "the commonalities between the circumstances of the Smallman/McRae assaults and the Henry offences are . . . not so strikingly similar as to permit a conclusion that Mr. McRae (or another third party) committed the Henry offences. In this regard," Crossin continued, "the Court may consider the report prepared by Detective G. Gabriel in relation to the Smallman offences." Noting that the report "outlines the generic characteristics and/or traits possessed by 'power reassurance' rapists," Crossin wrote:

> Detective Gabriel's report describes how many of the characteristics submitted by Mr. Henry to be relevant in terms of establishing identity are common amongst power reassurance rapists and, arguably, hold little probative value with respect to identifying the perpetrator.[2]

A careful review of the Gabriel report shows, however, that the question Gabriel was asked had nothing to do with Henry. Rather, Detective Gabriel was asked whether Donald McRae, having been linked through DNA to three of the twenty-five sexual assaults not ruled out by the Project Smallman investigators, had likely committed the other twenty-two.

In addressing that question, Gabriel described the "typology" of the Smallman crimes:

- Most occur indoors;

- The assaults are ritualistic and, in general, non-violent (a knife being used only to enforce compliance); if met with resistance, the offender will often flee;

- The offender is a loner; often living with one or both parents [Henry lived, albeit intermittently, with his wife and children; McRae, with his mother and stepfather]; and lacks personal hygiene [Jessie described Henry as "clean"];

- He resorts to "peeping" so as to make mental notes of available targets—meaning that, typically, the victim lives on the ground floor; the offender surprises her while she's sleeping—between midnight and 5:00 am;

- The offender may have a sexual dysfunction; may apologize for his behaviour and/or offer advice on how not to be an easy target "next time"; and

- The offender will continue to reoffend until he is either arrested, incarcerated, or some other barrier presents itself.

Gabriel concluded that, in all likelihood, McRae committed the other twenty-two sexual assaults:

All of the behaviours exhibited—including the dates, times and places of attacks, the interaction between victim and offender including the negotiation and compromise that took place, the use of a knife, the attempts at disguising identity—are all consistent with the behaviour exhibited in the (three) target cases.

The display of pseudo-unselfish behaviour and the arrogant attempts at blaming the victim for having unlocked doors, joined with the advice he provides in relation to those doors, are also consistent with the target cases.

Of significance in this series . . . is the fact that McRae was observed in 1987 by VPD surveillance units peeping into ground-level windows. Several attacks in this series occurred in the same vicinity. McRae was also in possession of a motorcycle. This provided him with the mobility required to cover vast distances. This offender typology, much like a B & E artist (which he is), engages in "mental mapping." (Kim Rossmo; *Geographical Profiling*; page 89; CRC Press, 2000 Washington).

In brief, this means that he makes mental notes of locations and potential victims as he moves through a specific area. This mental mapping provides him with target-rich recall and a vast array of selected victims to choose from.

In these peeping cases . . . McRae was compiling a mental map of potential victims . . . In McRae's case, it is evident there were three pockets of offending locations. They came in handy in that they were close to main arteries and provided for quick access and escape.

I am not aware of any press associated to these attacks. However, it is likely that McRae was able to follow the media both in print and TV, and was savvy enough to change locations when things heated up.

It must be considered that the similarities in the temporal, behavioural, verbal and geographic aspects of these offences appear to mirror one another. In simple terms, if you've read one case, you've read them all.

There are deviations in MO, this is obvious—(for example, the theft of personal items or not.) However, the significant portions of the offences themselves or the "ritual" aspects such as the selected victim, the negotiation and compromise that took place, and the sex acts, all suggest that there is a common offender.

When compared to the three target cases, it is my opinion that this common offender is more likely to be Donald McRae than anyone else.

In his report, Gabriel concluded that McRae's crimes did not possess a "signature"—signature being a "combination of MO and Ritual such that the profiler can say that he/she has never seen this combination before." That conclusion is not surprising; Gabriel would have been privy to the (identical) "Henry MO."

The Crown argued, and the Court of Appeal agreed, that because all power reassurance rapists share the same qualities, it cannot be said that Henry didn't commit his set of crimes, nor McRae his.

Whereas McRae engaged in what Detective Gabriel called "mental mapping," there is no evidence that Henry did. Whereas Henry lived, albeit on and off, with his wife and children, for the most part in locations far from the crime scenes, McRae lived, at all material times, with his mother and stepfather in the "heart of the city."

Although no crimes involving the same MO occurred either while McRae was in custody or during the period between Henry's arrest in July 1982 and his conviction in March 1983, the sexual assaults resumed soon thereafter. When surveilled, McRae was observed roaming the streets between 1:00 a.m. and 5:00 a.m.—the same period in which the Henry victims were assaulted. McRae is eight and a half years younger than Henry, and many of the Henry complainants initially described a man in his mid-twenties. At the time, the two men bore a remarkable resemblance.

Asked about the apparent coincidence between the lifting of surveillance (twice) and the sexual assaults on Miss Fields and Miss Kavanagh, Detective Witt said, "Donald McRae lived directly across the street from Henry's wife on East 17th. Given McRae's criminal record, he'd have been accustomed to doing "heat checks"—checking for police surveillance. You say Henry saw a ghost car upon his release? Well, McRae would've seen it, too. Furthermore, he'd have witnessed it leave before that first midnight."

"Miss Fields was assaulted in Mount Pleasant around 1:00 a.m., just a short while later," I pointed out. "Could he have acted that quickly?"

"Ah," said Witt, "but the address was in close proximity. Assuming McRae had been stalking the neighbourhood for days, he'd already have lined up his next prey. Once opportunity arose, he'd have gone for it. Ditto, Miss Kavanagh."

"It was suggested that Henry has a police scanner, something he denies. Would such a scanner have made a difference?"

"No," said Witt. "Scanners don't work on surveillance vehicles. Besides, McRae wouldn't have needed such a thing to keep track of the movements of the Strike Force. He could've done it simply by looking out his window."

Had Detective Witt agreed to meet with me a second time, I would have asked him whether the police deliberately protected McRae from the early 1980s to the early 2000s and beyond—and, if so, why. Although Henry is convinced that the police protected McRae because his birth father was a high-ranking VPD officer, I have been unable to confirm or rule out that hypothesis.

•••

CONTRARY TO THE Court of Appeal's conclusion that the Smallman evidence does not necessarily mean that Henry "is innocent of the offences for which he was convicted," the similarities between the two sets of crimes suggest that Donald McRae is the perpetrator of the Henry crimes.

As early as November 1980, the police, concerned about a "rip-off rapist" in Vancouver, knew that Henry lived and worked nowhere near the three Vancouver neighbourhoods—Mount Pleasant, Marpole, and Kitsilano—where the crimes took place. In March 1982, Jessie Henry moved, for reasons never explained, from Richmond, a suburb of Vancouver, into a home directly across the street from McRae (See insert 1, bottom.)

Shortly thereafter, she began informing on Henry to the police.

CHAPTER 59

McRAE

I n January 2009, Court of Appeal justice Mary Saunders dealt with an application by the Crown for a one-month publication ban on McRae's name. In granting it, she noted that the Crown wanted "an opportunity to contact him before his name is broadcast in connection with the reopening, thereby to provide him an opportunity to address the issue if he wishes to do so." On February 26, she extended the ban "until further notice of this Court." Noting that "Mr. X" was on parole and living in a halfway house (in fact, the Parole Board had dispatched him, after two parole breaches, to live in a high-security community correctional centre), she said that he was entitled, unless charged and convicted of the Henry crimes, to the presumption of innocence:

> The reporting of Mr. X's personal circumstances, combined with inflammatory demands by the media that his parole be revoked and statements that he is a "prime suspect" and a "dangerous sexual predator" being allowed to "live anonymously among us," mean that Mr. X's privacy and even security interests will be at risk if his name is published—more so than in the usual case of persons suspected but uncharged.
>
> If our society takes seriously the proposition that a person in Mr. X's position is presumed innocent until proven guilty, it seems to me that the deleterious effects, both on his privacy interests and on the administration of justice, of the publication of his name do outweigh the public interest in knowing that fact.

In 2012, Court of Appeal chief justice Lance Finch granted my application to lift the publication ban.[1] He wrote: "Many individuals are in a similar position to Mr. McRae and yet are unable to shield themselves from media attention. Mr. McRae has received a three-year reprieve from such attention, but I can see no reason why it is necessary for that reprieve to continue."

In March 2013, the Parole Board of Canada sent me a copy of McRae's parole documents. The panel that granted him day parole in September 2008 expressed a number of reservations:

> While [the three sexual assaults to which McRae pleaded guilty in 2005] are your only convictions for sex-related crimes, file information suggests you were a suspect in several more sexual offences committed between 1980 and the early 1990s . . . Your criminal record confirms that you have remained criminally active for over thirty years, and incurred almost 50 convictions for mostly property-related offences . . . Your community supervision history is not positive . . . You have little regard for court-imposed sanctions or community supervision conditions.
>
> Risk factors include: though purporting to have no memory of the sexual assaults, the claim of amnesia is not supported by other professionals; behaviour indicates little care for the law or the rights or feelings of others; though possessed of marketable skills, you chose to resort to property crimes and petty thefts; a 2005 psychological assessment indicates that, although the index offences predate the head injuries, the factors leading to those crimes "might still be present and, as such, the level of risk remains."

Twice, McRae's parole had been suspended—once, when a urinalysis test revealed that he had used cocaine, and a second time when he breached the condition that all his friendships with females must be reported.

In granting him day parole in September 2008, the board took the unusual step of imposing a residency requirement. As noted, rather than installing McRae in a halfway house, the board required him to live in a secure facility without leave privileges of any kind. In so doing, the board said:

You require the structure, support, and close monitoring that a CCC or CRF provides, in order to keep you free of substances and to assist in monitoring your relationships with women.

Without close monitoring and residing in a structured environment, your risk to reoffend is high.

You have no visible community support or employment prospects, and accordingly leave privileges will not be allowed.

From all accounts, McRae spent the remainder of his sentence housed at CSC's Regional Treatment Centre—a maximum-security facility in the Fraser Valley east of Vancouver. He was released only when the law required it—June 14, 2010, the day his warrant expired.

Since then, he has been a free man. Despite my efforts, I have been unable to locate him. His last known whereabouts is Surrey, BC.

CHAPTER 60

THE QUESTION OF INNOCENCE

The civil suit that Ivan Henry launched in 2011 against the City of Vancouver, various VPD members, the Crown, the Province, and the federal government alleges malicious prosecution, negligence, and *Charter* breaches. It seeks unspecified damages, including for loss of liberty; loss of reputation; loss of privacy while in prison; humiliation and disgrace; pain and suffering; loss of enjoyment of life; loss of usual, everyday life experiences; loss of developmental experiences; subjugation to prison life; physical, emotional, and psychological harm; past loss of income; loss of opportunity to earn income; and lost benefits. In response, the defendants have constructed every roadblock imaginable—most galling to Henry, the suggestion that he is almost certainly guilty as charged. In its statement of defence, the City of Vancouver emphasizes that "acquittal" does not equate to factual innocence.

The 2010 Court of Appeal expressly declined to declare Henry factually innocent. It said that even if the Smallman material were to be admitted in a new trial regarding the "propensity of another suspect," the Crown could lead evidence about Henry's attempted-rape conviction in 1976 and his self-admitted break and enter in 1982. It also said this:

> [I]t cannot be said that the Smallman evidence . . . leads one to conclude that [Mr. Henry] is innocent of the offences for which he was convicted. It does not exonerate him. At best, it is evidence that might be admitted at a new trial under the law relating to other suspects, not on the basis that it disproves the element of identity, but on the basis that it is capable of raising a reasonable doubt on that issue . . .

It is not at all clear that a trial judge would find it to be relevant and admissible, in whole or in part, as "other suspect evidence."

Even if it had been so inclined, the Court of Appeal would almost certainly not have declared Henry innocent. Indeed, no court in Canada has ever declared a person claiming actual innocence to be factually innocent. Without legislative change empowering our courts to make such findings, they will likely continue to view their jurisdiction as being confined to decisions of "guilty" or "not guilty."

Yet how do we square that with the presumption of innocence, the bedrock of our criminal justice system? The *Canadian Charter of Rights and Freedoms* says that "any person charged with an offence has the right to be presumed innocent until proven guilty according to law in a fair and public hearing by an independent and impartial tribunal."

Once an accused is convicted, though, that presumption seems to disappear forever, even if the conviction was unlawful. The best hope for a wrongly convicted person—in the absence of either a ministerial pardon or a finding of innocence by a public inquiry commissioner—is to have a not-guilty verdict substituted for a guilty one. Why, when a wrongly convicted person is merely acquitted, must he wear forever the scarlet letter of guilt?

In the 1985 Supreme Court of Canada case *Grdic v. The Queen*, the court said that "an acquittal is the equivalent to a finding of innocence."[1] Further, "to reach behind an acquittal, to qualify it, is in effect to introduce the verdict of 'guilt not proven,' which is not, has never been, and should not be part of our law." The decision appears to say that being acquitted returns a person to his/her original state of innocence.

Asked about the *Grdic* case, the respected former Supreme Court of Canada justice Ian Binnie told me that, while the courts regard "not guilty" as equivalent to innocence for some purposes, as a general principle it is not equivalent. "All an acquittal says is that the Crown has failed to meet its onus of proof beyond a reasonable doubt," he said. "All sorts of people are acquitted whom the jury thinks are probably guilty but, because of lurking doubts, refuse to find guilt beyond a reasonable doubt. There have been suggestions to change the *Criminal Code* to provide for a verdict of factual innocence, just as there are proposals for a Scottish 'not proven' verdict. But, in the end," Judge Binnie said, "the acquitted person is protected by the presumption of innocence, not by a finding of innocence."

When Justice Binnie speaks of the acquitted person being "protected by the presumption of innocence," he is speaking in a narrow legal sense. For instance, a person cannot be charged with a crime for which he has already been acquitted.

However, for practical purposes, a (merely) acquitted person enjoys no such absolution, both in terms of compensation and in the eyes of the public. Hence, for many wrongly convicted people—most of whom have endured additional years of incarceration for the simple fact of maintaining their innocence—a post-release finding of (only) acquittal is unacceptable.

Steven Truscott's dogged pursuit of his "actual innocence claim is a testament to the man's endurance. Scheduled to hang on December 8, 1959, for the murder of Lynne Harper, Steven Truscott, then fourteen years old, was granted a temporary reprieve a month before his execution date. After serving ten years, he was found not guilty and released. Not content with anything short of proof of factual innocence, Truscott finally succeeded, in 2006, in having Harper's body exhumed. Tragically, too much time had passed to yield useful DNA. A year later, after reviewing nearly 250 fresh pieces of evidence, the Ontario Court of Appeal declared that, though Truscott's conviction represented a miscarriage of justice, it could not declare him innocent:

> Counsel for the appellant acknowledge that a declaration of innocence has no statutory basis.
>
> They accept that it would be most extraordinary for an appeal court to make a finding of factual innocence. Indeed, counsel have not pointed to any instance in which a Canadian appellate court has ever made such a declaration.
>
> Counsel submit, however, that criminal courts in the United Kingdom have from time to time, where justice demands it, pronounced an accused to be factually innocent, if the evidence justifies that declaration . . . They argue that the miscarriage of justice occasioned to the appellant can only be properly redressed by a declaration of his innocence.

(Mr. Truscott) has not demonstrated his factual innocence. To do so would be a most daunting task absent definitive forensic evidence such as DNA. Despite (his) best efforts, that kind of evidence is not available.[2]

Like Truscott, Henry has been deprived of forensic evidence—not just definitive forenisic evidence, but any forensic evidence—to categorically prove his innocence.

However, my hope is that an accumulation of factors explored in this book are proof enough. If not, how high a bar must one jump to erase the taint of guilt that clings to the merely acquitted?

CHAPTER 61

PROVING INNOCENCE

In 1935, the US Supreme Court said that, while a prosecutor "might strike hard blows, he is not at liberty to strike foul ones" or use "improper methods calculated to produce a wrongful conviction." The difficulty usually lies in defining prosecutorial misconduct.[1] As with defence lawyering, the criminal-procedure standards are, as Brandon Garrett says, "extremely forgiving" to prosecutors as well[2]—whether the claims involve the alleged concealment of evidence or the misleading of the jury in opening or closing arguments.

In a 1989 decision involving Susan Nelles—a nurse charged with, but ultimately vindicated of, poisoning four babies at the Hospital for Sick Children in Toronto—the Supreme Court of Canada rejected the rule of absolute immunity of prosecutors:

> There is no doubt that the policy considerations in favour of absolute immunity have some merit. But in my view those considerations must give way to the right of a private citizen to seek a remedy when the prosecutor acts maliciously in fraud of his duties with the result that he causes damage to the victim.[3]

Ten years later, the Supreme Court of Canada said that to succeed in an action for malicious prosecution, it must be shown not only that the prosecution was undertaken without reasonable and probable cause, but also that it was motivated by malice or a primary purpose other than carrying the law into effect.[4] Such "malice" does not include recklessness, nor does it include gross or poor judgment. It requires proof of either an "abuse of prosecutorial power" or the perpetuation of a "fraud on the process of criminal justice."

Although the BC Court of Appeal confirmed that high bar in a 2013 decision in the context of Henry's civil suit, the Supreme Court of Canada has recently allowed Henry to appeal that decision.[5] The hearing is scheduled for November 2014.

• • •

PART OF THE state's defence in Henry's malicious prosecution suit is that his innocence has not been established. But how easy is it to establish one's innocence beyond a reasonable doubt, on the balance of probabilities, thirty years after the fact? And if it cannot be so established, does that mean that the claim of malicious prosecution must fail, regardless of any fraud perpetrated by the Crown?

Without the presence of at least one of the following three things, proving innocence is virtually impossible for the wrongly convicted:

- DNA evidence excludes the plaintiff as the perpetrator;
- the plaintiff has a bulletproof alibi; and/or
- the actual perpetrator has confessed.

In Henry's case, medical records of the semen samples collected from four of the complainants were withheld from him at trial. The samples have since gone missing.

Prior to trial, the Crown failed to instruct the police to investigate Henry's alibi statement, which showed him to be nowhere near many of the crime scenes. While his evidence should have been enough to raise the reasonable doubt required for acquittal, Judge Bouck's jury charge was so confusing, it left the jurors mystified.

Although the future is finally looking brighter for Romeo Phillion, a man convicted in the 1967 murder of Ottawa firefighter Leopold Roy, Phillion spent thirty-one years in jail trying to prove that he was nowhere near the crime scene. After a suppressed 1968 police report came to light years later—a report providing material support to his alibi claim, his case was reopened and, in 2009, he was acquitted. In July 2014, the Ontario Court of Appeal allowed him to pursue a civil action against the police and the Crown.[6]

Regarding confession by a third party, it is unlikely to happen in this case. Although Donald James McRae was a suspect in the Henry crimes and went on to sexually assault an untold number of women after Henry's incarceration, the police, for reasons known only to them, closed their file on him. Whereas the possibility of his being the real perpetrator in the Henry crimes was front and centre in Henry's 2010 appeal—indeed, it was the discovery of the link between the Smallman and Henry crimes that led to the reopening of that appeal—the court based its acquittal decision on judicial error and flawed identification evidence.

CHAPTER 62

SILENT WITNESS

G iven that DNA exclusion, iron-clad alibi, and confession of
the actual perpetrator are not available to Henry, his case for
innocence is twofold: first, no physical evidence links him to a
single one of the crimes, and second, the actions of the state—both in
investigating and in prosecuting his crimes—strongly suggest that they
knew he was not the culprit.

Dr. Edmond Locard (1877–1966), known as the Sherlock Holmes
of France, formulated a basic principle—known as Locard's "Exchange
Principle"—of forensic science:

> Wherever he touches, whatever he leaves, even without
> consciousness, will serve as a silent witness against him—
> his fingerprints or his footprints, his hair, the fibers from
> his clothes, the glass he breaks, the tool mark he leaves,
> the paint he scratches, the blood or semen he deposits or
> collects.
>
> All of these and more bear mute witness against him.
>
> This is evidence that does not forget. It is not confused by
> the excitement of the moment. It is not absent because human
> witnesses are. It is factual evidence. Physical evidence cannot be
> wrong, it cannot perjure itself, it cannot be wholly absent. Only
> human failure to find it, study and understand it, can diminish
> its value.[1]

When a crime is committed, fragmentary (or trace) evidence—
any type of material left at, or taken from, a crime scene, or the

result of contact between two surfaces, such as shoes and the floor covering, or fibres from where someone sat on an upholstered chair—needs to be collected. Specialized police technicians seal the crime scene off. They shoot video and take photographs of the victim (if there is one) and items of evidence. If necessary, they undertake a firearms and ballistics examination. They check for shoe and tire-mark impressions, examine any vehicles and check for fingerprints.

In the Henry case, no physical evidence was found linking him to any of the crimes. Such exculpatory evidence as was found was concealed from him. Whoever the perpetrator was, he ejaculated, shed tissue, left fingerprints (and possibly footprints). Tool marks indicated that the doors had been jimmied open, but the police, who had Henry's work knife, ruled it out as the offending implement.

When identification officer Corporal Foster testified about the difficulty of obtaining fingerprints at crime scenes, the trial judge questioned the relevance of the evidence. When Crown counsel Judith Milliken said that "two identifiable prints" had been obtained from a broken glass in Miss Horvath's kitchen, Judge Bouck said, "But they don't relate to these crimes . . . Let's try to move it along." Corporal Foster then testified that despite an effort to match the recovered fingerprints with six sets of known prints, they remained unidentifiable.

Although Judge Bouck said that the fingerprints "don't relate to these crimes," they were relevant in their failure to incriminate Henry. They suggested a perpetrator other than him. As Peter Neufeld, co-founder of the Innocence Project in New York, told me during the 2013 Innocence Network Conference, the terms "non-identifiable" or "unidentifiable" are unscientific. "What we have found," Neufeld said, "is that police marginalize evidence when it is not helpful to their case. Police suffering from a cognitive bias and/or tunnel vision are inclined to label otherwise identifiable fingerprint evidence as unidentifiable when it tends to exclude the suspect." As Henry's counsel argued in 2010, Judge Bouck should have underscored the exculpatory potential of the fingerprint evidence; he should have made it clear that although the prints may well have belonged to the perpetrator, they were not those of the accused.

While the full extent of the recovered physical evidence is unknown, we do know the following:

- Fields said that her assailant "jimmied the window"—popped it out of its rails. The plants lining the window ledge had been moved . . . "The police dusted for fingerprints."

- When O'Reilly's attacker left, both gates were left open. "They dusted for fingerprints everywhere."

- The Identification Squad investigating Miss Simpson's assault took a print of an angled knife mark on the casing.

- Constable Esme Adams made a silicon cast of the fresh tool-mark impression he'd found on Kavanagh's door.

- In addition to the sperm samples listed in a later-disclosed, heavily redacted document excerpt, the following physical evidence—"seized, obtained, and/or collected" from the victims—was later disclosed:

  - 81-25598 (May 5, 1981): Possible prints on door and screen.
  - 81-39111 (July 6, 1981): PC 768 attended for prints and photographs.
  - 81-62146 (October 17, 1981): Ident attended, took possible prints.
  - 82-15245 (March 10, 1982): Prints visible on window.
  - 82-30158 (May 14, 1982): T-shirt worn by victim, pubic hairs from bed of victim, gripping fingerprints, thumbprint.
  - 82-36128 (June 8, 1982): Property initialed and tagged by PC 644, science locker no. 10. Examination for possible seminal stains.
  - Property evidence: < > (expurgated) < > (expurgated)

The document further states: "82-14452 (March 6, 1982): Suspect taken into custody and questioned." Undisclosed was the identity of the suspect in question.

When I told Detective Montgomery that the state had nothing, other than the lineup identification, on Henry, he shook his head in disbelief. "It can't be," he said. "Not after all those crimes."

"It's true," I said. "The police 'lost' the semen samples. Not a hair or fingerprint or fibre—nothing was found linking Henry to the crimes." Montgomery just sat there, head bowed in his hands.

CHAPTER 63

THE LEGAL TRACK

For the wrongfully convicted in Canada, the road to compensation is a long, hard one. As of fall 2014, Ivan Henry has received no compensation for the horrific waste of half his life. Powerless as ever, he waits while the defendants' high-priced legal team argues that he's the author of his own misfortune and otherwise attempts to block or minimize his claim. As noted, the Supreme Court of Canada has agreed to hear his claim that prosecutors may be sued—not just for malicious prosecution, but for negligence as well.

Other positive changes are afoot in the area of wrongful conviction. In 2007, prosecutor George Dangerfield, the man many believe to be responsible for the wrongful conviction of James Driskell, moved unsuccessfully to strike certain pleadings from Driskell's statement of claim for malicious prosecution. Calling the law "unsettled" as to whether malicious prosecution applies when the police or Crown have conducted a "flawed investigation resulting in a wrongful prosecution or conviction," the court declined to strike the claim in negligence.[1] Following that decision, the defendants settled with Driskell for $4 million.

I earlier recounted the recent victory in the Phillion case, and, in March 2014, the Supreme Court of Canada granted Réjean Hinse leave to appeal a decision of the Quebec Appeal Court that denied him compensation for what the trial court judge had called "institutional indifference."[2] Convicted in 1964 of aggravated robbery, Hinse presented justice minister after justice minister with an affidavit from his fellow accused saying that Hinse had nothing to do with the brutal crime for which they had been convicted. Time and again, notwithstanding those affidavits and his claim that he was two hundred kilometres away from the crime scene, he was met with a closed door.

After the Quebec Police Commission concluded in 1989 that Hinse was the victim of "a botched investigation," his conviction was quashed by the Quebec Court of Appeal. In 1997, he was acquitted by the Supreme Court of Canada. In 2011, before a judgment was delivered, the province settled for $4.5 million. At the end of the trial involving Hinse's claim against the federal government, the Quebec Superior Court ordered the defendant to pay nearly $5.8 million.

In her lengthy reasons for judgment, the trial judge castigated the federal government for what she called its "institutional indifference":

> Need we recall that, for three decades Hinse sought the help of at least eight different Federal Justice Ministers, a number of Solicitor Generals and their deputies, several officials from the Canadian penitentiary service and the Parole Board, various officials, Minsters' advisors and other people in authority within the Federal Government. None of them were ever worried about the alarm bell he was ringing.
>
> Considering the foregoing, the Court is of the opinion that, as a result of its negligence, the federal government has failed to grant, to the numerous and insistent requests of Hinse, the seriousness and diligence that they merited. This wrongful conduct, which is spread over a period of forty years, is the fruit of an irresponsible attitude. If the [Justice Minister] had acted promptly and competently, the miscarriage of justice would have been rapidly identified.
>
> This legal bungling is enough to give one vertigo!
>
> What more to ask of an individual who has been wrongfully convicted, and who has unceasingly protested his innocence? To whom else can he inquire to find an outlet while he is still imprisoned?
>
> Regardless of who will provide the solution, Hinse begs: the light must be shone on this. While time is slipping through his fingers, and while documents are sent to the wrong people, the authorities do not act. It is particularly noteworthy that, around 1971, he charges forth once again only to see his requests for

clemency denied: however, he will never be told why. In 1980, when Hinse asked the Justice Minister to "reopen" his legal file, the latter would demand that he specify the steps he had taken up until then, making abstraction of 13 years of toil. He would rebuild his life piece by piece. As all the doors closed before him, he would then request a Royal Commission of Inquiry from three succeeding Justice Ministers.

Nobody would take him seriously.[3]

In summary, Canadians are standing on the brink of possibly sweeping changes in the area of wrongful conviction law. The highest court in the land has the opportunity to breathe much-needed oxygen into the "life, liberty, and security of the person" guaranteed to every person by Section 7 of the *Charter of Rights and Freedoms*.

Like Hinse, Ivan Henry pleaded with numerous federal justice ministers over a quarter century—Mark MacGuigan, Donald Johnston, John Crosbie, Ray Hnatyshyn, Joe Clark, Doug Lewis, Kim Campbell, Pierre Blais, Allan Rock, Anne McLellan, Martin Cauchon, Irwin Cotler, Vic Toews, and Rob Nicholson—to review his file and in particular the lineup photo. Not a single judge, bureaucrat, or politician took his claim of evidence fabrication seriously.

If this book aids in a just, fair, timely settlement of Henry's civil lawsuit or contributes to the development of the law in a positive way, it will have served an important purpose. In addition, I would urge Parliament to consider the establishment of an independent body whereby convicted persons claiming innocence may be heard and, if successful, receive compensation appropriate to the circumstances of their case.

CHAPTER 64

DIRE STRAITS

H ow just is a system that fails to accord every accused—rich or poor, with or without a criminal record—the presumption of innocence? What does it say when a society cares more about hockey scores and celebrity breakups than about an innocent man being unjustly convicted, the keys to his freedom thrown away?

Many innocent people "confess" to crimes to shorten jail time or avoid it altogether. Others, like Henry, refuse to back down. How just is a system in which innocent people who refuse to confess fare worse than either guilty offenders or innocent people who confess to crimes they did not commit?

How fair is a system that requires a wrongly convicted person to prove his innocence—after three decades of incarceration due to egregious conduct on the part of the state—before he receives compensation?

Better safeguards are in place today than existed in Henry's time. Police are held to stricter standards for the composition and conduct of lineups and interviews. Yet, police are still prone to tunnel vision. There will always be prosecutors who, cloaked in near-immunity, place winning ahead of justice, and there will always be judges, especially where the accused is unrepresented, who align themselves with the Crown early on in the trial.

At this writing, Ivan Henry is in dire straits.[1] A senior citizen, adrift, with no résumé, he's landed nothing but a few odd jobs. Four years after his release, he barely makes do on an old-age pension that takes no account of the decades he spent toiling in prison kitchens and laundries, sewing shops, and warehouses. Every cent he earned behind bars—at most, $5.25 per eight-hour shift, plus the little he received from other inmates for helping with their cases—went into his fight to regain his freedom: photocopies, court filing fees, stamps.

Entrenched in institutional thinking, traumatized by having been treated as guilty, he's left to his own devices. He receives no official help in finding employment and housing, building meaningful relationships, or becoming financially self-sufficient. Without a credit rating or job history, he faces the long, dismal, usually impossible task of clearing his name. And he faces an uphill battle to obtain reasonable compensation for his years behind bars. As retired Supreme Court of Canada justice Peter Cory wrote in *The Inquiry Regarding Thomas Sophonow*, this situation is intolerable:

> As a result of confinement in a penal institution, an individual is deprived of personal liberty. Liberty is at the core of the essential rights of a citizen of a democratic country. The *Magna Carta*, the Great Charter of 1215, provides in essence that no free man is to be arbitrarily deprived of his liberties. This concept has been a cornerstone of democracy for nearly 800 years.
>
> Freedom and liberty are the bedrock concepts of Canadian rights, as they are of all democracies. The *Canadian Charter of Rights and Freedoms* provides in Section 7 that no Canadian is to be deprived of that freedom without a fair trial before an impartial judge and jury.
>
> Capricious imprisonment deprives citizens of the State of their most basic right of liberty.
>
> Wrongful conviction has dire consequences for the individual. The wrongfully convicted must experience the same sense of outrage, frustration, isolation and deprivation as those capriciously imprisoned by tyrants. The result is the same for both victims.
>
> It must have very serious consequences for the State when it wrongfully takes away from one of its citizens that basic and fundamental right to liberty. It demonstrates the failure of our system of justice. Failures lead to a lack of confidence in police and the courts. That, in turn, can lead to a fear that anyone may be wrongfully convicted and imprisoned.

Society must do all that is humanly possible to prevent wrongful convictions and, when they occur, to adequately and fairly compensate the victim.[2]
[ITALICS ADDED FOR EMPHASIS.]

In their 2003 book, *Actual Innocence*, authors Barry Scheck, Peter Neufeld, and Jim Dwyer point out that the criminal justice system is alone in exempting itself from self-examination. "Wrongful convictions are seen not as catastrophes but topics to be avoided."[3]

On March 30, 2000, then-Conservative backbencher Peter MacKay, exhorting the government to act quickly on the Steven Truscott file, said in Question Period in the House of Commons:

> The Truscott case, as we know, has been a festering wound on the psyche of this nation and casts a shadow over the entire criminal justice system.
>
> The case against Truscott was based on ambiguous, circumstantial and inconsistent testimony from children, impossible medical analysis of the murder victim and Mr. Truscott himself.
>
> It seems obvious that the irregularity surrounding the investigation and subsequent trial and the new evidence warrant a full inquiry. In the pursuit of justice and public confidence, will the Minister of Justice commit to conducting a full public inquiry upon receipt of Mr. Truscott's application?

Hopefully, Peter MacKay, now Canada's justice minister, will soon apply that same principled position to the case of Ivan Henry.

Whether it be the courts or the justice minister who makes the ultimate decisions regarding Henry's actual innocence and malicious prosecution claim, one can only hope that justice is finally served—that the defendants acknowledge Henry's actual innocence and apologize to him and that he is paid the compensation he deserves.

EPILOGUE

On instructions from his lawyers, Ivan Henry refused to talk to me for several months as this book was nearing completion. "Anything I say to you," he said, "might be subpoenaed by the other side." I held my tongue and waited for him to come around. Then, early one morning, he phoned out of the blue and said he'd meet after all. "You're worse than a dog with a bone," he said, half-playful, half-growling. "What do you want to ask me?"

"Just this and that, I said, eyeing my growing list of questions. "Nothing to cause you upset."

Minutes later, by coincidence, I got an email from Tom Sophonow— asking, as usual, if I'd heard from Ivan. Before long, the three of us had agreed on a plan. After picking up Henry in North Vancouver, I'd drive us out to meet Sophonow at one of New Westminster's tonier pubs.

For months, I'd been trying to orchestrate this get-together. Unlike Ivan, who keeps to himself, Tom stays in touch with many wrongly convicted people: David Milgaard, Romeo Phillion, Guy Paul Morin, Norman Fox, Steven Truscott. True to Sophonow's vow when he was exonerated in 2000, he has continued to act as an advocate and spokesperson for people wrongly convicted of crimes. As he recently told me, "I offer my services by testifying on behalf of other victims of wrongful conviction. I want to help people in a similar situation keep the justice system's feet to the fire."

When Ivan was released in 2009, Sophonow offered to put up his $10,000 bail money. After Henry was acquitted, Tom offered him a job helping to restore the heritage house he'd bought ten years earlier with part of his $2.6 million settlement. When that job didn't work out, Ivan, feelings bruised, broke off contact. Ever since I met Tom, his wife, and his daughter in 2013, I'd been trying to reconnect the two men—Henry with his stormy past, and Sophonow with his quiet, contemplative nature belying the fact he is seven years Henry's junior.

At the pub, two minutes into ice water, half-price ribs, and other appetizers, the men were acting like best buddies. "I got my learner's licence today," said Ivan. "Yup, on the second try—first time I failed 6 out of 15—they said I passed 14 to 15. Some joke. I didn't answer two of the questions."

Reminiscing about the penitentiary at Prince Albert, Tom said, "If only you'd got there sooner, you could have gotten a cooking job like I did—in the kitchen, five dollars a day."

"Yeah, bad timing," chuckled Ivan. "The only thing left was a kitchen cleaner position—$1.60 a day."

The stories came spilling out—the crazies in prison, the suicides, the murders, the jailhouse informants like the one responsible for Tom's conviction. An inmate testified under oath that Tom had confessed to murder, a total fabrication.

"Did you ever consider prison your home?" asked Tom.

"Never," said Ivan. "Two weeks before my release date—it hadn't sunk in that I'd soon be leaving—my bags were packed and ready to go. Though I accepted my sentence, never once did I make myself feel comfortable."

"I know what you mean," said Tom. "When I got to Stony Mountain, some goof pressed me to sign a form saying if I didn't admit to my crime, there'd be no privileges: no visitors, no canteen, no access to the yard. Though I scrunched up the paper and threw it to the ground, I got the privileges anyway."

When talk turned to my book, Tom threw his arm around Ivan and said, "Go on that book tour with Joan, you hear? You need to be there, rekindling all the old memories, the experiences you went through. It's you the public will want to see, not her. Man, oh man, you'll end up, just like me, running from TV station to radio station. You'll be running around like crazy! Hell, in one place I spoke—some kind of panel discussion with lawyer Peter Wilson and a bunch of prosecutors—I got a standing ovation. Nothing feels better than that, man. Never in my life did I think I'd get a standing ovation."

When I asked Tom if he'd come to the book launch, he said, "That's Ivan's time. I wouldn't want to rain on his parade."

"Hey, man," said Ivan, "none of that 'rain' talk. You'd be there for support."

I asked Ivan—almost five years to the day after his release—how he was doing. "I guess I'm finally moving on," he said, "like getting my learner's licence. But I want to get rid of the baggage I've been dragging along. I never want to see another goddamn judge in my life. Just pay me what's fair and reasonable, and I'll close that chapter."

When Tom went to put more coins in the parking meter, I asked Ivan: "You having fun?"

"Why not?" he said, grinning. "They say that he who belly laughs has no time to bellyache."

"If you do get a ton of money," said Tom, sliding back into his seat, "what will you do?"

"Move to Alberta," Ivan said. "Lots of cattle, flat land. Hell, you can look down the road and see eighty miles straight out."

"Why not move to Saskatchewan, or Manitoba?"

"No," says Henry. "Let the ashes lie where they lie."

Hunched over my computer, Ivan showed Tom pictures of the two doctored lineup photos. "I'm not there, you see," he said. "It's just my head. And you know what that bastard judge did? He hung it in the judges' lunchroom so they could all have a great laugh."

During Ivan's early days in prison, he wrote his first appeal submissions using dried-up felt pens dipped in ink mixed with kerosene. Not long after I began work on this book, he gave me a gift—a brand-new rollerball pen. The symbol, he said, of freedom fighters everywhere. At the pub, I took notes with that pen. After Tom headed home in his vintage Mustang, and I was driving Ivan back to Vancouver to visit an old kitchen-steward friend from his Mountain prison days, I asked if he remembered what he'd said when he gave me that pen.

"I sure do," he said, eyes twinkling. "I said, 'Let's go after McRae. Hire a private detective, whatever it takes. After all the years I spent profiling perverts, I'm betting that bastard is still on the prowl.'"

"Three and a half years later," I said, "are you still keen?"

"You can bet your life on it."

NOTES

PROLOGUE

1. R. v. Henry, [2009] B.C.C.A. 12 (British Columbia Court of Appeal).
2. R. v. Henry, [2010] B.C.C.A. 462 (British Columbia Court of Appeal).

CHAPTER 3—CAT AND MOUSE

1. Skogman v. The Queen, [1984] 2 S.C.R. 93, p. 105 (Supreme Court of Canada).

CHAPTER 7—KILL ALL THE LAWYERS

1. R. v. Demers, [1926] 4 D.L.R. 991 (Quebec Superior Court).
2. R. v. Cleghorn, [1995] 3 S.C.R. 175 (Supreme Court of Canada).
3. Richard Peck, recipient of a Q.C. (Queen's Counsel) designation in 1987, is today one of the country's pre-eminent criminal lawyers. Mr. Peck is also a founder of the UBC Law Innocence Project, an organization that advocates on behalf of wrongly convicted prisoners.

CHAPTER 16—DOWN BUT NOT OUT

1. Michael Yates, *Line Screw: My Twelve Riotous Years Working behind Bars in Some of Canada's Toughest Jails* (Toronto: McClelland & Stewart, 1993), 173–74.

CHAPTER 18—CON-AIR

1. Adam Gopnik, "The Caging of America," *The New Yorker*, January 20, 2012.
2. Charles Dickens, *American Notes for General Circulation* (London: Bradbury and Evans, 1842).

CHAPTER 19—GARBAGE

1. R. v. Henry, [1984] CA001505 (B.C.C.A.).
2. Section 690 of the *Criminal Code* provided that the minister of justice may review a conviction if new evidence of a compelling nature emerges. Under this appeal of last resort, the minister can uphold the original conviction, order a new trial, or issue a pardon. The success rate of such applications is, and always has been, extremely low.

CHAPTER 23—THE RAZOR'S EDGE

1. Nelson Mandela, "Nelson Mandela's Address to a Rally in Cape Town on His Release from Prison," February 11, 1990. anc.org.za/show.php?id=4520.
2. The report, authored by Chief Justice T. Alexander Hickman (Chairman), Associate Chief Justice Lawrence A. Poitras (Commissioner), and the Honourable Mr. Gregory T. Evans, Q.C. (Commissioner), was published in December 1989.
3. August 10, Prisoners' Justice Day, commemorates all the men and women who have died of unnatural causes inside Canadian prisons.

CHAPTER 25—YELLOW PAGES

1. Henry v. Canada (Minister of Justice), [1992] 54 F.T.R. 153 (Federal Court of Canada).

CHAPTER 28—A FRIEND IN NEED

1. Palmer v. The Queen, [1980] 1 S.C.R. 759 (Supreme Court of Canada).
2. R. v. G.H. Weber, [May 6, 1997] (unreported), Registry number CA022409, 4.
3. R. v. Henry [1997] B.C.J. No. 2792 (Q.L.); leave to appeal refused [1998], S.C.C.A. No. 77.

CHAPTER 29—GONE IN A FLASH

1. Peter MacKay, March 30, 2000, openparliament.ca/debates/2000/3/30/peter-mackay-2/only/.
2. Julian Sher, "Rubin 'Hurricane' Carter and Steven Truscott Refused to be Condemned by History," CBC.ca, April 21, 2014. cbc.ca/news/canada/rubin-hurricane-carter-and-steven-truscott-refused-to-be-condemned-by-history-1.2616843

CHAPTER 31—A RAY OF HOPE

1. "Ontario Man Wants Assault Conviction Overturned after Bernardo Confession," CBC.ca, June 20, 2008. cbc.ca/news/canada/ontario-man-wants-assault-conviction-overturned-after-bernardo-confession-1.719749.

CHAPTER 33—FREE AT LAST

1. McEwen v. BC (Attorney General), [2013] BCSC 517 (BC Supreme Court).

CHAPTER 36—DETAINED FOR QUESTIONING

1. R. v. Wade, [1967] 388 U.S. 218 (Supreme Court of the United States).
2. "Clifford Olson," allserialkillers.com/clifford_olson.htm.

CHAPTER 37—LINEUP IDENTIFICATION

1. Robert J. Stewart, "The Buck Stops Nowhere: A Discussion paper," December 18, 2006. bannerline.net/pdf/rjs-police2007-1.pdf

CHAPTER 38—TEN WEEKS

1. R. v. Regan, [2002] 1 S.C.R. 297 (Supreme Court of Canada).

CHAPTER 39: TATTERED SCARECROW

1. Wallace Gilby Craig, *Short Pants to Striped Trousers: The Life and Times of a Judge in Skid Row Vancouver* (self-published, 2003).
2. William Shakespeare, *Measure for Measure*, 2.1.1–4.
3. U.S.A. v. Shephard [1977] 2 SCR 1067 (S.C.C.).

CHAPTER 40—WHITEWASH

1. *The Report of the Governor's Commission on Capital Punishment*, submitted to George H. Ryan, Governor of Illinois, April 15, 2005, 105.
2. Jerome P. Kennedy, "Writing the Wrongs: The Role of Defence Counsel in Wrongful Convictions," *Canadian Journal of Criminology and Criminal Justice* 46, issue 2 (2004), 198.
3. In R. v. Jewitt [1985] 2 S.C.R. 128, the leading case on the subject, the Supreme Court of Canada stated that judicial stays of proceedings are "tantamount to a judgement or verdict of acquittal" and subject to appeal by the Crown.

CHAPTER 41—CONTAMINATION

1. Elizabeth Loftus and Katherine Ketcham, *Witness for the Defense: The Accused, the Eyewitness, and the Expert Who Puts Memory on Trial* (New York: St. Martin's Press, 1991), 20–21.
2. Elizabeth Loftus, *Eyewitness Testimony* (Cambridge, MA: Harvard University Press, 1996).

CHAPTER 42—MEMORY IMPLANTATION

1. Council on Scientific Affairs, American Medical Association, "Scientific Status of Refreshing Recollection by the Use of Hypnosis," *Journal of the American Medical Association* 253 (1985), 1918–19.
2. R. v. Trochym, [2007] 1 S.C.R. 239 (Supreme Court of Canada).
3. Section 649 of the *Criminal Code* prohibits jurors from disclosing the content of their deliberation. It does not prohibit them from passing on their personal impressions of the trial.
4. Loftus and Ketcham, *Witness for the Defense*, 117.
5. William Saletan, "The Memory Doctor," *Slate Magazine*, June 4, 2010. slate. me/KyxWOV.

CHAPTER 43—I WAS WRONG

1. Brandon L. Garrett, *Convicting the Innocent: Where Criminal Prosecutions Go Wrong* (Cambridge, MA: Harvard University Press, 2012).
2. R. v. Atfield, [1983] 25 Alta. L.R. (2d) 97 (Alberta Court of Appeal).
3. R. v. Smierciak, [1946] 87 C.C.C. 175 (Ontario Court of Appeal).
4. FPT Heads of Prosecutions Committee, *Report of the Working Group on the Prevention of Miscarriages of Justice* (Department of Justice, 2012), 50.
5. Loftus and Ketcham, *Witness for the Defense*, 13.
6. Jennifer Thompson, "I Was Certain, but I Was Wrong," *New York Times*, June 18, 2000.
7. Jennifer Thompson-Cannino, Ronald Cotton, and Erin Torneo, *Picking Cotton: Our Memoir of Injustice and Redemption* (New York: St. Martin's Press, 2009).

CHAPTER 44—BLUE 3

1. R. v. Thursfield, [1838] 173 E.R. 490 (British House of Lords).
2. R. v. Boucher [1955] S.C.R. 16, 23–24 (Supreme Court of Canada).
3. Neal Hall, "Veteran Prosecutor Spotted Similarities between Sex Cases," *Vancouver Sun*, January 17, 2009.
4. Michael Naughton, *The Innocent and the Criminal Justice System: A Sociological Analysis of Miscarriages of Justice* (Basingstoke, UK: Palgrave Macmillan, 2013).
5. R. v. Stinchcombe, [1991] 3 S.C.R. 326, 333–36 (Supreme Court of Canada).
6. Pierre v. Lil'Wat Nation, [1999] B.C.J. 17 (British Columbia Supreme Court).

CHAPTER 45—THE TROPHY

1. Ian Mulgrew, "Trial Judge Defends Ivan Henry's Conviction," *National Post*, January 16, 2009.

CHAPTER 46—TUNNEL VISION

1. *The Inquiry Regarding Thomas Sophonow: The Investigation, Prosecution and Consideration of Entitlement to Compensation* (Manitoba Justice, 2001), 37.
2. R. v. Feldman, [1994] 42 B.C.A.C. 31, paras. 34–35, 66; affirmed, 93 C.C.C. (3d) 575 (Supreme Court of Canada).
3. R. v. Miaponoose, [1996] 110 C.C.C. (3d) 445 (Ontario Court of Appeal).
4. R. v. Khelawon, [2006] 2 S.C.R. 787 (Supreme Court of Canada).
5. R. v. Handy, [2002] 2 S.C.R. 908 (Supreme Court of Canada).
6. Offutt v. United States, [1954] 348 U.S. 11, 14 (Supreme Court of the United States).
7. MaDonna Maidment, *When Justice Is a Game: Unravelling Wrongful Convictions* (Black Point, NS: Fernwood Publishing, 2010), 47.
8. *The Lamer Commission of Inquiry Pertaining to the Cases of: Ronald Dalton, Gregory Parsons, Randy Druken.* (St. John's, NL: Office of the Queen's Printer, 2006), 75.

CHAPTER 47—ELSEWHERE

1. R. v. Blackmore, [1971] 2 O.R. 21 (Ontario Court of Appeal).
2. R. v. Cleghorn, [1995] 3 S.C.R. 175 (Supreme Court of Canada).

CHAPTER 48—MEDICAL EVIDENCE

1. *Report of the Commission of Inquiry into the Wrongful Conviction of David Milgaard* (Regina: Queen's Printer, 2008), 519.

CHAPTER 49—MORE JUDICIAL ERRORS

1. United States v. Burkhart, 458 F.2d 201, 204 (10th Cir. 1972).
2. Canada Evidence Act, R.S.C., s. 12 (1) (1985) (Canada).
3. R. v. Corbett, [1988] 41 S.C.C. (3d) 385 (Supreme Court of Canada).
4. Marcoux and Solomon v. The Queen, [1976] 1 S.C.R. 763 (Supreme Court of Canada).

CHAPTER 50—FRIEND OF THE COURT

1. Joan McEwen, "Ivan Henry: Self-represented Accused and the Trial Judge's Duty to Assist," *The Advocate* 70, part 4 (July 2012).

2. The right to silence is protected under sections 7 and 11 (c) of the *Charter*. Because an accused may not be compelled as a witness against himself in criminal proceedings, only voluntary statements made to police are admissible as evidence. Prior to an accused being informed of his/her right to legal counsel, statements made to police are considered involuntarily compelled and are inadmissible as evidence.

3. See, for example, Elliott C. Crawford's excellent blog post: okdefense.com/pros-cons-defendant-testifying/.

4. United States v. Burkhart, 458 F.2d 201, 204 (10th Cir. 1972).

5. Leonard T. Doust, Q.C., *Foundation for Change: Report of the Public Commission on Legal Aid in British Columbia* (Vancouver: Public Commission on Legal Aid), 2011.

6. R. v. Smierciak, [1946] 87 C.C.C. 175 (Ontario Court of Appeal).

7. R. v. Ryan, [2012] N.L.C.A. 9. (Newfoundland and Labrador Court of Appeal).

8. Brandon L. Garrett, *Convicting the Innocent: Where Criminal Prosecutions Go Wrong* (Cambridge, MA: Harvard University Press, 2012).

9. Naughton, *The Innocent and the Criminal Justice System.*

10. Garrett, *Convicting the Innocent.*

CHAPTER 52—CUT AND PASTE

1. FPT Heads of Prosecutions Committee, *Report of the Working Group on the Prevention of Miscarriages of Justice* (Department of Justice, 2012), 115.

CHAPTER 53—THE MAY 13 PHOTO

1. F. Lee Bailey, *The Defense Never Rests* (New York: Stein and Day, 1971), 179.

CHAPTER 54—WANT OF PROSECUTION

1. Criminal Appeal Rules (June 30, 1972), as noted in B.C. Supreme Court Rules, B.C.S.C., s. 9 (1) (1975) (Canada).

2. R. v. Henry, [1997] B.C.J. No. 2792 (Q.L.).

3. R. v. G.H. Weber, [May 6, 1997] (unreported), Registry number CA022409, 4.

CHAPTER 55—CONFESS OF FORFEIT

1. Kim Bolan, "Ivan Henry Exposed Himself to Female Prison Staff," *Vancouver Sun*, January 21, 2009.

CHAPTER 56—WRONGFUL LIBERTY

1. Frank Baumgartner, "The Mayhem of Wrongful Liberty: Documenting the Crimes of True Perpetrators in Cases of Wrongful Incarceration" (paper presented at the Innocence Network Conference, Portland, OR, April 11–12, 2014).

2. R. v. McRae (unreported, June 15, 2005); File No. 161766-2-DC; Vancouver registry (Provincial Court of BC).

CHAPTER 58—THE GABRIEL REPORT

1. Ronald M. Holmes and Stephen T. Holmes, *Profiling Violent Crimes: An Investigative Tool, 3rd edition* (Thousand Oaks, CA: SAGE, 2002), 145–48.
2. G. Gabriel, *Case Analysis: Project Smallman*, April 8, 2004.

CHAPTER 59—McRAE

1. R. v. Henry, [2012] B.C.C.A. 374 (BC Court of Appeal).

CHAPTER 60—THE QUESTION OF INNOCENCE

1. Grdic v. The Queen, [1985] 1 S.C.R. 810 (Supreme Court of Canada).
2. *Re Truscott*, 2007 ON.C.A. 575, paras. 252 ff (Ontario Court of Appeal).

CHAPTER 61—PROVING INNOCENCE

1. Berger v. United States, 295 U.S. 78 (1935) (Supreme Court of the United States).
2. Garrett, *Convicting the Innocent*.
3. Nelles v. Ontario, [1989] 2 S.C.R. 170 (Supreme Court of Canada).
4. Miazga v. Kvello Estate, [2009] 3 S.C.R. 339 (Supreme Court of Canada).
5. Henry v. British Columbia (Attorney General), [2014] B.C.C.A. 15 (BC Court of Appeal; leave to appeal to the Supreme Court of Canada was granted on May 15, 2014.)
6. Phillion v. Ontario (Attorney General), [2014] ONCA 567 (Ontario Court of Appeal).

CHAPTER 62—SILENT WITNESS

1. Paul L. Kirk, *Crime investigation: Physical Evidence and the Police Laboratory* (New York: Interscience Publishers, 1953).

CHAPTER 63—THE LEGAL TRACK

1. Driskell v. Dangerfield et al., [2007] M.B.Q.B. 142 (Manitoba Court of Queen's Bench).
2. Hinse v. Quebec (Procureur general), [2014] CarswellQue 1568 (Supreme Court of Canada.
3. Hinse v. Quebec (Procureur general), [2011] R.J.Q. 794 (Quebec Superior Court, District of Montreal).

CHAPTER 64—DIRE STRAITS

1. Joan McEwen, "Vancouver's Ivan Henry Finally Released," *Vancouver Magazine*, October 2012. vanmag.com/News_and_Features/Vancouvers_Ivan_Henry_Finally_Released.
2. *The Inquiry Regarding Thomas Sophonow*.
3. Barry Scheck, Peter Neufeld, and Jim Dwyer, *Actual Innocence: Five Days to Execution, and Other Dispatches from the Wrongfully Convicted* (New York: Doubleday, 2003).
4. Peter MacKay, House of Commons Hansard, March 30, 2000.

INDEX

Cardozo, C., Miss: assault, 247, 285, 289, 291; case reinvestigation, 169, 288; testimony, 37, 72–73, 291

Carrothers, A.B.B., Justice, 128, 278

Carter, Rubin, "Hurricane," 171

Charter of Rights and Freedoms. See Canadian Charter of Rights and Freedoms

Chessman, Caryl, 144–45

civil lawsuit (Henry's): allegations, 14, 188, 302; and the Crown, 315; and proving innocence, 307, 309; response to, 206–7, 255

complainants: crime scenes, 246, 285; effort to contact, 226–27; identity of, 10; and memory, 203, 216–22; re-interviews, 85–86, 199, 216–19; use of term "ripped off," 291–92

Connor, Jean, 219, 231

Connor, Patricia, 231

Conroy, Chris, 19, 20, 86, 99

Conroy, John, 279

Cooper, Bob, Constable, 47

Correctional Service of Canada (CSC), 123, 139, 170, 171, 301

Cory, Peter, Justice, 240, 318-19

Cotton, Robert, 228–29

Court of Appeal. *See* BC Court of Appeal

Craig, Wallace, Judge, 34–39, 46, 47, 52, 56, 74, 103, 208–10, 212–15, 271

credibility, 10, 107–8, 112, 116, 159, 224, 247, 251

criminal justice system: and claim of innocence, 257–58; and legal aid, 112, 256; and oath-binding, 236; and presumption of innocence, 303–5; and wrongful conviction, 145, 232, 234, 317–19

criminal record (Henry's), 15, 22, 26, 88, 94, 103, 105, 108, 112, 131, 251, 255

Crossin, David, 294

Crown counsel: duty of disclosure, 230–35; liability of, 315; misconduct of, 306–7; and VPD, 205–6. *See also* Luchenko, Michael; Milliken, Judith

Cullen, Manfred: friendship with Henry, 19, 113, 131–33, 136–38, 165–68; letter from Henry, 140–41

Cunningham, Sandy, 197

Dangerfield, George, 313

dangerous offender (DO) designation, 13, 109, 112, 115–20, 125, 132, 135, 160, 161, 162, 238, 274, 276

Davies, G., Miss, 37

DNA exoneration, 165, 168, 170, 171, 173, 175, 178, 209, 223, 228–29, 304–5, 307, 309, 328

Doust, Leonard (special prosecutor): 180, 181, 184; on legal aid, 256

Driskell, James, 175, 313

Driver, Terry, 185

Edwards, Kent, 276, 277

Exhibit Five, 79, 91, 97, 245, 272. *See also* photo array

Exhibit One: changes to, 268; pretrial, 36, 66; scientific testing application, 114–15; switching of photos, 260–63; testimony on, 48, 85, 96–97; at trial, 265. *See also* photographs of lineup

eyewitness testimony, 145, 203, 216–29

Federal Court judgment (1992), 154–55, 164, 265–66

Fields, A., Miss, 39, 101, 165, 201-2, 227, 242, 286, 297, 311

Finch, Lance, Justice, 278, 299

Fisher, Larry, 170

Flannigan, Miss (female guard), 175–76, 183–84, 280–81

Foster, Gary, Corporal, 72, 310

Foxx, Lloyd, Constable, 47, 48, 76, 77, 78, 269, 270, 271

Frankl, Viktor, 162–63

Gabriel, G., Detective, 294–96

Garrett, Brandon, 223, 257, 306

geographical profiling, 175, 185; crime scenes, 246, 285

Goldie, Michael, Justice, 168, 278

Grdic v. The Queen, 303

Gronmyr, Lars, Detective, 198, 289

guilty mind argument, 107, 109, 252, 253; and lineup photo, 271

habeas corpus application, 55

Hall, Neal, 197, 231

Hanemaayer, Anthony, 178, 308

Harkema, William, Detective, 46, 51, 132, 197, 198, 202-4, 205, 206, 207, 271; and photo array, 43–44, 203; and re-interviewing, 199, 204, 217, 226, 233; report of, 218, 219; testimony, 78–79, 85–86, 202–3, 241; visit to Henry, 115–16

Heggie, Constable, 84

Henry, Darwyn (brother), 170, 182

Henry, Gerry (father), 152

Henry, Ivan William Mervin: childhood, 25, 58; conspiracy theory, 15, 34, 36, 38, 41, 57–58, 63, 181, 213, 271; distrust of lawyers, 22, 54, 112, 181; distrust of police, 32, 33, 131; family, 28–29, 124, 150–52, 169–70; interviews, 14–15, 320–22; letter to Cullen, 140–41; ordeal of prison, 126–27, 129, 131, 139, 149, 163, 171–72, 174, 176; post release, 13, 186–88, 317–18; psychiatric reports, 59, 117–19, 162–63

Henry, Jessie (wife): as informant against Henry, 192–194, 298; box sent from prison, 150, 157; death of, 151; death-bed confession, 192, 194; lack of testimony, 92, 194; move to Mount Pleasant, 40, 84, 247, 285, 298; police interview, 19, 28–29, 83–84, 191–93

Henry, Kari (daughter), 31, 157–58, 161, 169, 192

Henry, Mrs. (mother), 150–51, 169–70, 181–82

Henry, Tanya (daughter), 13, 28, 150, 157, 186, 192, 194

Henry crimes: and McRae, 184–85, 233, 282–85, 296–97; and Smallman crimes, 231, 282, 285

Hinse, Réjean, 168, 313–14

Holloway, Rod, 57

Horvath, P., Miss, 41–42, 70–72, 105, 132, 219, 246, 271, 285, 286, 291, 310

Howland, Gordon, Sergeant, 31, 32, 51, 205

hypnosis, 44, 46, 203, 220–21, 271, 289

identification: and memory, 203, 216–22; and wrongful conviction, 223–28

ineffective assistance of counsel (IAC), 212

innocence: alibi statement, 244–47; and criminal justice, 257–58; and DNA exoneration, 165, 168, 170, 175, 223; factual, 168, 209, 302–5; and lack of remorse, 118, 160; legal, 209; and parole, 160–61, 279–81; and pleading guilty, 112, 178, 317; proving of, 306–8

Innocence Project, 12, 173, 310

Jacobsen, K., Miss, 42, 75–76, 219, 246, 285, 289, 291

Johns, Freddie, Detective, 47

judicial process. See criminal justice system

jurors: on trial proceedings, 221, 245, 252, 256, 265

Kajander, Esko, Detective, 47

Kaplan, William, 113

Kaufman, Fred, Justice, 168, 240, 252

Kavanagh, J., Miss, 42, 74, 79, 88, 94, 97, 104, 132, 165, 177, 186, 201, 202, 215, 218, 247, 285, 292, 311; absence from trial, 60, 78, 204; hypnosis of, 203, 217, 221, 289; interview, 203; re-interview, 85–86, 202, 204; testimony, 43–45, 46, 77, 225, 292

Keen, Daryl, Constable, 76, 133

Kent Institution, 123–25, 129, 130, 167

Kerr, Clifford, Dr., 118–19

Kitchen, William, Judge, 283, 284–85

Kitsilano crimes, 247, 285, 298

Lamer, Antonio, Justice, 243

Larson, H., Miss, 45–46, 68–70, 104, 219, 233, 247, 261, 271, 291

Laskin, Bora, Chief Justice, 129

Layton, David, 180

legal aid, 54, 57, 112, 127, 129, 135, 154, 156, 159, 164, 168, 169, 239, 254, 256–57, 274, 277, 317

Lévesque, Francis (pseudonym), 214–15, 270

lie detector test, 26, 28, 83, 88, 95, 103, 108, 117, 196

lineup. See physical lineup

Locard, Edmond, Dr., 309

Lockyer, James, 171

Loftus, Elizabeth, 216–17, 221, 222, 227–28

Luchenko, Michael (Blue 3): about, 34, 38, 231, 236; lack of disclosure, 55, 81, 232–34, 276; and lineup photo, 36, 69, 97, 142, 212–13, 260–62, 271; and off-indictment charges, 242; opening statement of, 62–63, 252; role in charges, 205; tactical interruptions, 67, 76, 235, 242, 265

MacCallum, Edward, Justice, 249

MacKay, Peter, 170, 319

Maidment, MaDonna, 243

malicious prosecution, 240, 302, 306–7, 313, 315

Marcoux case, 23, 87, 252

Marpole crimes, 247, 250, 285, 289–90, 298

Martin, Arthur, Mr. Justice, 205

McCarthy, R., Miss: testimony, 48, 101

McClellan, Edward, Sergeant, 195, 272

McDaniels, Gary, 177

McEachern, Allan, Chief Justice, 59

McRae, Donald James: appearance, 296; criminal history, 285–88, 299–301; and Henry crimes, 184–85, 233, 282–85; Henry/McRae as neighbours, 297, 298;

McRae, Donald James: *(continued)*
  as rip-off rapist, 292; and Smallman
  crimes, 294–96; and VPD, 308
medical evidence: lack of disclosure, 82–83,
  105, 232, 248–50; serology testing, 171,
  249–50
memory contamination, 203, 216–22
Miles, Kenneth, Staff Sergeant, 79, 272, 286
Milgaard, David, 154, 168, 170, 188, 249,
  250
Miller, Sarah, 259–60, 262–63
Milliken, Judith, 65, 66, 67, 70–71, 72, 73,
  75, 77, 78, 101, 103, 105, 205, 310
Mitchell, Bill, 276
modus operandi (MO): comparisons,
  294–96; of Henry, 26; post-Henry
  assaults, 289–90, 292; rip-off rapist,
  62–63, 201, 288–89, 291–92; Smallman
  crimes, 231, 288–89, 294–95; types of,
  293–94
Montgomery, Fred, Detective (pseudonym),
  193, 194, 195–96, 203, 205, 272, 290,
  311–12
Moon, Karla, 157–58
Morin, Guy Paul, 165, 168, 240, 250, 253,
  320
Morris, Barbara, Inspector, 218, 219
Mount Pleasant crimes, 247, 285, 298
Mountain Institution, 162–63, 167–68, 170,
  171–76, 183–84
Mulgrew, Ian, 237

Naughton, Michael, Dr., 232, 257
Nelles, Susan, 306
Neufeld, Peter, 310, 319
Nielson, K., Miss, 48
Noone, Joseph, Dr., 58
Norvell, Paul, 249

Oakalla, 32–33, 119
off-indictment crimes, 52, 59, 61, 63, 242
Olson, Clifford, 138, 196
Oppal, Wally, 231
O'Reilly, L. Miss, 50, 227, 242, 311

parole (Henry): application, 160–61;
  records, 279–81
Pavlovik, V., Miss, 48–49, 99
Peck, Richard, 57, 59
Philipson, Jerry, 99–100, 246
Phillion, Romeo, 306, 313
photo array: Exhibit Five, 79, 91, 97, 245,
  272; May 13 photo, 78–79, 91, 93, 97,

194, 195, 203–4, 212, 272–73; striated
  photo, 84, 191, 196, 241; unfairness of,
  225, 272
photographs: and memory, 221–22;
  taken from Jessie, 29, 78–79, 84, 93,
  194
photographs of lineup: Atkinson affidavit,
  155–56, 164, 266; as composite, 264–71;
  different copies, 77–78, 97, 242, 259–63;
  eight-by-ten, 259–60, 262, 267–68, 269;
  five-by-seven, 260–61, 263, 267, 268–69;
  Henry's testimony, 91; officers in photo,
  47–48; at preliminary hearing, 35–36,
  55–56; as proof of guilty mind, 271;
  scientific testing application, 114–15
physical evidence: and crime scenes, 309–12;
  fingerprints, 51, 72, 233, 310, 311; lack of
  disclosure, 181, 232
physical lineup (fall 1981), 42, 48–49, 50, 66, 75
physical lineup identification: use of,
  195–96, 198–99, 223
physical lineup (May 1982): denial of by
  Henry, 23, 87, 90, 270; details of, 47–48;
  and guilty mind argument, 107, 109, 252,
  253, 271; Henry's behaviour, 290; only
  redhead, 24, 94, 252; testimony on, 68,
  70, 76, 80, 85, 270–71; unfairness of, 225
Pickton, Robert William, 175, 231, 282
preliminary hearing: generally, 33, 34–52;
  and Judge Craig, 208–10; and judicial
  stay, 214–15; and lineup photo, 35–36,
  212–14; transcripts, 55–56. *See also*
  White, John
Prince Albert Penitentiary. *See*
  Saskatchewan Penitentiary
prison: access to bank account, 135; friendship with Cullen, 113, 131–33, 136–38,
  167–68; hiding lineup photo, 260; income,
  135, 141, 177; inmates, 124, 136, 139–40,
  165–67, 171–74; job as cook, 146–48; legal
  research, 134, 177–78; letter to Cullen,
  140–41; mailing costs, 143, 146, 177;
  preparing appeals, 134–35, 145–46; release,
  186–88; sexual behaviour in, 141–42;
  solitary confinement, 126–27, 148–49, 158;
  transfer request, 151–52, 161; violence,
  147, 153, 174, 183; Weird Ricci, 171–72
prison guards: female, 142, 175–76, 280;
  mind games, 138–39, 147–49; and
  prisoner's rights, 158, 165; strip searches,
  139, 142
prosecution. *See* Crown counsel
Rainsley, Constable, 84

ABOUT THE AUTHOR

J oan McEwen is a Vancouver-born lawyer, labour arbitrator, and writer.

Joan clerked for BC Supreme Court chief justice Nathan Nemetz from 1976–77, then articled with Farris and Company before clerking for Paul Weiler's newly minted BC Labour Relations Board. After practising labour law for twelve years, Joan—having adopted, with lawyer Irwin Nathanson, the first of their two (blood brother) sons—set up shop as a labour arbitrator in 1990.

Joan caught the writing bug in 2006 after enrolling in the Writer's Studio at Simon Fraser University. She has been writing ever since. Indeed, it was while working on her second novel—now tucked away, as is the first, in a bottom drawer—that she saw Ivan Henry on television for the first time.

Today, Joan is actively involved advocating for the post-convicted—innocent and guilty alike—by lobbying for prison and post-prison conditions conducive to rehabilitation and successful reintegration into society.